# Coaching and Mentoring Supervision Theory and Practice

Edited by

*Tatiana Bachkirova, Peter Jackson
and David Clutterbuck*

Open University Press

Open University Press
McGraw-Hill Education
McGraw-Hill House
Shoppenhangers Road
Maidenhead
Berkshire
England
SL6 2QL

email: enquiries@openup.co.uk
world wide web: www.openup.co.uk

and Two Penn Plaza, New York, NY 10121-2289, USA

First published 2011

MIX
Paper from
responsible sources
FSC
www.fsc.org
FSC® C013604

A catalogue record of this book is available from the British Library

ISBN-13: 9780335242986 (pb) 9780335242979 (hb)
ISBN-10: 0335242987 (pb) 0335242979 (hb)
e-ISBN: 9780335242993

Library of Congress Cataloging-in-Publication Data
CIP data applied for

Typeset by Aptara

Printed and bound by CPI Group (UK) Ltd, Croydon, CR0 4YY

The McGraw-Hill Companies

# Coaching and Mentoring Supervision Theory and Practice

## Supervision in Context series

Coaching & Mentoring Supervision: Theory and Practice by Tatiana Bachkirova, Peter Jackson and David Clutterbuck

Skills of Clinical Supervision for Nurses: A Practical Guide for Supervisees, Clinical Supervisors and Managers (Second Edition) by Meg Bond and Stevie Holland

The Social Work Supervisor: Supervision in Community, Day Care, and Residential Settings by Allan Brown and Iain Bourne

Psychotherapy Supervision: An Integrative Rational Approach to Psychotherapy Supervision by Maria C. Gilbert and Kenneth Evans

### *Forthcoming in 2012:*

Supervision in Action: A Relational Approach to Coaching and Consulting Supervision by Erik de Haan

Supervision in the Helping Professions (Fourth Edition) by Peter Hawkins and Robin Shohet

Clinical Supervision in the Medical Profession: Structured Reflective Practice by David Owen and Robin Shohet

# Contents

# Part III: Contexts and modes of supervision

# Part IV: Practical case studies in supervision

# Series editors' preface

We welcome this excellent new addition to the Supervision in Context Series. Supervision of coaches, mentors and consultants has grown up more recently than supervision in many of the people professions such as counselling, psychotherapy, psychology, social work and nursing. Although a minority of coaches had been receiving supervision for many years, this was mostly delivered by supervisors trained in counseling, psychotherapy or psychology and supervision in coaching lacked its own distinctive approach, relevant to its own unique challenges. This lack of specific coaching supervision was a major factor, as many in the field were reluctant to take up supervision and there was a good deal of resistance to its development (Hawkins and Schwenk 2006). It did not help address what the authors of this book describe as the "blurred boundary between coaching and counseling". The first research and the first book specifically on supervision for coaches, mentors and consultants was not published until 2006 (Hawkins and Smith 2006) and the first training specifically for supervisors of coaches and mentors did not start until 2003. Yet in the last ten years much has been done to develop this fast growing field, of which this book is the latest very welcome addition. This book brings together a remarkably rich array of contributions. These show how supervision has developed for coaches in a wide range of European countries (specifically UK, France, Denmark and Switzerland), for internal and external coaches; for mentors and consultants, and for those coaching individuals, groups, teams and wider systems.

Coaching supervision draws on many of the supervision models and approaches developed in other professions, as David Gray and Peter Jackson illustrate in chapter 1.1, and each of the chapters in section two elucidate. However, supervision of coaches has significant differences from those supervising other helping professionals. Whereas the counselor, nurse, or social worker have clear individual and group clients that they bring to supervision, those who are carrying out executive coaching, paid for by organizations, always have to serve multiple clients. Those coaching managers and leaders in organizations have the challenge of serving the individual coaching client, the organization in which the coaching takes place and the relationship between the two. It is all too easy for the coach to be more focused on the individual they are with in the coaching room and pay less attention to the organization and yet this organization has an investment in the coaching relationship and its outcomes. When the coach comes to supervision, the supervisor needs to hold in mind the coach and their development, the coach's individual and team clients, the organizations investing in the coaching and the systemic connection across all these different entities. This requires a sophisticated, systemic and sensitive form of supervision.

Tatiana, Peter and David also point out other extra challenges for the coach supervisor; namely that coaches are often less well trained to "identify mental-health issues impinging on the boundaries of coaching"; and "less prepared to identify the effect of their personal process on their work because they are not required ... to undertake ... counseling or other personal development." These put extra responsibility on the coaching supervisor who needs to combine expertise on the coaching craft, understanding of adult development and psychological process, a wide ranging understanding of business, systems and organizational dynamics. This requires specific supervision skills on top of the coaching skills they will have already acquired.

One of the great strengths of this particular book is that Tatiana, Peter and David have brought together contributions from practice, teaching and research as well as the growing body of theory in the field, while providing a lively and practical text that help both the new coaching supervisor and those who have been practicing for many years.

This new edition sits proudly alongside the other books in this series, which include:

> *Supervision in the Helping Professions* by Peter Hawkins and Robin Shohet (now in its 3rd edition)
> *Clinical Supervision for Nurses* by Meg Bond and Susie Holland (now in its 2nd edition)
> *The Social Work Supervisor*, by Allan Brown and Iain Bourne,
> *Psychotherapy Supervision* by Maria Gilbert and Ken Evans.

Shortly we will adding to this series with new books on "Supervision in Medical Settings" edited by David Owen and Robin Shohet and a book on "Supervision in Schools" by Elizabeth Holmes.

This whole series focuses on how to create, develop and sustain helping relationships, through providing quality supervision to those who work broadly in the people and helping professions. Quality supervision is the key link in helping practitioners link what they learn in theory, with what they learn and do in practice and is therefore the core of all continuous personal and professional development. At its best it serves and benefits the professional being supervised, their clients, the organizations in which they work (and work for) and the development of the profession. In today's world no helping professional can afford to be without supervision and this book also provides an excellent frame for coaches, mentors and consultants to know what they should be demanding as part of sustaining the quality and development of their practice.

We are confident that this new edition will significantly take forward the development of supervision in these new and developing professions.

Professor Peter Hawkins and Robin Shohet Series Editors April 2011

# Introduction

The initial impetus for this book was a conversation at the annual conference of the European Mentoring and Coaching Council. Two of the editors had attended several sessions that addressed directly or indirectly the role and importance of supervision. It was clear to us that, while there seemed to be near-universal support for the role and importance of supervision in coaching and mentoring, there was also considerable variation in perspective as to what was meant by supervision. These differences arose from multiple sources – among them context (e.g. supervision for internal or external coaching), purpose (e.g. for the primary benefit of the coach, or that of the organizational client), professional background of the supervisor (e.g. psychology/counselling or business and coaching experience) and their theoretical orientation (e.g. solution-focused, psychodynamic, etc.).

This impression of diversity, so common in an emergent profession, was recognized as an opportunity to capture the richness of theory and approach to supervision and to provide an overview of current themes in coach/mentor supervision. Gradually the idea of this book developed into the intention to create a comprehensive guide to this developing area of complex, multidisciplinary professional practice. So our aim was to:

- reflect the evolving status of supervision;
- clarify what good coaching/mentoring supervision looks like in different contexts;
- provide practical case examples to complement and shed light on the theoretical bases for coaching/mentoring supervision;
- reflect the diversity of perspective on supervision in coaching and mentoring;
- explore alternative ways of delivering and using supervision;
- address the complex issue of evaluating the effectiveness and quality of supervision.

We were very pleased that so many carefully selected international authors from different theoretical backgrounds and with different contextual experience responded to our invitation to contribute to this ambitious project. It is their generosity with ideas and time and their willingness to engage with our expectations for a particular vision and structure of the book that gives us hope that this book will fulfil our intention of providing a comprehensive overview of current practice, the issues arising and contributory theory of coaching supervision.

## What do we notice as changing in relation to coaching supervision in the professional communities?

The idea of supervision in helping professions is not new (see Chapter 1 for an overview). However, in relation to coaching we are still at the stage of building an understanding of what its role, status and potential are. This understanding is developing along with the development of coaching as a professional practice. As the coaching world is becoming better organized and gradually more professionalized, coaches are able to engage with clearer pathways in education and professional development. They become more aware that, because of the nature of coaching, access to feedback for self-improvement is naturally limited, unsystematic and infrequent. Although we collect regular feedback from our clients it is not the same as from those who can look at our work from an informed position of a specialist in this area. It could be argued that the lack of this type of feedback can represent significant risks to the interests of the client.

From another angle, there is a growing pressure from client organizations for systems of continuous quality assurance (as opposed to one-off accreditation of coaches and mentors). In response to these external expectations, the principal professional bodies in coaching in Europe have begun to establish a broad consensus about the requirements for executive coaching. Many organizations require that coaches they employ have a solid supervisory provision. In many cases organizations provide supervision for internal coaches and for managers providing coaching or mentoring. So supervision in coaching is rapidly evolving from a 'nice to have' to a 'need to have'.

Having a supervisor seems to be essential now for professional coaches working in Europe and the focus of attention is moving onto the quality of supervision provided and the skills of using supervision. Some universities now offer postgraduate certificates, diplomas and MA programmes in coaching/mentoring supervision and there is also a variety of non-university-based training courses available. With attention to quality of education and training of supervisors, the field of knowledge on coaching supervision is now emerging as a discipline separate to, but informed by, supervision in other contexts such as therapy or counselling.

## What is still debated and what is our position in relation these debates?

At the same time we are aware that the above perspective on the situation is not universal. There are concerns that the introduction of supervision into coaching communities may add to the existing confusion around the blurred boundary between coaching and counselling. Some concerns are expressed that supervision may lead to cloning of coaching styles and stultify diversity and creativity. Others question the value of supervision on the basis of lack of evidence that it actually improves the quality of coaching (Rogers 2004). The term 'supervision' in itself causes unfortunate associations in the minds of some coaches. Strong views about the need for supervision to be made mandatory also add to tensions in relation to this topic. Perhaps these and other concerns may in fact contribute to the situation which shows that integration of supervision in coaching practice is currently less widespread outside of Europe.

Acknowledging the legitimacy of the above concerns, we would like in this introduction to indicate our position in relation to some of the debates about coaching supervision. We also intended that every chapter of the book should make its own case, helping readers to form their own views on these dilemmas, as well as to learn about supervision in practice.

While the book is intended to help readers make up their own mind, there is, nevertheless, some boundary to the scope. Before engaging with some of these debates, therefore, it is important to give three examples of the definitions of coaching supervision that in combination describe what is meant by it in the book:

> Supervision is a forum where supervisees review and reflect on their work in order to do it better.
>
> (Carroll 2007: 433)

> Supervision is the process by which a coach/mentor/consultant with the help of the supervisor, who is not working directly with the client, can attend to understanding better both the client system and themselves as part of the client-coach/mentor system, and transform their work.
>
> (Hawkins and Smith 2006: 147)

> Coaching supervision is a formal process of professional support which ensures continuing development of the coach and effectiveness of his/her coaching practice through interactive reflection, interpretative evaluation and the sharing of expertise.
>
> (Bachkirova 2008: 16–17)

## Do coaches really need supervision?

It is no news that different paradigms colour what we see and value. The question that is posed here can be seen from the perspective of two different paradigms. First, practitioners from a business background may be inclined to look for the 'bottom line': is there hard data that suggests substantial benefits from introducing supervision? In contrast, practitioners with roots in psychology and counselling may be more inclined to look first at the ethical questions of helping relationships and at the subtle influences at play in the coaching process.

From the first perspective, we should be clear that, looking at coaching supervision as a business case, not much evidence exists as yet to insist on its value. It is incredibly difficult to design research that would allow exploring a direct link between the process or even the fact of supervision and the effect of this on the practice of the coach – and even more difficult to demonstrate its impact on the work of the client. It should be noted, however, that on the same basis the value of many managerial practices and even education as a whole could also be questioned.

Looking at this issue from the second angle brings to the fore the complexity of coaching and its many functions and purposes. For example, those arguing against the need for supervision often object to the idea of coaching following the footsteps of therapy (Slater 2008) on the basis that the context and particularly the clientele of these practices are significantly different. However, even agreeing that some differences exist, a case can be made that supervision is more important for coaches than for counsellors (Bachkirova 2008). Coaches have more than one client in each coaching engagement and so have a greater need to see the complexity of the relationship and the many perspectives of the various stakeholders in their work. Coaches are less equipped than counsellors to identify mental health issues impinging on the boundaries of coaching, so they would benefit from another pair of eyes to check their concerns. Coaches may also be less prepared to identify the effect of their personal processes on their work because they are not required, prior to coaching others, to undertake compulsory counselling or other personal development work themselves, as are counsellors. With a similar appreciation of complexity the emerging research also shows many developmental benefits and positive influences that coaches report as a result of being supervised (Butwell 2006; Slater 2008; McGivern 2009).

### Should supervision be compulsory?

We are not advocating that coaching supervision should be mandatory. Different professions struggle in different ways with the task of ensuring the continuing quality of their service. Accreditation was designed as one of such methods, but it is far from perfect in practice and in principle, because it is static, past oriented and inevitably oversimplifies the complexity of coaching practice. We believe that in a search for the best approach of ensuring the dynamic quality of what we do we can lead the way, even for other professions, by conceiving the role of supervision as our professional conscience in practice. It is our professional conscience that should make us regularly reflect and question our work. There are many implications of this conception of supervision and the first and obvious one is that it cannot be mandatory. Indeed, we hope and believe that discretionary supervision is likely to work better than if it were mandatory.

### Does the supervisor need knowledge and skills over and above those of a coach?

Yes, we believe that there are essential, additional skills and knowledge. Hawkins and Smith (2006) describe typical functions of supervision as qualitative, developmental and resourcing. With the variety of coaching approaches and styles, coaches are not necessarily equipped to fulfil this role. Also, according to the vision that we indicated above, supervisors have the additional function of looking after the health of the profession as a whole. At the same time, we must be somewhat accepting that the knowledge base of the discipline and the skills of its practitioners are both still developing – a programme to which this book is intended to contribute.

## What is our position in relation to development of knowledge in this book?

The three editors of this book are all involved in research, teaching and practice in both supervision and coaching (and/or mentoring). Through these activities and over time, we have become aware of some fundamental principles or commitments. These commitments have shaped our approach to this book and we feel it is important to state them as an aspect of the context in which the book is offered and might be read.

First is a commitment to the flow of information through research/theory, practice and teaching. It is no accident that we are each involved in all of these activities as we each believe that they feed from each other. The whole is greater than the sum of the parts. Hence, this book is intended neither as abstract philosophy, nor as bluffer's guide. It is intended to help people reflect on their practice, extend their theories in use, develop their professional identities and add value to their clients.

Second is a commitment to the idea that our knowledge of supervision is complex and emergent. It is complex insofar as it is a real-world activity that is influenced by very many conditions. It is emergent insofar as among those multitudes of conditions there *may* be key conditions which predict effective practice, though the availability of evidence to guide us is, and is likely to continue to be in the short term, partial and contradictory. The consequence of this is the third commitment to diversity.

Hence, third, we recognize the diversity of models, of practice and of guiding theory and we urge 'students' (by which we mean practitioners and academics as well as 'consumers of teaching') similarly to engage with the diversity of thinking in the field.

It is as a result of these commitments that we present this book – as we do with our teaching and supervision – primarily as an opportunity for the reader to learn from an engagement with the breadth of ideas available and from reflecting actively on that engagement.

## Overview of the sections of the book

### Part I: Models and professional issues of supervision

The purpose of this section is to introduce the reader to a variety of both well-established and novel models of supervision practice. Our intention is to provide practical solutions to the general issues of coaching supervision and also to explore important professional issues such as ethics and professional standards. Each chapter introducing a model starts from a rationale for its practical importance and value. The reader will be engaged with a question: why would I need to adopt this model? The authors demonstrate that each model is different from others and has a particular value in some specific contexts. They describe roles and responsibilities of the supervisor, potential pitfalls when this model is used and illustrate the model with a short case illustration. Although some of the models are highly original, the authors recommend the literature that could stimulate further thinking in relation to the model and offer suggestions for further learning.

The model presented in the first chapter is of a slightly different character from the others in this section insofar as it is proposed as a systemic meta-model that allows classification of other models of coaching supervision and is based explicitly on a historical overview of supervision models in psychotherapy. In Chapter 2 the reader will be able to have a fresh perspective from two of its proponents on the well-known 'Seven-eyed' model of coaching supervision. Chapters 3 and 4 both address different aspects of supervision allowing a rich perspective on a supervision process; these are the 'three worlds – four territories' model and the 'seven conversations in supervision'. Michel Moral has contributed a specifically French perspective, extending supervision practice to working with a coaching team engaged in a single organizational project. In Chapter 5 a model of working with the self is suggested for supervisors. This section concludes with a discussion of the many important issues related to professional standards of supervision and ethics of the professional practice. As a whole, this section illustrates many different ways of making sense of the complexity of information that the supervisor has to deal with. It also shows the richness and multiplicity of angles that could be taken on the supervisory process.

## Part II: The use of theoretical approaches in coaching supervision

The purpose of this section is to present different theoretical perspectives useful in coaching supervision. Our intention is that these discussions will help supervisors to deepen their understanding of their own practice, and will provide coaches and sponsors with a critical insight into the range of practices available. Each chapter explores the main features of the approach relevant to coaching supervision; the role and responsibilities of the supervisor; when and where this approach is most useful or least useful; and how to evaluate the quality of the supervision from the angle of this approach. These perspectives are built on complex histories of theoretical exploration and development which command whole volumes in their own respect. Each author has drawn on a comprehensive literature relating to those theoretical concerns in order to highlight the peculiarities and opportunities offered by that particular approach. We recognize that on some topics this can only open the door for readers to a whole world of further reading. For this reason, at the end of their chapter each author has suggested starting points for further study.

In this section we have covered some of the most significant theoretical approaches as they have developed in the history of counselling and psychotherapy – psychodynamic, Gestalt, person-centred and transactional analysis – in addition to two theoretical areas which seem particularly pertinent to the contexts in which coaching takes place: organizational psychology and systems theory. There are inevitably omissions: why have we not included a chapter on cognitive-behavioural theory and its derivatives? Could we have said more about adult learning? Rather than reflecting preferences in our own practices (and given the constraints on the overall length of the book) we have been guided here by which topics appeared to us to have the most relevance to the practice of *supervision*. In those two, illustrative, examples, we took the view that they were more relevant as theories applied to *coaching* rather than *coaching supervision*. We recognize that every choice to do something implies a choice not to do something else, but a choice to do nothing is no choice at all. Apologies to any readers, whose special area of interest is not covered in the chapters we selected.

## Part III: Contexts and modes of supervision

This section explores a number of specific contexts and modes of coaching supervision, and is intended to help the reader make comparisons between them. We start by reviewing a range of issues relating to supervising internal coaches – either coaching direct reports or operating as an internal executive coach – where the relationship dynamics between coach, client, supervisor and organization can become highly complex. We then examine the concept of group supervision, which has become an increasingly popular option, both because of cost considerations and the wider perspectives that may be brought from observations and questions from coach peers. Next, we branch aside into supervision for mentors, a relatively recent innovation that is rapidly gaining traction.

Chapter 17 in this section blurs the definition of coach and organizational consultant, in a case study from Ashridge, which provides valuable lessons for wider applications of coaching supervision. We continue by delving into the concept of peer-supervision. Peer supervision, as commonly practised, is potentially controversial, on the basis that often neither party may have much specific knowledge or skills of supervision per se. Yet, as our authors point out, it can be a very powerful resource to support coaches in their practice. The final chapter in this section looks at the media of supervision. The tacit assumption that supervision is a face-to-face activity is being challenged by increasing use of email and telephone supervision, with the suggestion that these media are neither inferior nor superior to face-to-face supervision, but different. The diversity of these examples of different modes of supervision reinforces the impression of an emerging discipline, where innovation and experimentation will be a dynamic force for at least the next few years.

## Part IV: Practical case studies in supervision

Engaging with the case studies in this section, the reader will be able to consider models, theoretical perspectives and contexts in relation to a particular application. The case studies illustrate a range of discussions introduced in earlier sections, thereby providing both real-life examples and a study resource for critical reflection. Each chapter includes a description of the context for the case study and comprehensive description of the supervision programme/scheme. The authors are explicit about what can be learned from each and particular issues that they highlight.

The section starts with the chapter that explores mentoring supervision for doctors and dentists in a UK National Health Service (NHS) Deanery. It gives a rich picture of how this service evolved and changed as the result of mentors' development and understanding of what they need from supervision. This is followed by an exploration of how supervision works within the context of mentoring in Denmark, and an account of a group supervision process from Switzerland. In the chapter on supervision of maternity coaches the reader will engage with the nuances and challenges of supervision in the service of coaches in this particular context and examine the solutions that worked for them. The final case study tracks the implementation of supervision in a professional service firm, looking in particular at the decision-making process and learning from the programme.

## Overview of important issues emerging from the book

### Tendency for system approaches

A number of our authors have referred specifically to the systemic nature of coaching and of coaching supervision. Some of the models, such as Hawkins and Smith's seven-eyed, are firmly rooted in a systemic perspective. Others recognize that all issues brought to coaching have a systems dimension. Sustainable change cannot normally occur within a client without some change in their environment or relationships with others; indeed, client, coach and supervisor are part of a complex adaptive system – constantly evolving and reshaping as they interact with each other and with external forces. Our authors recognize the risk that linear, cause and effect thinking in supervision may be highly misleading for both coach and supervisor, and hence unhelpful to the client.

### Tendency for the group mode of work

We have noticed an increasing interest in the group mode of work in coaching as well as in supervision. There are various explanations for this trend in different chapters, with the two most powerful reasons being cost and the opportunity to gather multiple perspectives on a client issue. An emerging trend is for executive coaches to undergo both individual and group supervision.

### Multi-supervision and networks

One of the growing trends in mentoring is the shift from reliance on a single mentor at a particular career point, to multiple mentors overlapping in time. Our chapters reflect a similar transition in coach supervision. Having a single supervisor, who provides all the supervisory functions required, is no longer the only option. It is quite common, for example, to have one supervisor, who is a very experienced coach and has learned supervision skills, and one who is less experienced as a coach, but highly trained in counselling supervision or, say, supervision using Gestalt. Each provides a different perspective and source of challenge. We have also encountered a small number of cases where supervisors network with each other and encourage clients to take ad hoc issues to a colleague, who may provide a different perspective.

### The dark side of supervision

The contributors to this volume are all in some sense pioneers in the field of coaching supervision, and there is a sense across the groups of academics, professional bodies and practitioners involved in this field of considerable opportunity: opportunity to develop methods and approaches, to establish good practice, to help coaches and their clients; in short, to do good. It is easy in this pioneering mood to give relatively less weight to what we might call the 'dark side' of supervision.

From our work with practising coaches, we are aware that some supervision relationships do involve some or all of the following: collusion (mutual self-congratulation), dependency, and even abuse (for example, the supervisor having an agenda of their own). The potential for these phenomena is strong, suggest our authors, in peer-supervision between relatively inexperienced coaches, or when the supervisor has assumed the role solely on the basis of many years experience as a coach. However, we have little real evidence of the prevalence of the dark side of supervision, nor in what contexts it occurs. It is an area where more research is needed before we can feel comfortable in making any pronouncements!

### Sense-making

The discussions presented here take a broad view of different conceptualizations of function, process, role and tasks in supervision. The differences in the choice of vocabulary and explanatory structures can obscure at the micro level a feature which becomes very apparent at the macro level. This is the fact that supervision is about making sense of the experience in the room with the coach. 'How', and even 'why' might vary with approach (and 'what' will be different in every session), but sense-making is at the core. It is perhaps for this reason that theory from applied psychology as well as psychotherapy and counselling can be so informative. But supervision is also human, experiential and inter-subjective. So the concept of sense-making helpfully highlights to us the inevitability that we might, from time to time, feel lost, take wrong turns, and take a punt on the wrong hunch. And none of this detracts from being a 'good' supervisor.

**Lack of research**

It's hardly surprising in an emerging profession that there are many gaps in our knowledge. In some ways, this is a boon, in the sense that 'not knowing' encourages experimentation and 'knowing' discourages it. However, we could not permit ourselves to avoid the responsibility to make at least some suggestions for further research. Among the areas we suggest for future studies are:

- What are useful criteria for effectiveness in coach supervision, and in what contexts? (Note that we are not suggesting generic, all-purpose criteria here!)
- What enables a coach to make most effective use of a supervisor?
- What strategies and practices can supervisors employ to maintain their own continuous professional development; and what support would be helpful to them?
- What role does the 'fit' between supervisor and coach play?
- What are the appropriate methodologies for undertaking research in a context of such complexity?
- What are the typical challenges that coaches bring for supervision and what topics are avoided?
- What is the nature of the developmental function of supervision?

Finally we would like to remind the reader that the authors have tried to structure their chapters providing as many examples, case illustrations and suggestions for further learning as possible. We hope that the case illustrations will be useful as a learning resource for courses on coaching supervision. Whether you are an experienced supervisor or a novice we hope that the book provides an opportunity for you to engage with various approaches and models of supervision, extend your skills, identify important issues and critically evaluate your practice. If you are a coach or mentor, we hope you will be able to learn about different approaches to supervision, to identify those from which you can mostly benefit and to learn how to use supervision better. If you are an organizational sponsor, we also hope this book is useful for you in developing a better understanding of supervision so that you can ensure the best value practice when engaging coaches or establishing your own supervision scheme.

# References

Bachkirova, T. (2008) Coaching supervision: reflection on changes and challenges, *People and Organisations at Work*, Autumn edition.

Butwell, J. (2006) Group supervision for coaches: is it worthwhile? A study of the process in a major professional organisation, *International Journal of Evidence Based Coaching and Mentoring*, 4(2): 43–53.

Carroll, M. (2007) Coaching psychology supervision: luxury or necessity? in S. Palmer and A. Whybrow (eds) *Coaching Psychology Handbook*. London: Routledge, pp. 431–48.

Hawkins, P. and Smith, N. (2006) *Coaching, Mentoring and Organizational Consultancy: Supervision and Development*. Maidenhead: Open University Press.

McGivern, L. (2009) Continuous professional development and avoiding the vanity trap: an exploration of coaches' lived experiences of supervision, *International Journal of Evidence Based Coaching and Mentoring*, Special Issue 3: 22–37.

Rogers, J. (2004) *Coaching Skills*. Maidenhead: Open University Press.

Salter, T. (2008) Exploring current thinking within the field of coaching on the role of supervision, *International Journal of Evidence Based Coaching and Mentoring*, Special Issue No. 2, November: 27–39.

# Part I

# Models and professional issues in supervision

# 1 Coaching supervision in the historical context of psychotherapeutic and counselling models: a meta-model

*David Gray and Peter Jackson*

## Introduction

This chapter is somewhat different from other chapters in this section of the book. A proportion of it has already appeared, along with a more general discussion of supervision, in an article in the *Australian Psychologist*, under the title, 'Towards a systemic model of coaching supervision – some lessons from psychotherapeutic and counselling models' (Gray 2007). The historical perspective and 'systemic model' is included in the present volume because of the opportunity it affords to students, coaches and supervisors to assess and integrate models and theories described in other chapters. It is for this reason that it is here referred to as a 'meta-model'.

This chapter, then, sets out to identify what kinds of models of supervision are available to coaches. In undertaking this objective, models and lessons from the supervision of counsellors and psychotherapists will be explored. There are three reasons for this. First, many current practising coaches are professionally trained and have practised, or are practising, as counsellors or psychotherapists. Second, there have been over 30 years of debate and analysis of alternative models of supervision from which lessons for coaching supervision can be drawn. Third, even when coaching focuses ostensibly on business issues, personal, experiential and problem-based themes often flow out of the coaching process. These include 'red flag' issues when the coachee may be experiencing psychological difficulties. As Whybrow and Palmer (2006) suggest, even non-clinical populations contain potentially vulnerable clients. It seems, therefore, that (arguably) supervision models from a counselling or psychological background may have some relevance for all business and evidence-based coaches.

## Some models of supervision

Carroll (1996) describes three phases in the evolution of models of supervision within the fields of counselling and psychotherapy. Phase 1 was associated with psychoanalytic models. In the days of Freud, supervision was largely informal, but in 1922 the International Psychoanalytic Society formulated a set of standards within which personal analysis of the trainee[1] was the cornerstone. Thus began the tension between supervision and therapy that, according to Carroll (1996) remains unresolved to this day. In other words, in some models of supervision, the supervisor provides both supervision and personal therapy to the supervisee – a kind of blurring of roles. The second phase of supervision, based on counselling models, emerged in the 1950s with an emphasis on skills development and a rather didactic framework in some supervisory approaches. As in phase 1, the supervisor remained firmly fixed within their parent theoretical orientation and taught through this view of the world. Phase 3, beginning in the 1970s, was associated with developmental and social role models that emphasized the roles and tasks of the supervisor and the learning stages of the supervisee. The discussion that follows relates primarily to this third phase.

Is it necessary, though, to have a model of supervision? Hess (1986) takes a somewhat phlegmatic view that the work of supervision probably gets done, irrespective of the particular theory or model used by the supervisor. This is partly because reality demands it. If the supervision misses core problems, these will return to irritate the supervisor–supervisee relationship until they are resolved. It also happens because the essential elements of supervision while addressed, are being given different terms by people with different theoretical orientations. Hence, what a psychotherapeutically orientated supervisor may call a therapeutic alliance, a client-centred supervisor may call positive regard. What is clear however, is that while, for example, psychotherapy can be seen as helpful to the process of supervision, it is not in itself a *theory* of supervision. A theory of supervision has to address issues that are those of the supervisee, not those of the client. The remainder of this section outlines some of these theoretical models. Note that while it is recognized that group supervision is possible, the focus here will be on *individual* supervision, primarily because it is, at least currently, probably the most widely adopted format.

## Developmental models of supervision

A developmental model of supervision has dominated counsellor–psychotherapist supervision for many years, focused primarily on a *stages* model of development (Ronnestad and Skovholt 1993). Indeed, Holloway (1987) comments that developmental models of supervision have become the 'zeitgeist of supervision thinking and research' (1987: 209).

One of the first developmental models was suggested by Hogan (1964) who outlined a four-stage process. At stage 1, the therapist tries to apply everything they have learned, demonstrating high degrees of dependence (on the supervisor) and insecurity. One of the supervision methods at this level is direct teaching. At level 2 the therapist's growth is characterized by what Hogan terms a dependency-autonomy conflict, with the therapist oscillating between being overconfident to being overwhelmed by the responsibilities involved in working within the profession. This period also involves considerable fluctuations in levels of motivation.

Level 3 is where the therapist becomes a master of his [sic] trade, with stable levels of motivation and increased professional self-confidence. At level 4 the therapist demonstrates an artistry and creativity that is characteristic of being at a 'master' level. Hence, they are both insightful but also aware of the limitations of insightfulness; personally secure but aware of insecurity. At this level, the supervisory relationship becomes more equal. Hogan makes it clear, however, that the four levels are not mutually exclusive or discreet and that within their own lifetime, the therapist may move from levels 1 to 4 many times. Subsequent models, however, tend to abandon this approach, preferring a more sequential, linear formulation.

Stoltenberg (1981) takes Hogan's (1964) model to develop what he calls the 'counsellor complexity model' with counsellors achieving more cognitive development as they progress through a series of developmental stages. Stage 1 is characterized by a process in which the counsellor is encouraged to develop personal autonomy but within a structured environment. At the next stage new skills and advice are offered by the supervisor whilst in Stage 3 more sharing and collegiality are encouraged. In the final, master, stage, consultation is provided but only when it is sought. This, then, is a developmental process in which the supervisee moves from a dependent to a more autonomous position and in which the interventions of the supervisor are largely determined by these stages of growth.

Stoltenberg and Delworth (1987) suggest a three-stage integrated developmental model (IDM) in which trainees [sic] move through a series of levels, progressing against three primary structures – self-awareness and other-awareness, motivation and autonomy. In terms of self- and other-awareness, what they term Level 1, trainees focus primarily on themselves, especially in terms of fears and uncertainties. This often clouds the trainee's ability to be empathetic and insightful about the needs of their clients. At Level 2, the trainee begins to focus more on the emotional and cognitive needs of the client. But by trying to see issues from the perspective of the client, the Level 2 trainee may become immersed in their problems and as confused and pessimistic as the client themselves. In contrast, Level 3 trainees are able to identify the impact a client's problems have on themselves and can move backwards and forwards between a focus on their own emotional responses to the client and what the client is experiencing.

The IDM model is dynamic in the sense that a trainee may be at Level 2 in some domains (such as intervention skills, assessment techniques or theoretical orientation) but at Level 1 in others. Stoltenberg and Delworth (1987) suggest, however, that a fourth, higher level occurs (the 'Level 3 Integrated Counselor') when the therapist has integrated Level 3 skills and knowledge across all the domains. This, however, is a stage not attained by most therapists and can be regarded as a 'master therapist' level, reflecting both horizontal movement across domains as well as depth.

The validity of developmental models has been questioned by Chagnon and Russell (1995) and Holloway (1987). Chagnon and Russell's (1995) study of 48 supervisors found that both low and highly experienced supervisors tended to be equally effective in assessing the developmental level of the trainees and most, regardless of experience level, had most difficulty in identifying development Level 2 in Stoltenberg's (1981) model. According to Chagnon and Russell (1995) this raises the possibility that levels are overlapping and interdependent, particularly at Level 2, where trainees exhibit characteristics of both Level 1 and Level 3. Hence, rather than a sequential process, trainees may 'ebb and flow from one developmental level to the next' (Chagnon and Russell 1995: 557). Analysing the results of numerous empirical studies, Holloway (1987) finds that differences between levels appear most pronounced at a very beginning level and among internee-level trainees, and that these are largely based on relationship characteristics. Hence, as we have seen, initial-level trainees seem to need more support, while interns demonstrate a sense of increasing independence.

## Social role supervision models

Social role models emphasize the roles and tasks of the supervisor as well as the stages of development of the supervisee. One of the most influential is the six focused model developed by Hawkins and Shohet (2000). This was subsequently developed as the 'seven-eyed model' and is described in full by Hawkins and Schwenk in Chapter 2 of this volume.

### *The six focused model*

Hawkins and Shohet (2000) originally presented what they called a 'double matrix' model of supervision, arguing that it differs to other models because it concentrates on the *process* of supervision, but within an organizational context, constraints and social norms. Far from supervision moving through a series of stages, supervision involves, at any time, operating at many different levels. Four elements are involved: a supervisor, a therapist (supervisee), a client and a work context. While usually only the supervisor and supervisee are present during the supervision, Hawkins and Shohet (2000) argue that both the client and work (social) context are carried into the supervision session (both consciously and unconsciously). Indeed, Turner (2010) points to a consideration of unconscious processes, as one of the prime reasons that supervision exists. Hence, the supervision process involves two interlocking matrices:

- a therapy/coaching system connecting the supervisee and the client (modes 1 to 3 in Hawkins and Schwenk's model);
- a supervision system connecting the supervisor and supervisee (modes 4 to 6 in Hawkins and Schwenk's model).

The purpose of the supervision system is to pay attention to the therapy/coaching system. This can happen in two ways – through discussing reports, viewing written notes or viewing videotapes, or observing how that session is reflected in the here-and-now experiences of the supervision process.

### The discrimination model

The discrimination model (Bernard and Goodyear 1998) is another example of a social role supervision model. It purports to be 'a-theoretical', and focuses instead on the supervisor who has three roles: teacher, counsellor and consultant and for each of these can adopt three different types (foci) of supervision:

- intervention, where the supervisor concentrates on the supervisee's intervention skills;
- conceptualization, that is, how the supervisee understands what is occurring in the session;
- personalization, or how the supervisee adopts a style of approach which is uncontaminated by personal issues and counter-transference responses.

For example, in the role of teacher, the supervisor might adopt an intervention focus that didactically teaches the supervisee a therapeutic technique. Again as a teacher, but this time adopting a conceptualization role, the supervisor might use transcripts of sessions to help the supervisee to identify themes within the client's statements. In the role of counsellor, and adopting a focus of intervention, the supervisor might help the supervisee to identify how the client is impacting on them and undermining their ability to use their skills in therapy sessions.

It is called a discrimination model, precisely because it requires the supervisor to tailor their responses to the supervisee based on their individual needs. It is also a social model because it requires the supervisor to tailor their intervention, depending on the situation they face. Hence, at any one moment, the supervisor might be responding in any one of nine ways (three roles multiplied by three foci). As in other models, there is a recognition that for novice supervisees, there may be more of a focus on the teaching role of the supervisor. For more advanced supervisees, greater emphasis is placed on the consultant role, or a balance across all roles. Implicit, then, is the acceptance that supervisees do pass through developmental stages.

## Towards a meta-model of coaching supervision

Although the models of counselling and psychotherapeutic supervision just described illustrate a range of debates and arguments, a number of themes (for coaching supervision) appear most relevant:

- Supervision involves facilitating the development of the supervisee in terms of confidence, motivation and knowledge.
- The relationship is complex and includes paying attention to what is happening both between the supervisor and supervisee and the supervisee's relationship with their client.
- The supervisee's development is not necessarily linear and can involve progressing at varying speeds for different functions and processes. It can also include regression (for example, in confidence).

- Teaching (or more accurately, learning) is at the heart of the relationship, both for the supervisee but also for the supervisor.
- The supervisor/supervisee relationship is influenced by social and organizational contexts within which it occurs.

As Carroll (2006) warns, supervising coaches is not the same as supervising counsellors, in part, because coaches are often working in and for organizations, and it is the organization that sets the coaching agenda, particularly if they are sponsoring the coaching intervention. The role of the supervisor becomes one of handling the tensions between the coach, the coachee and their organization (Paisley, cited in Carroll 2006) and coping with complex dynamics such as maintaining professional boundaries, managing contracts and being aware of the needs and responsibilities of each player (Carroll 2006). Towler calls the organization the 'invisible client' (2005: 309), which imposes unconscious influences in the supervision room. The supervisors of coaches, therefore, need to add the systemic and cultural aspects of organizations to their knowledge sets, as well as their understanding of an individual's perspectives. The influences of organizational culture become a significant rather than an incidental factor in the process of supervision (Towler 2005).

Figure 1.1, then, offers a systemic model of coaching supervision that highlights some of the elements necessary within a supervisor–supervisee relationship (contracting, the relationship itself, teaching and evaluation) but one which is bounded

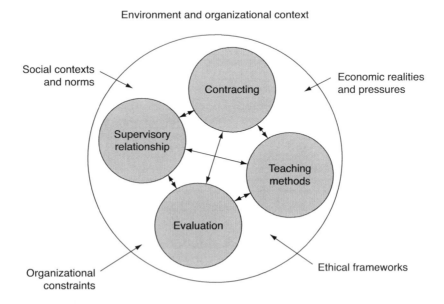

**Figure 1.1**  A systemic model of coaching supervision

within organizational and social contexts, and within ethical norms. What follows is offered in the spirit of discussion, rather than as a definitive model.

## Contracting

Supervision starts with defining and structuring the supervisor–coach relationship. This, then, is the entry point to the systemic model. Applying the work of Ronnestad and Skovholt (1993) to coaching, contracts can serve to identify and clarify:

- the supervisee's (coach's) developmental needs including their education and work experience;
- the supervisor's competencies, making these explicit in terms of their professional skills and experience (including knowledge of organizational behaviour);
- opportunities (and limitations) provided by work settings so that goals set are practical and realistic;
- supervisory goals, methods and focus which are made explicit.

It is important that both supervisor and coach explore each other's expectations to see if they match. It there is a mismatch, these differences must be explored and negotiated.

The contract should deal with the expectations and needs of third parties such as the client or their sponsoring organization (Copeland 1998; Hawkins and Shohet 2000). It is essential that the boundaries between operational and any clinical issues that arise are described (Towler 2005). Organizations may have their own policies on supervision, but even if they do not, they are likely to have clear expectations about the quality of the work. As Copeland (2006) also warns, the culture and values of supervisors and the organizations in which they operate, may often be diametrically opposed.

Whatever the supervision approach, ground rules need to be established. Hawkins and Shohet (2000) suggest that these include the frequency, duration and timing of the supervisory sessions. Boundary issues should also be made explicit, including the essential issue of confidentiality. They warn, however, that confidentiality is easier to promise than always keep. When reporting on the progress of a coaching intervention, for example, supervisors (and coaches) will have to take care in defending the anonymity of individual coachees. Some organizations, of course, may insist that individuals (for example those who are under-performing) are named. The degree of anonymity, then, needs defining explicitly in the contract. Counsellors, psychotherapists and others then have a choice of whether to take part in such a programme or withdraw due to ethical reservations.

## The supervisory relationship

According to Bernard and Goodyear a supervisory relationship is 'a product of the uniqueness of two individuals, paired with the purposes of meeting for supervision and modified by the demands of the various contexts that are the subject or content of the experience' (1998: 34). This complex, unique, yet evolving relation-ship, is, of course, influenced and shaped by many internal and external factors and processes. One is the self-presentation of the coach, that is, their behaviours, confidence (or anxiety) and expectations. Belief systems, theoretical orientation and cultural differences (including both racial and gender differences) are all likely to play a significant role in the relationship. In each of those areas benefits such as ease of communication must be weighed against the risk of reduced challenge (or to put it another way, the pros and cons of diversity weighed against the pros and cons of homogeneity).

A more pluralistic approach may go some way to overcoming this, particularly in the way in which supervisors may be prepared to critically challenge the orthodoxy of a model. In general, however, Feltham and Dryden (1994) warn that a pluralistic model is probably more suited to those at the 'journey person' or 'master craft person' stages of development than to those who are still trying to consolidate their understanding.

## Teaching methods

We have seen that direct teaching or instruction does not play a particularly prominent role in the psychotherapeutic models described earlier. Nevertheless, there may be times when a supervisor wishes (or needs) to pass on skills, knowl-edge or ideas in a fairly didactic way. There may, however, be different ways of approaching this.

### Instruction

During the early stages of supervision, the supervisor may need to provide direct instruction to the coach, especially in terms of building their skills. Bernard and Goodyear (1998) outline four steps in what they call microtraining: teach one skill at a time; present the skill; practise the skill (e.g. through role play); allow for mastery. Sometimes, the supervisor may even recommend books or other reading matter (Carroll 1996).

### Promoting reflection

Reflection may be focused on either of the interlocking systems referred to earl-ier, that is, attention can be directed and encouraged by the supervisor towards the coach's reflections on their own actions, thoughts and emotions and second towards the interaction between the supervisor and coach themselves. In so do-ing, not only is the content of practice understood better, but the 'capability of reflection' is also developed (Jackson 2004: 63). Indeed, one of the functions of supervision is to teach them *how* to reflect (Armstrong and Geddes 2009) and for many coaches, supervision is the only place where they can reflect on and dis-cuss their coaching experiences. The reflective process needs to avoid defensive self-protection and look to changing perceptions and practice, and the capability to make meaning out of experience. Hawkins and Shohet (2000) recommend that this self-reflection can be used to identify the strengths and weaknesses of the current support system, decide whether the contract with the supervisor requires some renegotiation, or whether alternative forms of supervision (such as peer supervision) needs to be arranged.

Taking the systemic perspective, it is also important to stand back and to reflect on the dynamics occurring within the supervision process itself, particularly in relation to whether it is fulfilling personal needs and goals. Such reflectivity may improve the supervisee's work with their clients as well as their overall professional judgement (Neufeldt et al. 1996). This reflective process is triggered by causal conditions, often the supervisee's feelings of uncertainty, dilemma or surprise. Before moving towards understanding phenomena, intervening conditions mediate between the problem and reflective processes. These include the cognitive capabilities of the supervisee (some will be more capable of reflection than others) and the organizational environment.

## Modelling

Modelling involves the coach observing the supervisor engaged in the process of professional practice, and can provide a useful means of demystifying the process and providing the individual with a template for their own work (Stoltenberg 1993). As Ronnestad and Skovholt (1993) point out, one of the hazards of modelling is that even experienced supervisors may demonstrate inappropriate model characteristics. Senior practitioners, for example, may tend to operate from their own expert experience base, while novice practitioners under supervision may prefer a more structured, simple and step-by-step modelled procedure. So, supervisors may need to reflect on (or discuss through their own supervision), what kinds of modelling behaviours they are going to demonstrate, and how.

## Feedback

Feedback is part of the coach's learning process because it comprises an evaluative quality or judgement by the supervisor. For the coach to learn from feedback it must be clear, concise and honest. This may sometimes mean that the feedback is critical and even confrontational. When provided in an organizational context, feedback might include a focus on how the coach is dealing with organizational objectives and needs during the coaching process. It may be prudent to prepare coaches at an early stage by indicating in the contract that feedback of this kind may occur. Feedback is also a form of evaluation. So not only may evaluation influence the coach's choice of teaching interventions, it may even trigger a recontracting process.

## Evaluation

According to Gray (2004), coaching should be evaluated, because it allows us a critical window into professional practice. It also allows us to develop self-knowledge, and the opportunity to identify how personal interactions, processes and outcomes can be improved. But if evaluation is appropriate for coaching, then it must be equally valid for the supervision of coaching. According to Loganbill et al. (1982), evaluation is the final function of the supervision process, but one that may suffer from a tension with the goal of other functions such as promoting the development of the supervisee. One approach might be to ignore or deny this judgemental element of evaluation. A better approach, however, would be to encourage an ongoing dialogue involving the effects of evaluation upon the supervisor–supervisee relationship. Indeed, as Hawkins and Shohet (2000) argue, evaluation should be a two-way process and needs to be scheduled into the arrangements for supervision.

A first, and obvious, question, however, is: what should be evaluated? Bordin (1983) suggests that this will be determined by the specific goals identified at the beginning of the supervisor–trainee relationship. Feltham and Dryden (1994) suggest three key areas for evaluation. The first is how the supervisee is progressing. Feedback on performance may be important to inexperienced supervisees who are anxious to know if they are attaining an appropriate standard. Supervisors may wish to provide feedback on both their perceived strengths and weaknesses. A second evaluation theme is: 'how are we getting on?' with a focus on the supervisory alliance itself. This may include an evaluation of the original contract to see if it still holds. The third theme is to identify and discuss some of the recurring concerns that have emerged during the supervision process, such as the supervisee's lack of challenge to the client when necessary. It is also important that trainees evaluate some of their less successful interventions (Brown 1985). If supervision is taking place in a work-based context, then an important focus of evaluation will have to be whether the organization's objectives have been fulfilled and the problems that were encountered in meeting them.

### Ethical issues

As Figure 1.1 shows, all the systemic elements within supervision are bounded by ethical framework and constraints. While there may be a congruence between the ethical codes of each supervisor and coach, complications may arise when they come from different professional backgrounds, or adopt the standards of different professional associations. This issue is discussed in more depth in Chapter 7 of this volume.

## Conclusion

We have seen, then, that many of the developmental models of supervision, drawn from psychotherapy and counselling, have been largely superseded by alternative and somewhat more socially rooted approaches. What most of these models have in common, however, is at least some notion of progress, development and change on the part of the supervisee – whether this takes place through distinct, sequential stages or not. For the supervision process to succeed, it needs to commence with a clearly defined set of principles in the form of a contract. This is the bedrock of the supervisor–supervisee relationship and should define the expected outcomes, process and methodology that is going to be used. Even how the contract can be modified to meet changing circumstances should be described.

The nature of the supervisor–supervisee relationship within coaching, however, is much harder to define, particularly if each party is working from different theoretical models. This may occur when the supervisee is, for example, an evidence-based business coach, while the supervisor is professionally trained as a psychotherapist. They may exhibit different cognitive styles, belief systems and differences in ethical perspectives. Both parties, then, need to be sensitive to their potential similarities, but seek to work to resolve any differences. How they do this, of course, could be specified in the contract. The relationship between the supervisor and supervisee will involve one or several approaches to teaching, ranging from didactic instruction (probably not a common occurrence) to collective reflection, modelling and feedback. All elements will be subject to evaluation (including the evaluation process itself).

As noted in the introductory paragraphs of this chapter, this material is included in the present volume because of the opportunity it affords to all students, whether coaches or supervisors, whether currently on a formal educational programme or not, to assess and integrate models and theories described in other chapters. Students (thus defined) will find different models and theories concentrating on different aspects of the meta-model presented here. This may be a conscious and overt choice on the part of the originators; it may be implicit in the model rather than explicit; or it may be a blind spot. As the reader engages with each, the meta-model suggests holding the following questions in mind:

- Is it more useful to be more consistent in approach, or more flexible?
- What function/concern/focus is most effectively dealt with by a particular model or theory? What is not dealt with?
- How could this model or theory help me to develop?

## Note

1  In this discussion we have generally used the term 'trainee' to reflect the assumptions and usages in the original sources. In the modern coaching context we see supervision as part of ongoing professional development.

## References

Armstrong, H. and Geddes, M. (2009) Developing coaching supervision practice: an Australian case study, *International Journal of Evidence Based Coaching and Mentoring*, 7(2): 1–17.

Bernard, J.M. and Goodyear, R.K. (1998) *Fundamentals of Clinical Supervision*, 2nd edn. Needham Heights, MA: Allyn & Bacon.

Bordin, E.S. (1983) A working alliance based model of supervision, *The Counseling Psychologist*, 11: 35–41.

Brown, D. (1985) The preservice training and supervision of consultants, *The Counseling Psychologist*, 13(3): 410–25.

Carroll, M. (1996) *Counselling Supervision: Theory, Skills and Practice*. London: Cassell.

Carroll, M. (2006) Supervising executive coaches, *Therapy Today*, 17(5): 47–9.

Chagnon, J. and Russell, R.K. (1995) Assessment of supervisee developmental level and supervision environment across supervisor experience, *Journal of Counseling & Development*, May/June, 73: 553–8.

Copeland, S. (1998) Counselling supervision in organisational contexts, *British Journal of Guidance & Counselling*, 26(3): 377–86.

Copeland, S. (2006) Counselling supervision in organisations: are you ready to expand your horizons? *Counselling at Work*, 51: 2–4.

Feltham, C. and Dryden, W. (1994) *Developing Counsellor Supervision*. London: Sage.

Gray, D.E. (2004) Principles and processes in coaching evaluation, *International Journal of Mentoring and Coaching*, 2(2): online.

Gray, D.E. (2007) Towards a systemic model of coaching supervision – some lessons from psychotherapeutic and counselling models, *Australian Psychologist*, 42(4): 300–9.

Hawkins, P. and Shohet, R. (2000) *Supervision in the Helping Professions*, 2nd edn. Buckingham: Open University Press.

Hess, A.K. (1986) Growth of supervision: stages of supervisee and supervisor development, *The Clinical Supervisor*, 4: 51–67.

Hogan, R.A. (1964) Issues and approaches in supervision, *Psychotherapy, Theory, Research & Practice*, 1: 139–41.

Holloway, E.L. (1987) Developmental models of supervision: is it development?, *Professional Psychology: Research and Practice*, 18(3): 209–16.

Jackson, P. (2004) Understanding the experience of experience: a practical model of reflective practice for coaching, *The International Journal of Evidence Based Coaching and Mentoring*, 2(1): 57–67.

Loganbill, C., Hardy, E. and Delworth, U. (1982) Supervision: a conceptual model, *The Counseling Psycholgist*, 10: 3–42.

Neufeldt, S.A., Karno, M.P. and Nelson, M.L. (1996) A qualitative study of experts' conceptualization of supervisee reflectivity, *Journal of Counseling Psychology*, 43(1): 3–9.

Ronnestad, M.H. and Skovholt, T.M. (1993) Supervision of beginning and advanced graduate students of counseling and psychotherapy, *Journal of Counseling & Development*, March/April, 71: 396–405.

Stoltenberg, C.D. (1981) Approaching supervision from a developmental perspective: the counselor complexity model, *Journal of Counseling Psychology*, 28: 59–65.

Stoltenberg, C.D. (1993) Supervising consultants in training: an application of a model of supervision, *Journal of Counseling and Development*, November/December, 72: 131–8.

Stoltenberg, C.D. and Delworth, U. (1987) *Supervising Counselors and Therapists*. San Francisco, CA: Jossey-Bass.

Towler, J. (2005) A grounded theory study of organisational supervision of counsellors: The influence of the invisible client. Unpublished PhD thesis, University of Surrey.

Turner, E. (2010) Coaches' views on the relevance of unconscious dynamics to executive coaching, *Coaching: An International Journal of Theory, Research and Practice*, 3(1): 12–29.

Whybrow, A. and Palmer, S. (2006) Taking stock: a survey of coaching psychologists' practices and perspectives, *International Coaching Psychology Review*, 1(1): 56–70.

# 2 The seven-eyed model of coaching supervision

*Peter Hawkins and Gil Schwenk*

## Introduction

The purpose of this chapter is to introduce the seven-eyed model of coaching supervision which is probably the longest established and most widely used coaching supervision model. We will describe the history of the model, consider the key elements and provide a case illustration of the model in action. We will continue by defining the roles and responsibilities of the supervisor and potential pitfalls when this model is used.

The origins of the model date back to the mid-1980s when Peter Hawkins created a systemic and integrative model of supervision (Hawkins 1985), which later was developed along with his colleagues, Joan Wilmot and Judy Ryde and particularly Robin Shohet at the Centre for Supervision and Team Development and became known as the seven-eyed supervision model (Hawkins and Shohet 1989). This has been used across many different people professions in many countries in the world (Hawkins and Shohet 1989, 2nd edition 2000, 3rd edition 2006 and translated into Greek, Swedish, Czech, Chinese and German). Since 1995, with his colleagues at Bath Consultancy Group, he has further developed the model for the world of coaching, mentoring, team coaching and organizational consultancy (Hawkins 1995; 2006, 2010, 2011a, 2011b; Hawkins and Schwenk 2006, 2010; Hawkins and Smith 2006).

The model was developed to include all the different aspects that can be focused on in supervision and the range of supervisory styles and skills needed for each area of focus. It is based on a systems understanding of the ways things connect, interrelate and drive behaviour (see Chapter 13). It integrates insights and aspects of inter-subjective psychotherapy (Stolorow and Atwood 1984, 1992) focusing on the interrelationship between the internal and relational life of individuals.

The model points out the way in which the systemic context of the coachee can be mirrored in the coaching relationship and how the dynamics of the coaching relationship can be mirrored in the supervisory relationship. These seven areas of potential focus can be useful to both supervisor and supervisee in reviewing the supervision that they give and receive and can help them discover ways they can expand their supervision practice. The seven foci, which are commonly referred to as seven eyes or seven modes, are numbered 1–7 for the ease of reference and learning.

## The seven-eyed model of supervision

> While Socrates' contemporary, Protagoras, declares at this time, 'Man is the measure of all things', the exciting, the difficult, the inconvenient truth of Socrates' philosophy is its plangent suggestion that 'man's relationship with man' and 'man's relationship with the world around him' is the measure of all things.
>
> Bettany Hughes 2010: 164

### Contracting

Before exploring the seven modes in a supervision session, it is critically important to develop a mutual contract for both the supervisory relationship in general as well as each specific session. At the beginning of each supervisory conversation it is essential to clarify the reasons that the coach is bringing this client situation to supervision and what the coach wants as the outcome. This helps the supervisor anchor the session to the coachee's expectation so that it is in service to the coachee and their context. Typical questions include:

- We will be thinking about your coaching situation in detail in a few minutes. As we get started, what is it about this coachee/coaching relationship that is motivating you to bring him/her to supervision today?
- What is the outcome that you would like from focusing on this client/client relationship?
- What would be the benefit of this outcome for you, the coachee, their organization, and their wider systemic context?

It is important to summarize your understanding and get confirmation of the purpose and desired outcomes prior to progressing with the seven modes. This is far more than just agreeing the logistic details of the session. From our experience of supervising and training hundreds of supervisors, the supervision starts from the moment that the coach and supervisor come together. It is important to listen carefully to the contracting since it will illuminate the coachee's perspective and aspects of the coach–client relationship. It is especially important to listen for the verbal and non-verbal expressions and metaphors that the coach uses since they are all important clues to guide the supervisory conversation. The contracting can also clarify which modes might be most important for this particular supervision.

### Seven modes of supervision

The seven-eyed model reinforces the interpersonal aspect of coaching and supervision since it is based on two complimentary systems. As indicated in the Figure 2.1, the first relationship is the coach–client system and the second, the

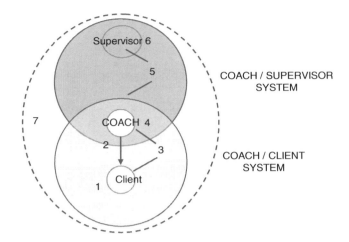

**Figure 2.1** Seven modes of supervision

coach–supervisor system. Each of these relational systems are nested in a wider organizational and systemic context, including the organizations that all three parties work for, the stakeholders of those organizations and the professional and/or training bodies that the coach and supervisor may belong to. We set out in more detail the seven modes for the supervisor and supervisee below.

### Mode 1: the coachee and their context

As described above, we have two interrelated systems in the supervisory room but an important part of the coach–client is not actually present – the coaching client! In order to work in service to the coaching client and their organizational context, we refer to mode 1 as 'getting the client(s) into the room'. The way we understand the 'client' is important here as it distinguishes executive coaching from other person-centred approaches. For us there is always a minimum of three clients – namely the coachee, their organization and the relationship between the two. All of these need to be attended to in mode 1.

The objective of mode 1 is to refresh the coach's awareness of the clients so that we are able to metaphorically create a 'hologram' of the coachee and their organizational context in the supervisory room. We want to develop a 'felt' understanding of the coachee and the client organization and how they are presenting and framing the issues.

The supervisor's skill in this mode is to help the coach accurately return to what actually happened in the session with the coachee – what they saw, what they heard and what they felt – and to try and separate this actual data from their preconceptions, assumptions and interpretations. It is also useful for the coach to be helped to attend to what happened at the boundaries of their time with the coachee, their arrival and exit, for it is often at the boundaries that the richest unconscious material is most apparent.

Typical mode 1 interventions include:

- Think back to the last session with this client and revisit what happened just before the session fully got underway.
- What did the client look and sound like as they came into the session?
- How did the session start?
- Describe this client. What comes to mind when you think of him/her?
- How did the coachee present him/herself during the session? Become the client and show me how they were.
- What did you see, hear and feel during the session?
- What is the coaching contract with this client? What are they and their organization wanting to achieve from the coaching?

## Mode 2: the coach's interventions

Mode 2 looks at how the coach works with the coachee, how they work through each stage of the coaching process and the interventions the coach made, including alternative choices that might have been used. It might also focus on a situation in which the coach is about to intervene, exploring the possible options and the likely impact of each. Often mode 2 will be initiated by the coach raising a dilemma or impasse that they have arrived at in the coaching process. They will often present this impasse in the form of an 'either-or' dilemma such as: 'Should I confront the issue or should I let it go?'

The skill of the supervisor is to avoid the trap of debating the either/or options, and instead to enable the coach to realize how they are limiting their choice to two polarized possibilities and facilitate a shared brainstorming that frees up the energy and creates new options. Then the benefits and difficulties of these options can be explored and some possible interventions tried out in a 'fast forward rehearsal' (Hawkins and Smith 2010).

Mode 2 interventions by the supervisor might include:

- You seem to have a dilemma here! On one hand, you want to x whilst on the other hand you want to y.
- What is the interest or intent behind both parts of the dilemma? What could you do that would enable both interests/intents to be honoured?
- What is the wildest intervention you could use?
- Who else do you know who would handle this well? What would they do?

## Mode 3: the relationship between the coach and the coachee

The focus of mode 3 is the relationship that the coach and the coachee are co-creating together. It is here that the relational aspect of supervision first comes to the fore by moving the focus from (1) the coachee and their world, and (2) the activity of the coach, to attending to both the conscious and unconscious relational field in the coaching (see Hawkins and Schwenk 2010).

The supervisor has to facilitate the coach in standing outside the relationship that they are part of so that they can see and experience it afresh, from a new angle. The Chinese have a proverb that the last one to know about the sea is the fish, because they are constantly immersed within it. In this mode the supervisor is helping the coach to be a flying fish, so they can see the 'relational water' in which they are normally swimming.

In mode 3, we want to have the coach reflect on the relationship with the coachee. This can be both logical descriptors and more spontaneous descriptors that tap into the unconscious. We might ask:

- If you were a fly on the wall, how would you describe your relationship with this client?
- What other relationship does this remind you of?
- If you and this client were marooned on a desert island, what would happen?
- If this relationship was a colour, a piece of music, a type of weather, a country, etc., what would it be?

To a great extent, the answer to these questions is an indicator of what is probably already happening in the relationship. If a coach answers the question about being marooned on an island by saying they would set up separate camps at either end, there may be distancing and unexpressed opposition in the relationship that can now be opened up and explored. If on the other hand, the coach says that they would enjoy sitting around the fire talking until all hours, there may be a cosiness which can be inquired into.

Mode 3 can parallel the relationships that key contacts have with the coachee. For example, one coach recently answered the question about the nature of the dance between her and the coachee by saying 'I (the coach) am standing on the side applauding the coachee whilst feeling a bit useless.' As we subsequently explored the coachee context a bit further, it was evident that she was a very competent individual performer who was appreciated for her ability to get things done in the organization. However, there were concerns about how she worked largely independently and there were some concerns about her ability to work effectively with others. Her contact with others colleagues often resulted in conflict situations. In this way, we often want to observe the pattern that the coach has become part of, as an indicator of how others might be relating to the coachee. It is important to pay attention to this easily overlooked aspect of mode 3.

These mode 3 questions can also be used to achieve a better understanding of the coachee's relationships. The supervisor could use similar questions to understand the relationships with key individuals in the coachee's relational web. So, if the focus of the coaching is about the relationship of the coachee and their manager, the supervisor could ask:

- From what you have heard and understand from the client, what does their relationship with their manager remind you of?

- From what you have heard and understand from the client, if the coachee and their manager were marooned on a desert island, what would happen?

## Mode 4: the coach's awareness

In mode 4, the focus is on the coach's self-awareness. We want to enable the coach to notice what is being re-stimulated in them by the coachee's material, and to use themselves as an instrument for registering what is happening beneath the surface of the coaching system.

In this mode the supervisor helps the coach to work through any re-stimulation of their own feelings that have been triggered by the work with this client. Having done this, the coach can be helped to explore how these feelings may relate to what the coachee is experiencing but is unable to articulate directly. The coach also explores how their own blocks may be preventing them from facilitating the coachee and their system to change.

Questions in this mode could be:

- What are you experiencing in your body as we discuss this client?
- What emotions or thoughts do you have?
- Who do they remind you of?
- When have you been in a similar relationship dynamic? What did you need to say in that situation, which may give you a clue to what needs expressing here?

## Mode 5: The supervisory relationship

In mode 5 we focus on what is happening in the relational field between the coach and the supervisor. In this mode, we notice the 'us-ness' of the relationship that has been co-created as we discuss this coaching scenario.

We can use similar questions to the ones that we use in mode 3. Alternatively, we can simply ask, 'what do we notice about how this (supervisor–coach relationship) is similar or different to the coach–coachee relationship?' We can also pick up on a specific characteristic of any dynamic that has come into awareness. For example, if we had noticed that the coachee was responding to his manager or colleagues as a compliant-resistant child, we could explore how this is being played out in the ego states of parent, adult or child transaction of the supervisor–coach relationship (Berne 1964).

Frequently, this will highlight similarities between the supervisor–coach relationship that replicate (or sometimes replicate by opposing) the relationship between the coach and the client. This 'parallel process' includes both the conscious aspects (which include the feelings) of how they are relating as well as the unconscious feelings and ways of relating that have been absorbed from the coachee system (Hawkins and Shohet 2006; Hawkins and Smith 2006). The coach can therefore unwarily treat the supervisor in the same way that their coachee treated them or, indeed, demonstrate the way in which the coachee engaged them, by engaging the supervisor in the same way.

Having acquired this skill, the supervisor can then, at times, offer their tentative reflections on the impact of the presented material on the supervisory relationship to illuminate the coaching dynamic. When done skilfully this process can help the coach bridge the gap between their conscious understanding of the coaching relationship and the emotional impact it has had upon them.

In mode 5 a supervisor might say:

- When you discuss this client we become very argumentative and both our voices speed up and get louder – and I wonder whether this reflects something about the coaching relationship.
- I am wondering how 'that dynamic' (whatever has been noticed) is happening between us. How are we 'xing' in this relationship?' e.g. 'So, we've noticed that the coachee constantly defers to you, the manager and others, I'm wondering how we are deferring in this relationship here and now and what deference is occurring here.

### Mode 6: The supervisor self-reflection

The focus for mode 6 is the supervisor's 'here and now' experience while with the coach and what can be learned about the coach/coachee relationship from the supervisor's response to the coach and the material they present.

In this mode the supervisor has to attend not only to presented material and its impact on the 'here and now' relationship, but also their own internal process. The supervisor can discover the presence of unconscious material related to the coaching relationship by attending to their own feelings, thoughts and fantasies while listening to the presentation of the coaching situation.

It is important for the supervisor to learn to avoid self-censorship but to speak their 'here and now' awareness out loud in a non-judgemental and non-interpretative way. If the supervisor can muse and tentatively speak their awareness out loud, it may help the coach to reflect upon and spark further inquiry and dialogue. For example, the supervisor might say:

- I am aware that my heart is beating faster as I hear you telling this and I am feeling quite agitated by the situation.
- I feel sad and empty as I listen to this.

One of us was supervising a coach and every time they talked about a specific client, found it very difficult to keep their eyes open and stay awake. At first they felt guilty and embarrassed by this phenomenon and even tried changing the time of these supervision sessions in the hope that not having them straight after lunch would improve their capacity to be attentive! After several sessions and exploring this in their own supervision, they plucked up the courage to mention that every time this client was mentioned they could not keep their eyes open and wondered why this was. The coach replied with: 'It is funny you should say that, but that is exactly what happens to me when I am with this client but I was too embarrassed to mention it!' Not only had the sleepiness been somatically transferred, but the embarrassment and self-blame had also been parallelled. Following this the coach was able to confront what was happening in the coaching relationship, unearth deep patterns of passive aggression and help the coachee express their issues far more directly.

## Mode 7: The wider context

The focus of mode 7 is on the organizational, social, cultural, ethical and contractual context in which the coaching and supervision is taking place. This includes being aware of the wider context of the client organization and its stakeholders, the coach's organization and its stakeholders and the supervisor and their organizational and professional context. It also includes the power and cultural dynamics that lie within the various relationships. One of the purposes of mode 7 is to develop the coach's understanding of the coachee's organizational context in order to illuminate the shift that the coachee may need to make a sustainable impact on their wider system.

Mode 7 also includes an attention to the wider systemic context of the supervisory relationship (see Chapter 13) which includes the organizations that both the supervisee and supervisor work for and their ambitions and expectations, as well as the professional context and organizations that both parties belong to. The developmental context of the supervisee is also an important aspect of the context that needs attention. They may still be in professional training or seeking accreditation or a thought leader in the field.

The supervisor has to be able to bring a whole system's perspective to understand how the systemic context of the work being presented is affecting not only the behaviour, mindsets, emotional ground and motivations of the coach and coachee, but also themselves. The skill is to attend appropriately to the needs of the critical stakeholders in the wider systems, and also to understand how the culture of the systemic context might be creating illusions, delusions and collusions in the coach and in oneself. Attention to mode 7 also requires a high level of transcultural competence (Hawkins and Shohet 2006; Hawkins and Smith 2006) and awareness of one's own cultural assumptions and prejudices (Ryde 2009).

Some mode 7 inquiries might include:

- What have you learned from the client about the values and assumptions operating in the organization? How is this demonstrated in the relationship between coachee and the manager/peer/customer, etc.?
- How is conflict handled in the organization and by this particular coachee?
- Who are the main stakeholders that you heard about in the sessions? How would you describe the coachee's relationship with each?

- How are these stakeholders connected?
- How are wider political, economic and social pressures being enacted in the relationships you are working with?
- What is the shift needed in the wider system for it to fulfil its purpose, and what shift needs to happen in the coachee to better serve that purpose?

## Roles and responsibilities of the supervisor

To be a competent practitioner of the seven-eyed model, it is important to develop a deep understanding of it through reading and experiential learning. However, practice with specific and detailed feedback is the most important aspect to develop competence and confidence. In training coaching supervisors in the seven-eyed model we make extensive use of practice trios so that the supervisor is able to get feedback from both the supervisee and the observer. We also find that video is an excellent tool to enable the supervisor to see how they are working and make adjustments in style and approach.

We constantly learn from each cohort of new trainees about the fascinating craft of supervising coaches and the lifelong journey to develop this craft. Increasingly we are reminded that at the heart of being a good coach or a good coaching supervisor is not only academic knowledge of theories and models, or an armoury of tools and techniques, but a constant dedication to developing one's human capacity to be fully present for another, acting with what we term 'ruthless compassion'. For it is the ruthless compassion we can bring, not only for our client, but also the work they do in the world and for our craft, that ultimately allows the fear and anxiety that pervades so many work situations to be overcome, and for our clients to find new strength to act courageously.

## Case illustration

Each mode of supervision can be carried out in a skilful and elegant manner or ineffectively, but no matter how skilful one is, a single mode will prove inadequate without the skill to move from one to another. A typical supervision session does not normally follow a chronological progress from mode 1 to mode 7. Rather the conversation progresses from mode to mode based on the flow of the coach or as facilitated by the supervisor towards modes that may be beneficial in helping the coach to gain a 'super vision' of the coaching relationship and the choices that are available to them to better facilitate the coachee.

Table 2.1 indicates the most common way of moving through the modes with some example questions and interventions that could be used for each mode.

**Table 2.1** Examples of moving through different modes

| Mode | Typical questions or interventions |
| --- | --- |
| Contracting for the session | • What is important about this client situation that motivates you to focus on it today?<br>• What do you want to get from reflecting on this situation? |
| Mode 1: Get the client into the room | • In your mind's eye, replay the first five minutes of the first time that you met this client, what do you notice?<br>• What comes to mind as you think of this client? |
| Often this will lead to mode 3: The coach–client relationship. | • How would you describe the dance that is happening between the two of you?<br>• If you and this client were going to a fancy dress party in some way that symbolizes the coaching relationship, what/who would you both be? How would you both appear? |
| This may be a good time to check how this lands with the coach using mode 4. | • Invite the coach to notice what is happening for them right now. What is the body reaction, how are they feeling, what metaphors or comparators are used? |
| Now the conversation could move into several modes. It might stimulate some awareness in you as the supervisor – mode 6. | • I feel overwhelmed as I hear how much this client is facing right now.<br>• I'm struck by the relative levels of confidence. It sounds like you are 'adoring' the client. |
| Often mode 6 is a door into mode 5: the supervisor–coach relationship. | • I wonder if 'adoring' is happening between us? How is this similar or different than the coaching relationship?<br>• What insights does this give about the coaching relationship? |
| At any point, the conversation may highlight a dilemma that the coach is facing. This flags mode 2: the coach's interventions. | • What are the choices or options going through your head regarding this dilemma?<br>• What is the interest or intent behind both parts of the dilemma? What could you do that would enable both interests/intent to be honoured? |
| At any point, the conversation may flag some aspect of the wider system or stakeholders which is an opportunity to explore mode 7: the wider system. | • What do you know about the client's stakeholders? How might they view this situation?<br>• From what you know about the way things get done in this organization, what would be a culturally acceptable approach? What would be a shift that the culture would tolerate? |

**Table 2.1**  (*Continued*)

| Mode | Typical questions or interventions |
|---|---|
| Typically, a supervision session finishes by returning to mode 2 to clarify and anchor the coach's next interventions with the coaching client. | • Given our exploration today, what is the shift that your client needs to make that will positively impact their wider system?<br>• What is the shift that you need to make in working with this client?<br>• Typically, this is an opportunity to do a fast-forward rehearsal of the desired state, behaviour and words. |
| Review the contract for the session. | • At the beginning of this time, you said that you wanted to (1, 2, 3). To what extent have you achieved this?<br>• How confident are you in implementing this insight with the client? |

Whilst this is a 'typical' flow, supervision, like coaching, is co-created by the participants in the conversation. The conversation will go 'where it needs to' and where either the supervisor (or coach) subtly facilitate movement from mode to mode.

## Evaluation of the model

Having worked with this model over many years we find that it stands the test of time. Because it is more about a *way* of looking than *what* to understand about the work, new models develop but they seem compatible with this model. In the same way we find that those with very different theoretical approaches can relate to this model and therefore coaches from different schools of coaching can learn together in training using the seven modes. The dialogue between them can be instructive as well and decreases rigid and limiting mindsets. The philosophy behind it is inquiring and dialogic and encourages this attitude between individuals from very different schools and approaches. Although it would be easy to place this approach within systems theory, we have found that it also is understood well within other, quite disparate, approaches such as psychoanalytic and cognitive behavioural.

We find that many supervisors vastly improve their practice if they extend their capability to include all seven of the modes. In fact we have discovered that different supervisors are often stuck in the groove of predominantly using one of the seven modes of working. Some focus entirely on the situation 'out there' with the coachee and adopt a pose of pseudo objectivity (mode 1). Others see their job as to come up with better interventions than the coach managed to produce (mode 2). This can often leave the coach feeling inadequate or determined to show that these suggested interventions are as useless as the ones they had previously tried. Other coaches have reported taking a problem with a coachee and having left supervision feeling that the problem was entirely their pathology (mode 4).

'Single-eyed vision', which focuses only on one aspect of the process, will always lead to partial and limited perspectives. This model suggests a way of engaging in an exploration that looks at the same situation from many different perspectives and can thus create a critical subjectivity, where subjective awareness from one perspective is tested against subjective data from other perspectives or modes.

As the model encourages an open, inquiring attitude, it is very effective in empowering the coach, who is, after all, our customer as supervisors. Through the use of the model they are better able to give feedback on the help they are being given and request a change of focus. An openness to hearing this feedback can model a similar openness in the coach with their coachee. It can thus be used as a framework for a joint review of the supervision process in which the coach and supervisor reflect together on which modes they have most focused on and to which they might need to pay more attention.

There is a danger that the sequence of the modes introduced in the case illustration can by taken literally by some supervisors and they will use the model too mechanically as opposed to when the supervisory dialogue requires them. We hope that this chapter will be used as a good resource preventing supervisors from falling into this trap.

## Learning more

It is important that supervision is not seen as an activity carried out by a supervisor, supposedly with 'super-vision'! Rather it should be seen as a joint activity between coach and supervisor that ensures that the quality of practice constantly develops the capacity and capability of the coach and makes sure they are adequately resourcing themselves for the work they undertake.

For additional information about the seven-eyed model, the key book that focuses specifically on coaching supervision is:

Hawkins, P. and Smith, N. (2006) *Coaching, Mentoring and Organizational Consultancy: Supervision and Development*. Maidenhead: MacGraw-Hill/Open University Press.

For additional information about the broader use of the seven-eyed model, see

Hawkins, P. and Shohet, R. (2006) *Supervision in the Helping Professions*, 3rd edn. Maidenhead: Open University Press.

# References

Berne, E. (1964) *Games People Play*. New York: Grove.

Hawkins, P. (1985) Humanistic psychotherapy supervision. A conceptual framework: self and society, *European Journal of Humanistic Psychology*, 13(2), 69–77.

Hawkins, P. (1995) *Shadow Consultancy*. Bath Consultancy Group working paper.

Hawkins, P. (2006) Coaching supervision, in J. Passmore (ed.) *Excellence in Coaching*. London: Kogan Page.

Hawkins, P. (2010) Coaching supervision, in E. Cox, T. Bachkirova and D. Clutterbuck (eds) *The Complete Handbook of Coaching*. London: Sage, pp. 381–93.

Hawkins, P. (2011a) Expanding emotional, ethical and cognitive capacity in supervision, in J. Passmore (ed.) *Supervision in Coaching*. London: Kogan Page.

Hawkins, P. (2011b) *Leadership Team Coaching*. London: Kogan Page.

Hawkins, P. and Schwenk, G. (2006) *Coaching Supervision*. London: CIPD Change Agenda.

Hawkins, P. and Schwenk, G. (2010) The interpersonal relationship in the training and supervision of coaches, in S. Palmer and A. McDowell (eds) *The Coaching Relationship: Putting People First*. Routledge: London, pp. 203–21.

Hawkins, P. and Shohet, R. (1989) *Supervision in the Helping Professions*. Maidenhead: Open University Press.

Hawkins, P. and Shohet, R. (2000) *Supervision in the Helping Professions*. 2nd edn, Maidenhead: Open University Press.

Hawkins, P. and Shohet, R. (2006) *Supervision in the Helping Professions*. 3rd edn, Maidenhead: Open University Press.

Hawkins, P. and Smith, N. (2006) *Coaching, Mentoring and Organizational Consultancy: Supervision and Development*. Maidenhead: MacGraw-Hill/Open University Press.

Hawkins, P. and Smith, N. (2010) Transformational coaching, in E. Cox, T. Bachkirova and D. Clutterbuck (eds) *The Complete Handbook of Coaching*. London: Sage, pp. 231–44.

Hughes, B. (2010) *The Hemlock Cup: Socrates, Athens and the Search for the Good Life*. London: Jonathan Cape.

Ryde, J. (2009) *Being White in the Helping Professions*. London: Jessica Kingsley.

Stolorow, R.D. and Attwood, G.E. (1984) *Structures of Subjectivity: Explorations in Psychoanalytic Nominology*. Hillsdale, NJ: The Analytical Press.

Stolorow, R.D. and Attwood, G.E. (1992) *The Context of Being – The Intersubjective Foundations of Psychological Life*. Hillsdale, NJ: The Analytical Press.

# 3  The three worlds four territories model of supervision

*Mike Munro Turner*

## Introduction

Awareness of self and other is at the heart of all coaching supervision, for both supervisor and coach, just as it is at the heart of all coaching. But what do we need to be aware of in our selves and in the other?

The seven-eyed model (Hawkins and Smith 2006; see also preceding chapter) provides one map of what we can attend to. In developing this model Hawkins and Smith took a research-based approach, reviewing different models of and approaches to supervision to develop a map of where people in the different approaches put their attention. I have found this model very helpful in directing my attention across the broad landscape of the supervision domain.

However, after using the model for some time, I found that it had some limitations and so started to modify it. I found it helpful to split mode 4 (the coach's experience) into what the coach was experiencing in the coaching session itself, and their experience in the here and now of the supervision session. Similarly I found it helpful to distinguish what the coachee was experiencing in the coaching session, and what was going on back in their life outside the coaching session (together represented in the seven-eyed model as mode 1, the coachee system).

Also, the more experienced I became as a supervisor, the more I found myself needing to make finer distinctions about the individual players' experiences. I already had developed a model which provided exactly these distinctions which I increasingly incorporated into my supervision practice. I first wrote about this model in 1996 (Turner 1996). Since then it has been further developed (Munro Turner and Wilson 2008; Newell and Munro Turner 2008).

This chapter describes the resultant coaching supervision model. It aims to help the supervisor bring the coaching session live into the supervision session, raise the coach's awareness, and so enable the coach to have new options in their coaching.

## Function of the model

Coaching supervision is generally seen to have three functions (Hawkins and Smith 2006):

1   resourcing – helping the coach manage the coachee emotions which they
    pick up when working with coachees;
2   development – developing the skills, understanding and capacities of the
    coach;
3   qualitative – ensuring the quality of the coach's work.

The model presented here focuses on the third of these areas – and in particular
on improving the quality and effectiveness of specific coaching relationships and
interventions by helping the coach have new choices in their client work. However, in focusing on the qualitative aspects, the model also leads the coach into
exploring and engaging with the resourcing and development issues they face.

This model is based on the belief that, by getting the whole system live in the
room, the supervisor can tune into the wider system and use the thoughts, feelings
and other experiences that arise to provide insight into the coaching, the coach and
the coachee. The system here is considered to consist of the supervision session
itself, the coaching, the coachee and their workplace, as well as the supervisor
and the coach. Getting the system into the room refers to evoking and bringing
into awareness all these aspects either directly because they are happening in
the moment or indirectly because they have been evoked through the memory,
imagination and intuition of the supervisee and supervisor. The model provides
a map of this system to help the supervisor direct their attention and that of the
supervisee to all the relevant elements of the system.

## The three worlds four territories (3W4T) model

The 3W4T model describes the three 'worlds' the supervisor can attend to – the
coachee's world, the coaching session, and the supervision session. Within each of
these worlds, the supervisor can attend to four territories of experience for each of
the players involved (themselves, the coach and the coachee). The four territories
are Insight, Readiness, Authentic Vision and Skilful Action.

### The three worlds

Effective supervisors ensure that they attend to what is happening across the whole
supervisory system. To do this they pay attention to three sub-systems or 'worlds'
(see Figure 3.1):

1   the Work World – which consists of the coachee in their workplace and
    wider life;
2   the Coaching World – which consists of the coach and coachee in the
    coaching session. Like the Work World, the supervisor has only in-
    direct experience of Coaching World, either through what the coach tells
    the supervisor overtly or through what is unconsciously evoked in the
    supervisor;

# Three Worlds

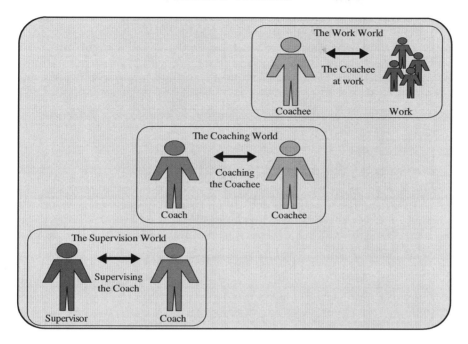

**Figure 3.1**  The supervisory system

3    the Supervision World – which consists of the supervisor and the coach in the supervision session, and which the supervisor has direct experience of (because of course they are part of it!)

These worlds are linked together in two principal ways:

- by the coach, who is present in the Coaching World and the Supervision World: it is they who bring the coaching world into the supervision session (and so provide the content for the supervisor to work with). It is they who then take the shifts they make and the insights they have back into the coaching session.
- by the coachee, who is present in the Work World and the Coaching World: they bring their experience of the work world into the coaching session in order to explore the challenges they face (and so provide the content for the coach to work with). They then take the shifts they make and the insights they have back into the workplace.

These linkages create resonances between the worlds which lead to aspects of the Coaching and Work Worlds being present within the supervision session. So when the coach enters the supervision session, they bring with them a whole network of conscious and unconscious knowledge, feelings, imaginings, perceptions, needs, desires and intuitions about what happened in the coaching and back in the coachee's world. By encouraging and amplifying these resonances, particularly those that the coach is unaware of, and by developing sensitivity to them, the supervisor is able to access information about, and generate insight into, what is occurring in the coaching session and the coachee's world. This information and insight can then be used to help the coach gain insight and develop new choices in their coaching work.

### A model of the person

The experience of each of the individuals involved (supervisor, coach and coachee) can be represented using the four territories model (also known variously as the Renewal Model and the Jericho Model) which maps the four territories of experience: Insight, Readiness, Authentic Vision and Skilful Action (Newell and Munro Turner 2008; see Figure 3.2). It is derived from a right relations model developed by Danielle Roux (private communications 1989–1992).

In using the four territories framework to reflect on our work and understand the various worlds involved, we are interested in what we attend to or focus on in the supervision session. For each of the four territories these are shown in Table 3.1.

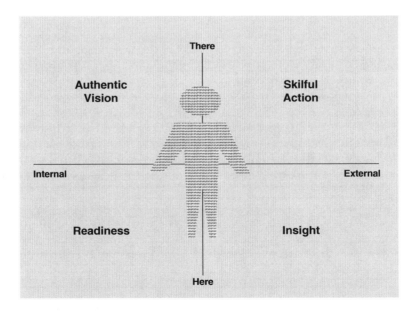

**Figure 3.2** The four territories

**Table 3.1** Focus and the four territories

| Territory | Aspect of the Self | Focus |
|---|---|---|
| **Insight:** seeing what is and what could be in my world. | Sensing, perceiving | What I sense and perceive as having happened, as filtered and moulded by my preconceptions, prejudices, projections and assumptions. |
| **Readiness:** attending to what constrains or enables me in my response to my world; developing my flexibility and resilience. | Feelings and concrete mind | My inner experience as evoked by my perception of what has happened, my meaning systems, personal history, habitual thoughts, etc. |
| **Authentic Vision:** clarifying the difference that I want to make; my desired way of being; my intent. | Creative mind | My imagined ideas about how things could be otherwise, my ability to think differently and explore possibilities. |
| **Skilful Action:** – transforming vision into action. | Body | My behaviours – what I did, or might do – guided by my vision of how things could be different. |

## Three worlds and four territories (3W4T)

Combining the four territories model with the three worlds models allows the perspectives the supervisor can attend to in the supervision session to be mapped. There are eight different perspectives. These are illustrated below with examples of the kinds of questions that might bring that aspect of the supervisory system into the supervision session.

1 The supervisor can ask the coach questions about the coachee:

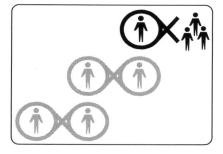

- Insight: 360 data, challenges they face, their life balance, the results they are creating;
- Readiness: psychometrics, ego strength, development stage, personal story and themes;
- Vision: coachee's purpose, the difference/change they want to make, the legacy they seek to leave, their work ambitions;
- Action: habitual behaviours, what have they tried already, what they focus on.

Depending on the particular issue the coachee is exploring in the coaching, it may also be relevant to ask about:

- the coachee's key relationships (using variants of the questions in perspective 4 below) and about the experiences of other players in the coachee's world;
- the wider organizational context: structure, vision, mission and values;
- the larger context – political, economic, social, technological, legal and environmental factors (which can be recalled using the PESTLE mnemonic).

2   The supervisor can ask the coach questions about the coachee in the coaching session:

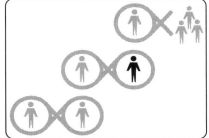

- Insight: how does the coachee perceive the coach?
- Readiness: what was the coachee thinking and feeling?
- Vision: what does the coachee want to get from the coaching?
- Action: how did the coachee behave, what did they say, how did they say it?

3   The supervisor can ask the coach questions to help them reflect on what they experienced and did in the session, and what they might do differently in future sessions:

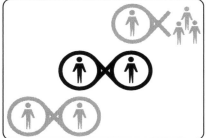

- Insight: what did you notice about the coachee, what themes and patterns did you notice in their story?
- Readiness: what were you thinking and feeling, what were you not able to say to or ask the coachee?
- Vision: what was your intent in the session, what was the difference you were trying to make?
- Action: what was your approach in the session, what did you do, what interventions did you make?

4   The supervisor can help the coach reflect on the coaching relationship and world:

- What kind of relationship do you and coachee have?
- What is happening in the space between you and the coachee?
- If you were observing yourself with your coachee what would you notice?
- If you and your coachee were cast away on a desert island, what would happen?

5   The supervisor can focus on the coach as they are in the supervision session:

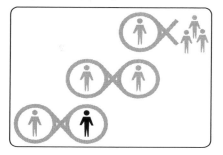

- Insight: what are you noticing about what is happening in the session, how do you see me and my role, what is the context you are sitting in at this moment?
- Readiness: what are you thinking and feeling; what are you keeping out of awareness, what is trapping you, what is the shift you need to make?
- Vision: what is your desired outcome from the supervision session, what are you feeling is your way towards?
- Action: what do you notice about how you are acting in the session?

6   The supervisor can use their own experience in the moment to be aware of what is going on for them:

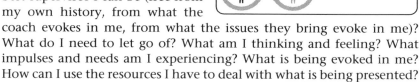

- Insight: what is really happening here? How do I see the coach be-having? Am I addressing Resourc-ing, Developmental and Qualita-tive areas? What do I see playing out? Do I see a shift in the coach?
- Readiness: how free am I to be the best supervisor I can be (free from my own history, from what the coach evokes in me, from what the issues they bring evoke in me)? What do I need to let go of? What am I thinking and feeling? What impulses and needs am I experiencing? What is being evoked in me? How can I use the resources I have to deal with what is being presented?
- Vision: what do I aspire to? What meaning and purpose do I need to embrace or allow in helping me create a shift in the coach?
- Action: how can I act to create a shift in the room?

7   The supervisor can notice what is happening in their relationship with the coach, and in the Supervision World as a whole:

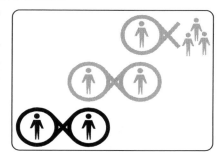

- What kind of relationship do we have?
- When I connect to my own ex-perience, that of the coach, and the space between us, what do I notice?
- Is there a parallel process operat-ing?
- What's worked well in our session today, and what might we have done differently?

8   The supervisor can notice and work with the relationship between the different systems, helping the coach make the shift in the supervision session that will lead them to being able to shift the coachee and so cause a shift back at work:

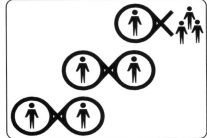

- Can I bring into my awareness all three systems simultaneously?
- How does what is happening in each relationship shed light on what is happening in the other ones (e.g. how does what is playing out in the supervision session shed light on what happens in the coaching session – the parallel process)?
- What is the shift I need to make to enable the coach to shift to enable the coachee to shift and so create a shift back in the workplace?

## Practising supervision – how to use the model

The four territory model introduced earlier can also be used to guide the supervisor in structuring the supervision conversation. In this context it takes the form shown in Figure 3.3. Having contracted with the coach, and identified a coachee to work with and the reason for bringing them to supervision, the supervision conversation can then cover the following:

1   **Bringing the whole system into the room.** Gather information on the whole supervisor-coach-coachee-work system by enquiring about or noticing across the three worlds and four territories. Generally attention will focus initially on the Work System, then the Coach System, and then the Supervisor System. The supervisor has access to information within themselves about the Coach and Work systems, as well as about the here and now of the supervision session itself, which they can contribute.

2   **Connecting what needs to connect.** Having got the system into the room, the coach can begin to see the gaps, contradictions, conflicts, blindspots, either-ors, etc. in what is present, either directly themselves or through interventions by the supervisor. Seeing these gaps may shift how the coach sees what is going on in their coaching and so free them up to have new choices – and sometimes they will need the help of the supervisor in making connections and filling in the gaps.

3   **Creating new possibilities and meanings.** A shift in seeing what needs to connect may be all that the coach needs to be able to return to their coaching with new options. Or they may need new ways of looking at the situation. This may involve reframing the situation so that new options appear. The supervisor seeks to discern and enable the shift the coachee needs to make to have new choices in their work.

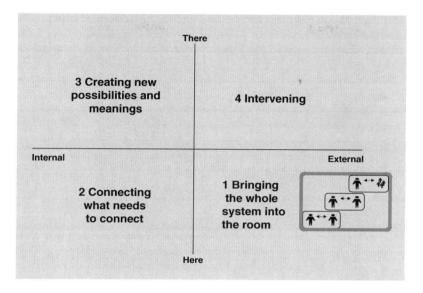

**Figure 3.3** Supervision process

4 **Intervening.** The final step is to help the coach ground the insights they have gained from the supervision and be clear about what they will do differently or how they will be differently in the next coaching session. If the coach has made a clear shift during the supervision session, then this stage may be less about designing specific interventions and more about helping the coach maintain their shifted state.

Whilst the above order reflects the broad flow of the supervision conversation, in practice the conversation will move back and forth between the various areas. The session can conclude with a review, exploring what worked and what could be improved.

The skills necessary to apply this model successfully are implied by the elements of the supervision conversation outlined above. Key among these are:

- bringing the system fully into the room – like spinning plates at the circus, the supervisor seeks to energize all elements of the system simultaneously so that a synthesis can emerge and the whole be seen;
- creating a space in which the coach can be aware of as much of this system as possible so that they are able to connect what needs to be connected;
- being sensitive to as much of the system that has been brought into the room as possible so that the supervisor is also able to become aware of what needs to connect and so, if necessary, help the coach make the connections themselves.

## Case illustration

One of the most interesting, and potentially powerful, phenomena that can arise in supervision sessions is that of parallel process. A parallel process is occurring when 'the pattern of relationship in one area is enacted in another, with no conscious awareness of what is going on' (Hawkins and Smith 2006: 167). It can therefore provide a rich source of information in the supervision session about what is happening in the coaching and back in the coachee's wider life. This illustration includes parallel processes operating between the worlds within the three worlds four territories model.

### Work World

Having contracted with the coach (Thomas), I start by asking about the coachee.

Thomas tells me he has had an initial session with the coachee (Jane). He describes her as being a well-regarded programme manager in the public sector. Jane feels she lacks the potential to progress further because of her lack of confidence, particularly around difficult personalities. Questioning by Thomas has established that 'difficult personalities' are people who are more senior than her and people she perceives as being stronger than her. As well as this being a problem at work, Jane mentions that this is an issue with her husband, a senior policeman with a powerful personality. She also says she thinks too much about what other people think of her, that she needs praise, and that she is afraid of being 'found out'. She wants the coaching to help her be more assertive with these senior, stronger people. Realizing I haven't heard about the Action quadrant of Jane's work life, I ask how specifically she acts in the presence of 'difficult' people. Thomas says that she's cautious and careful, and tries hard not to do anything controversial that might upset them.

### Coaching World

Thomas has brought Jane to supervision saying 'How do I get into this with her? Where should I go with this? I feel stuck.' Focusing on Thomas's inner dynamics (Readiness) I am curious as to why he's feeling stuck as I know him to be a competent coach who would typically not be stumped by a situation like this. It is likely therefore that there is something else going on here that is interfering with his normal competence. I make a mental note to return to this. To give Thomas a different perspective, I move his attention onto a different territory of experience, Vision, using the 'If you were marooned on a desert island together what would happen?' question. This shift in perspective frees him up to think differently and he immediately replies 'I'd be the one making the suggestions and leading, and Jane would be very cooperative – she'd want things to work.'

I point out this apparent contradiction to Thomas. On the one hand he doesn't know where to go in the coaching, and yet on the imagined desert island he sees himself as the leader. So Thomas finds himself in the bind of feeling he has to provide leadership – but not knowing what to do.

Thomas reflects on this – 'Yes, I'm taking the responsibility myself. I'm taking on being the stronger, more senior person where I know the answers and where Jane is cooperative, but not assertive.' It seems Jane has recreated in the session the reality she deals with in her day to day life by unconsciously coaching Thomas to play the role of a stronger, more senior person and he has unconsciously accepted this role, a clear example of a parallel process linking the coach's and coachee's Readiness territories.

However, this insight has not freed Thomas up as his next response is 'But I still need to know what questions to ask her.' Whilst this sounds like an Action issue, it seems likely that it is rooted in the opposite quadrant, Readiness, where some out of awareness process may be interfering with Thomas's ability to know where to go with Jane.

### Supervision World

Wondering whether my 'here and now' experience may shed some light on Thomas's dilemma, I turn my attention to the Supervision World. Focusing inwards on my own Readiness territory, I notice that I too am feeling a pressure to come up with some answers and uncertain as to where to go next. Thomas's feeling of stuckness and uncertainty about how best to coach Jane has communicated itself to me where it has emerged as a felt pressure to fix Thomas – a second parallel process.

Recognizing these linkages gives me the opportunity to use them to inform the supervision. I now have a direct experience of what may be going on, not just for Thomas in his coaching session, but also for the people around Jane back in her place of work, and at home. I turn my attention to my creative mind (Vision) and start to wonder what is the shift I need to make in this supervision session which might defuse the second parallel process and in turn defuse the first?

The parallel process between Jane and Thomas is a complementary one in which Jane's compliance has evoked Thomas's directing stance. But both are in a bind – Jane because she knows being compliant won't deliver what she wants at work, and Thomas because he doesn't know what direction to give!

By contrast, in the parallel process between Thomas and me, our experience is similar – we are both feeling a pressure to come up with answers. And then I realize (more clearly now with the benefit of hindsight) that this is true for Jane as well – it's just that her way of avoiding the discomfort of feeling incompetent is to be compliant and let others take the lead. If this hypothesis is right, then I need to step out from the parallel process and then enable Thomas to do the same so that he is freed up to in turn free up Jane. I hypothesize that this will involve each of us making a shift in our Readiness of being willing to not know, to feel uncertain, and to feel incompetent.

I realize that my focusing on coming up with solutions (Vision) for Thomas for him to use (Action) on Jane has been maintaining the parallel process. Parallel processes are usually rooted in the Readiness quadrant and, as I focus on my inner experience, I realize my need to appear to be the 'expert supervisor' has been driving my interventions. To break it, I need to stop searching for solutions within myself, drop my 'expert supervisor' persona, and switch my attention to clarifying my intent (Vision) – which I realize needs to be to focus on helping Thomas access his own insight. Turning my attention to my externally facing quadrants I realize that this will involve making interventions that keep pushing the thinking back to Thomas (Action), and that seeing that Thomas, rather than me, is working hard is what will tell me I'm being successful (Insight).

By seeing the chain of causality from the Work World, through the Coaching World, to the Supervision World I have been able to free myself up, I now need to help Thomas free himself up, so I turn our attention to the Coaching World.

### Coaching World

Recognizing that Thomas is stuck in a fixed pattern of thought with regard to Jane I try focusing his attention outside this coachee system by asking 'What would you do with a typical coachee?' Thomas gives an immediate and confident answer listing the questions he would ask and the approach he would take. 'So what's stopping you do that here?' He immediately replies 'She expects me to have the answers.' Thomas laughs as he sees the pattern and then says 'I don't feel confident to not know' (his Readiness quadrant). He pauses, reflecting on what he's said, and then commenting that this is what Jane also experiences (her Readiness quadrant). There is a palpable change in his energy which suggests his Readiness has shifted.

I ask him what has shifted for him. Thomas says that he's realized that wanting to feel confident is interfering with his ability to coach well. Further exploration of this shift in Readiness helps him recognize that, by allowing the feeling of not being confident, he can extend his range as a coach (since he can now coach Jane both when he is feeling confident – and when he's not). He recognizes that he needs to be willing to not feel confident (Readiness) – partly so that he can ask the questions that need asking – and partly to demonstrate to Jane that one can be confident despite not knowing (Action). Focusing on his Readiness, I wonder aloud if his feelings of 'unconfidence' can become an ally in his coaching, allowing him to use his own feelings of 'unconfidence' in the next session as an indicator that he's doing real work with Jane and enabling her shift back in the work place.

I ask Thomas to imagine himself in his next session with Jane. I ask about what his experience will be in each of the four territories to ensure that there is coherency between his territories. He says:

- Readiness: I feel comfortable about being 'unconfident' – and I can even see myself welcoming it as an indication that I'm really engaging with Jane.
- Vision: My intent is to help Jane engage with her unconfidence as a way of increasing her confidence in dealing with difficult people. I am holding a vision of myself, and of her, as people who are comfortable and even energized by feeling uncomfortable.
- Action: I will ensure that I don't intervene to offer Jane solutions but will hold back to create the space for her to be more assertive. I may even make a paradoxical intervention along the lines of 'Jane, you're a powerful woman – you can even get others to be assertive over you!' to help her reframe how she sees herself.
- Insight: I will be looking out for Jane's discomfort around not knowing so that I can help her get more used to being with this feeling.

## Evaluation of the model

The principal purpose of this model is to provide a map of what a supervisor can attend to so as to ensure that the whole system is brought into the room. It can be useful in a number of ways:

- For novice supervisors, it provides a framework to guide our interventions, enabling us to ensure that we cover the necessary ground. As we become more familiar with the model, so using it to guide our attention will become increasingly second nature.
- For coaches working in peer group supervision sessions, it provides a structure to our conversation, helping us to cover the territories effectively.
- For experienced supervisors, it provides an anchor point to which we can return when we feel lost or cast adrift in our supervision sessions. It also shows us where we prefer to focus as supervisors, and where our gaze does not fall.
- For all supervisors, after a supervision session it provides a framework for reflecting on the session and analysing what happened, and a structure for writing it up. After the session in the case illustration above had finished, I reflected using the 3W4T model on what had happened. Some of the movement described above only became apparent in this post-session sense-making process. And more became apparent only in writing this case illustration.

- For coaches using a two world (Work and Coaching Worlds) four territory model, it enables self-supervision and reflection after coaching sessions. The output from this can then be a useful input to our supervision sessions.

This framework separates out and makes explicit the variety of places the supervisor can direct their attention. This exhaustiveness is a strength – but it also means that the model is more complex to learn and apply than, for example, Hawkins and Smith's seven-eyed model. Indeed, when first developing this approach, I used the map for note taking but then found that I got distracted from the supervision process by trying to work out where to place particular notes on the map. Rather, the model is at its most powerful when it has been internalized and can be referred to live inside one's head during a supervision session, or is being used to learn about supervision either in post session reflections or whilst observing supervision sessions.

## Learning more

For further insight into how to use this model, the following will be helpful:

- To understand the wider context in which supervision occurs and for more information on the seven-eyed model see Hawkins and Smith (2006) and the preceding chapter in this book.
- For a more detailed understanding of the four territories model see Newell and Munro Turner (2008), Munro Turner and Wilson (2008), and various articles at http://mikethementor.co.uk

## References

Hawkins, P. and Smith, N. (2006) *Coaching, Mentoring and Organizational Consultancy: Supervision and Development*. Maidenhead: Open University Press.

Munro Turner, M.H. and Wilson, S. (2008) Developing leaders: coaching for renewal, *International Journal of Coaching and Mentoring*, 1/2: 39–48.

Newell, D. and Munro Turner, M.H. (2008) A model of coaching for renewal, *International Journal of Coaching and Mentoring*, 1/1: 94–100.

Turner, M.H.M. (1996) Executive mentoring, *Counseling at Work*, Spring: 5–6.

# 4    Using the seven conversations in supervision

*David Clutterbuck*

## Introduction

While most textbooks refer to the coaching conversation as if it were a single, discrete dialogue, in practice both coach and client carry out reflective dialogues in their minds before, during and after the spoken conversation. Each of these additional dialogues has an important role to play in the nature and the effectiveness of the coaching conversation. Within supervision, the seven conversations provide a practical method for bringing different perspectives to bear on how both coach and client approach the learning dialogue and the learning relationship. They also focus attention on the thoughts and behaviours of both parties in the coaching relationship.

The seven conversations of coaching (Megginson and Clutterbuck 2009) were originally conceived as a means of deconstructing the coaching dialogue, with the aims of identifying where the dialogue was most and least effective and helping coaches raise their awareness of what was going on in both their own minds and that of their client (and to a lesser extent what was occurring in the space between). The stimulus for development of this approach was that coaches frequently became 'stuck' somewhere between having a general sense that a coaching relationship was not working properly, or that they were not delivering sufficient value to the client, and having a clear understanding of what was going wrong. Very often, for example, they assumed that the problem lay with how they were engaging with the client within the coaching session, when the real issues related to unconscious conversations either they or the client were having internally before the formal coaching session. Expanding the coach's perspective of where the coaching conversations were taking place offered an alternative and arguably faster method of exploring the relationship and conversational dynamics.

The seven conversations have proved to be a practical and flexible tool within the supervisor's toolbox. Among the reported benefits reported by supervisees are the following:

- It provides a structure, against which to explore elements of the coaching conversation.

- It helps coach and supervisor identify issues for reflection between supervisory session.
- It provides a framework on which to hang a wide variety of techniques and approaches.

Observations show that it also shifts the emphasis of reflection and analyses away from what the coach said or did, and towards the dialogue between the coach and the client – and hence permits more of a systems approach to understanding the conversational dynamics. It therefore provides a practical framework, around which the supervisor can help the coach both identify development needs and resolve issues with current clients.

## Description of the model

The seven conversations have been presented at EMCC and Conference Board conferences and published in *People Management* (2010). They are:

1. the coach's reflection before dialogue (their preparatory thinking before the coaching conversation);
2. the client's reflection/preparatory thinking before the dialogue;
3. the coach's internal, unspoken reflections during the dialogue;
4. the spoken dialogue;
5. the client's internal, unspoken reflections during the dialogue;
6. the coach's reflections after the conversation;
7. the client's reflections after the dialogue.

Most coach development and support focuses on the middle of these – the spoken dialogue. Yet the effectiveness of the spoken dialogue depends heavily on the other six conversations. Building our competence in each of the conversations is essential in mastering the coaching role. In the next section, I explore each conversation in more detail and provide some pointers for the supervisor in attending to it.

### The coach's initial inner dialogue

The purpose of this dialogue is to ensure that the coach is mentally prepared for the coaching conversation. The quality of the conversation is dependent, to a significant extent, on the quality of thinking both coach and coachee put into their preparation. In this dialogue, the coach considers how they have helped so far and in what ways. Inevitably, this leads them to reflect upon their own emotions and motivations (e.g. Are they trying too hard to help? Do they care too much?). Other issues they reflect upon might include the following:

- *Context*. What is the 'big picture' for this client? What metaphors might I use to describe the client's situation? What metaphors does the client use? Do I understand what drives the client and why? Who else is present in our conversations and in what ways?

- *Avoidance.* What issues or emotions is this client avoiding? What issues is the coach avoiding? What collusion may be happening between them?
- *Attitude.* How the coach feels generally about this relationship can have a major impact on the subsequent conversations. Useful questions to ask include: am I looking forward to this meeting? (If not, what's the issue and what should I be doing about it?); what are my responsibilities in this relationship?

Of course, there are many other powerful questions coaches can ask themselves. But considering this kind of question in advance of the coaching session seems to help free up intuition, by raising awareness of the conversational and relational dynamics. It also helps prevent distracting thoughts such as 'I need to articulate this in order to file it away' from intruding into the main coaching conversation. And it gives the coach ammunition with which to address concerns about the relationship and the client's authenticity. This ammunition might otherwise have been lost in the ebb and flow of the main conversation around the issue the client brings to the table.

The supervisor's role is fundamentally to direct the coach's attention to this conversation and support them in reflecting on it.

## The client's initial inner dialogue

Preparation by the coachee is equally important and can be equally demanding. At least an hour's quality reflective space is typically required to prepare for an intensive coaching session. Particularly useful themes include:

- *What they have learned since the previous session, by conscious or unconscious consideration of questions raised by the coach, or by letting insights they gained within the session percolate.* Useful questions here include:
  - What has happened to me and my thinking since our last meeting?
  - How have I and my perceptions changed?
  - How have I made use of the insights I gained?
- *What issues they would like help with, in the next session and why.*
  - What issues have been resolved and what new issues have arisen?
  - What's the relationship between these issues and my overall goals?
  - What thinking have I already done around these issues?
- *Their own attitudes and motivations towards the coaching conversation and coaching relationship.*
  - Do I really want to resolve this issue? What are my motivations for introducing it *now*?
  - How prepared am I to be challenged on this issue?
  - What more could I do to help the coach help me?

Having this dialogue – even if they address only one or two of these questions – helps the coachee accept their responsibilities in the relationship. It also helps them to structure their thinking, so that they are better able to articulate the issue and how it affects them. And it reinforces what might be called 'conversational honesty' – the openness that underpins mutual positive regard.

As a supervisor, I find that many coaches are so concentrated on what they need to do for the client that they forget that a dialogue needs active participation by both parties. A frequent outcome of analysing this discussion is that the coach feels less guilt about lack of progress on the part of the client and becomes more courageous about confronting the client's lack of preparation.

### The coach's inner dialogue during the spoken conversation

This inner dialogue takes place in parallel with the process of listening and asking questions. Sometimes called 'reflection-in-action' (Schön 1983), it requires both coach and coachee to participate fully in the conversation and observe it as dispassionately as possible. The focus of this inner conversation shifts intuitively, in response to verbal, physiological and other triggers. At times the focus will be inner directed; at others outer directed. Inner-directed conversations relate to 'How am I helping?' and might address questions, such as:

- What is the quality of my listening?
- What am I observing/hearing? What am I missing?
- Is my intuition turned on?
- What assumptions am I making? How might these be acting as a filter on my listening and my understanding?
- Am I spending too much attention on crafting the next question?

Outer-directed conversations, in contrast, raise awareness of issues, such as:

- What is the client not saying?
- What is the quality of the client's thinking?
- How am I feeling in the moment? If I feel uncomfortable, what is making me so?

The role of the supervisor here is to help the coach verbalize their observations, so that they can begin the process of including them in their intuitive repertoire. On occasion, I have helped the coach design exercises aimed at making them more 'attentive to their attentiveness' – simple exercises they can apply within or outside the coaching context.

### The spoken conversation

This is the part that attracts the most attention. It's also the easiest conversation and therefore highly beguiling. Inexperienced or inexpert coaches frequently are aware only of this conversation, and oblivious to the inner conversations going on simultaneously in themselves and the client (if they have an inner conversation at all!). I would argue that effective coaches maintain awareness of all three, while instinctively reviewing the dynamics of the spoken conversation, asking themselves questions such as:

- Is there consonance between what is said and our body language?
- Is there a logical pattern of development to the conversation?
- Are we exploring issues from multiple perspectives?
- Are we exploring issues in sufficient depth?

From observation of coaches in assessment centres, it seems that inexperienced coaches often tend to feel they have to keep the conversation going, which puts them in the driving seat. More experienced coaches allow the conversation to find its own path and help the client make choices about which direction to follow, when there are forks in the road. An analogy is an orchestra, where the players decide what the tune will be and the conductor merely holds them together. Allowing the conversation to happen in this way enables the coach to notice so much more – the choice of words and phrases, the tone and energy of the conversation, non-verbal communication, particularly at the level of micro-expression, and the structure of the client's reasoning.

One of the biggest barriers to attending to this conversation can be the need by some coaches to constrain the conversation within a predetermined model or process – for example, GROW (Whitmore 2002), clean language (Sullivan and Rees 2008) or solutions focus (Jackson and McKergow 2007). If the constant, unspoken question is 'Am I keeping this conversation on track?' or 'Am I doing the process right?' then the coach's focus tends to be on the process, not on the client.

Part of the supervisor's role here is to help the coach feel less anxious about *controlling* the spoken conversation, which allows the coach to be more fully attentive to the client.

### The coachee's inner dialogue during the spoken conversation

The coachee can contribute more to the learning dialogue, if they are also process aware. The management of the conversation and its direction then become a shared activity.

It is unlikely, however, that many clients will be aware of their own inner conversations. Yet at some level they will be making choices about what they say, how honest they will be with the coach and how much attention they are paying to their own words and emotions. Part of the coach's role is to act as a mirror on this inner conversation, helping to surface unspoken thoughts and to heighten the client's self-awareness. Using approaches such as Gestalt can be very powerful in this context.

However, there is another aspect, which I find few coaches have considered – the coach's responsibility to help the client develop their own skills of self-observation. It may be more difficult for the client to reflect on their inner conversation in the full flow of the spoken conversation, but frequent pauses for reflection provide opportunities for them to consider questions, such as:

- What assumptions or filters am I applying in answering the coach's questions?
- How am I helping the coach understand my issues?

As in the second conversation above, the supervisor's role here includes helping the coach examine both their own and their client's responsibilities. On several occasions, for example, an outcome of analysis of this conversation is that the coach determines to confront the client, as with 'Why do you think I feel you are not being honest with me?'

## The coach's inner conversation after the meeting

'Reflection-on-action' is also a critical part of the coach's continuous improvement and personal growth. While the meeting is still fresh in their memory, the coach should review the five antecedent conversations, asking themselves questions about:

*How I helped*

- What did I do to enhance the quality of the client's thinking?
- Was I appropriately directive/non-directive?
- Did we create a 'bias for action'?

*What choices did I make?*

- What questions did I withhold and why?
- Was I sufficiently challenging?
- Did I give the coachee sufficient time to think?

*What did I learn?*

- What patterns can I discern from this and previous conversations with this client?
- What would I do differently another time?

*What concerns do I have?*

- Where did I struggle?
- What negative emotions am I aware of?

## The client's inner conversation after the meeting

One of the advantages of holding coaching sessions where the client has to travel subsequently is that it gives them space for reflection in the immediate aftermath of the coaching conversation. This post-meeting reflection is vital in terms of translating good thoughts into practical action. Failure here is often, in my experience, associated with coaching relationships where the client talks endlessly about their issues during the session, but makes little progress between sessions.

The coach's responsibility extends, in my view, to helping the client develop the skills, ability and motivation to reflect purposefully and hence gain full value from the session. This may mean discussing with them how and when they will reflect and contracting with them that they will do so.

Critical areas, on which this conversation can usefully focus include:

*Learning*

- What new ideas and insights have I gained?
- What do I need to think about more deeply?

*Intention*

- How am I going to put this learning into practice?
- What do I want to explore with other people?
- What changed expectations do I now have of myself?

*Process and behaviour*

- Was I sufficiently open and honest?
- What could I have done to extract more value from the conversation?
- What will I do differently in preparing for the next coaching session?

The supervisory conversation here often centres on what the coach might reasonably expect of the client in post-session reflection and follow up. A frequent conclusion by the coach is that they should be more assertive in making their expectations clear, event though it is up to the client to decide what to do!

## Using the seven conversations

The seven conversations are particularly useful:

- when the coach feels in some way inadequate or that they have 'failed' the client;
- when the client procrastinates constantly, leaving the coach frustrated;
- when the coach feels too close (intimate), or too distant from the client;
- when the coach has a sense that there are unidentified others in the room;
- when conversations are repeated, with no sense of significant progress in the client's thinking or behaviour;
- when the coach simply has the intuition that they are 'missing something important' in the conversation or the relationship;
- when the coach feels there is a moment (or longer) of disconnect in the conversation but can't pin down what was occurring (Clutterbuck 2008).

Analysing the conversation helps the coach firstly to identify the point in the conversation where they first became consciously aware of their concern, then to work back in the conversation(s) to try to identify earlier points, where there are clues to what is coming. These clues may, of course, be other than verbal – a conversation is made up of much more than just words. The discipline of conversation analysis, with an aim to 'reveal the organized reasoning procedures, which inform the production of mutually occurring talk' (Hutchby and Woolfitt 2008: 2), has much to offer here in terms of technique and process although it is not essential for the supervisor to be highly versed in analytic techniques.

It is also important to keep in mind that conversations are about a lot more than simply imparting information. According to Gee (2005: 2): 'The primary function of human language is . . . to support the performance of social activities and social identities and to support human affiliation with culture, social groups and institutions'. That sounds a bit like a definition of coaching!

There is a challenge for coaches in the potential conflict between attentiveness and reflection-in-action. If the coach is to be fully engaged with the client, can they at the same time allow part of their mind to be analytical and almost observing as a third party? It seems from dialogue with coaches, both within supervision and more generally, in group training sessions, that people have widely differing abilities to do this.

The seven conversations process enhances the seven-eyed model (Hawkins and Smith 2006). It examines the conversation from the perspective of the client, from the strategies and interventions used by the coach, and the relationship between the coach and the client. It can help contextualize the conversation and the coaching relationship, by revealing and exploring conversations the client is not having, or conversations that are antecedents to those occurring in the coaching session. It can also be used by the supervisor and supervisee to deconstruct their own conversations – for example, when the supervisor reflects back to the coach their feelings and observations about what is being said and how it is being said. I sometimes find myself asking 'Which bits of the conversation with the client have you transposed to *this* conversation, between us?'

## Supervising with the seven conversations

Choosing whether to attend to observations from each of the conversations, and whether to draw the client's attention to them, requires a combination of intuition and judgement. In supervision, I make similar choices. However, most of the dialogue using the seven conversations framework comes from the coach's post hoc recognition of unconscious observations, revealed by reviewing the conversations.

I find myself constantly experimenting with different ways of using the seven conversations to help the coach gain insights. Typically, I might begin by asking the coach questions such as:

- What is it about this particular coaching relationship that gives you a sense of unease or that something is not quite right?
- How clear in your mind is this feeling? How clear to you is what causes this feeling?
- What is at the edge of your awareness about this relationship?
- Does your concern relate just to the most recent session with the client or does it arise from several sessions?

Having identified the source of concern (which may simply be a general, unfocused feeling at this stage) we work through the seven conversations in whatever order the coach wishes. If I sense that they are avoiding reflecting on one of the conversations, I voice what I'm feeling and invite them to consider what they want to do with that piece of information. Sometimes they acknowledge the avoidance and change the order, in which we review each conversation; sometimes we 'park' the observation and agree to review it at a later point in the supervision dialogue. The seven conversations framework gives us a structure, with which to prioritize what we focus on and ensure we don't forget elements that we decide to park.

If we feel that an analysis of the verbal content would potentially be useful, an additional question set comes into play. These questions include:

- What words or phrases captured your attention then?
- With the attentiveness of recollection, what words or phrases capture your attention now?
- Do these words or phrases echo those from previous coaching conversations with this client? (Or – often even more revealing – with another client?)
- What makes these significant for you?
- What makes them significant for the client?
- Is the client aware of this significance?

Of course, analysis can be seductive and could potentially even be an avoidance tactic – focusing on the detail to avoid larger implications. It's a matter of judgement when the coach has acquired sufficient understanding of the conversational dynamics and their choices – both then and in future conversations – to move from deconstruction to construction.

## Case illustration

In the case below, the coach came to supervision with a specific client in mind. The stimulus for applying the seven conversations was a combination of an intuitive sense by the coach that the coaching relationship was not working as well as it could and a difficulty in pinpointing what the problem was and/or where the source of the problem lay. The initial dialogue explored what the coach's intuition was telling them both at the current time (as they sat in the supervision session) and as they recollected from the session(s) with the client. The decision to use the seven conversations as a framework for exploring this issue was taken jointly – suggested by the supervisor and agreed to by the coach, in the spirit of experimentation.

The coach felt a level of frustration that, while the dialogue with the client was open, energetic and positive, very little of substance emerged at the end. She felt that the client was not taking the relationship seriously enough. The spoken conversation was energetic and enjoyable, but the client seemed reluctant to commit to any firm course of action.

Two conversations gradually emerged as having particular significance. One was the client's reflections before the coaching session. It emerged that gathering information about the issue had been driven by the coach. The client's starting point was a general feeling of unease about his progression in the organization. He felt no urgency – he had brought the issue simply because the coaching session provided an opportunity to explore it.

The other conversation, which coach and supervisor explored in depth, was the conversation in her mind, during the coaching session. She had experienced increasing frustration at his apparent reluctance to engage with ideas about how he could move his career on, for example by being more proactive in managing his reputation.

The coach decided to work on the first of these conversations to begin with. An initial question was whether the client had even had this conversation. The coach had assumed that, because the client had chosen this issue, he had given it some thought already, but the recollected conversation suggested this was not so. A lesson the coach extracted here was the importance of identifying what pre-thinking a client has done, before plunging into the coaching dialogue.

At this point, she expressed the perception that she would feel more confident, if she had some approaches in her kitbag to help the client take a step back and have the inner conversation, as a precursor to the main conversation. Various alternatives were discussed, ranging from the simple questions 'What thinking have you done about this already?' or 'What conversation might you usefully have had about this with yourself in preparation for this meeting?', to giving the client a sheet of paper on which to write or draw everything they know and feel about the issue. We also briefly rehearsed a conversation she might have with the client to set expectations about his preparation for the next session.

We then moved on to her inner conversation during the spoken coaching conversation. An analogy emerged of sailing, where the direction of the wind and the angle of the rudder and sail are always partially or fully opposed and making headway is often a matter of moving sideways, rather than directly ahead. Her attempts to steer the conversation were diverted by his unwillingness to commit to a particular course. Reliving some of the points in the conversation, where she had felt this most strongly, a critical question evolved – 'Whose need was it to have an outcome from this conversation?' The coach quickly realized that the urgency to find a solution was hers, driven by her need to feel that she had helped, and that the client's need was to understand his situation and his motives more fully. What the client could do about career progress was less important to him at this point than deciding whether he wanted to progress and, if so, in what direction.

From analysing this specific conversation, the coach was able to explore with the supervisor a much wider range of issues, relating to potential conflict between her needs and those of her clients. In particular, she realized that her strong sense of responsibility for her clients and their welfare had both benefits and downsides and that she needed to manage this aspect of her practice more proactively. The value of the seven conversations approach was that it allowed supervisor and coach to focus their deconstruction of what was happening between the coach and the client and to view the coach/client interaction longitudinally (that is, as a series of recurring pre-session, during, and post-session events over time).

## Evaluation of the approach

Feedback from coach clients has broadly been that the seven conversations are efficacious in helping them think methodically about their coaching practice and to pinpoint when and where in the coaching dialogue issues of concern may be located. Coaches I have supervised also report that they have been able to use the approach in self-analysis, particularly to identify when coaching relationships do not seem to be progressing as expected.

However, as a relatively recent concept, there is neither a wide body of experience, nor any form of empirical review of how it works in practice. It is also difficult to link the approach to empirically researched supervisory practice. I hope that in future there will be opportunities to experiment with and compare use of the seven conversations in combination with more traditional approaches to supervision.

Comparison with other frameworks for supervision suggests that this approach addresses some but by no means all of the wide range of tasks associated with the supervisor role. For example, Harris (1983) identifies eight key tasks, which appear to have informed the frameworks created by Hawkins and Smith (2006), Proctor (1988) and Carroll (2004). The seven conversations framework helps the coach master specific skills (listening to the wider conversations), enlarge understanding of the client and of process issues, increase the coach's awareness of self and of their impact on the process, and help overcome personal and intellectual obstacles towards learning and mastery. However, it has relatively little impact in terms of developing understanding of concepts and theory or providing a stimulus to research. Nor does it necessarily encompass the ethical dimension of supervision.

## Learning more

If you decide to experiment with the seven conversations, the place to start is with your own practice. I have found it informative to compare the conversations that take place in one or more of my coaching relationships with those that occur in my supervision.

Perhaps the most valuable advice I have given myself in using the seven conversations is not to use it as a process for managing supervision sessions, but as a stimulus, reinforcement and balance for my intuition. 'Apply gently for best results!'

# References

Carroll, M. (2004) *Counselling Supervision. Theory, Skills and Practice*. London: Sage.

Clutterbuck, D. (2008) Moments of Disconnect, unpublished essay, Oxford Brookes Business School.

Gee, J.P. (2005) *An Introduction to Discourse Analysis: Theory and Method*. Routledge: London.

Harris, E. (1983) A working-alliance based model of supervision, *Coaching Psychologist*, 11(1): 35–45.

Hawkins, P. and Smith, N. (2006) *Coaching, Mentoring and Organizational Consultancy*. Maidenhead: McGraw-Hill.

Hutchby, I. and Woolfitt, P. (2008) *Conversational Analysis*. Cambridge: Polity.

Jackson, P. and McKergow, M. (2007) *The Solutions Focus: Making Coaching and Change SIMPLE*. London: Nicholas Brealey.

Megginson, D. and Clutterbuck, D. (2009) *Further Techniques for Coaching and Mentoring*. Oxford: Butterworth Heinemann.

Proctor, B. (1988) *Supervision: A Working Alliance* (videotaped training manual). St Leonards on Sea: Alexia Publications.

Schön, D.A. (1983) *The Reflective Practitioner: How Professionals Think in Action*. London: Temple Smith.

Sullivan, W. and Rees, J. (2008) *Clean Language: Revealing Metaphors and Opening Minds*. Carmarthen: Crown House.

Whitmore, J. (2002) *Coaching for Performance: Growing People, Performance and Purpose*. London: Nicholas Brealey.

# 5    A French model of supervision: supervising a 'several to several' coaching journey

*Michel Moral*

## Introduction: supervision in France

Very few books related to supervision have been published in France, even in the domain of psychotherapy (Malarewicz 1999; Delourme and Marc 2008). Less than five are available. Recent ones specifically related to coaching are Devienne (2010) and Darmouni and Hadjadj (2010).

In fact, it is assumed and accepted that a well-known therapist or coach, who is possibly the author of several reference books, who is involved in teaching and training, and who often delivers speeches in the symposiums, 'naturally' becomes a supervisor. No one asks if they have been trained, what their theories and frameworks are and what kind of logic drives their supervision practice.

But, slowly and surely, new supervision patterns are emerging and small communities of supervisors share how they work and how these processes can be improved. We cannot review all these different patterns but describe in detail only one: supervision of a team of coaches fulfilling an organizational coaching contract. Specific methodologies have been developed for this kind of supervision and the objective of this chapter is to explore the conceptual roots and show how the whole process is driven.

## Organizational and team coaching

If many books have been written addressing organizational change, only few mention organizational coaching. Very few provide frameworks and perspectives that can assist a team of coaches working with multinational companies or on cross-border challenges and using a true coaching process. Most approaches rely on either the Organization Development (OD) paradigm (Lewin 1951; McGregor 1971) or the Corporate Culture Change methods (Schein 1985). Such models are either 'commitment based', trying to convince employees and middle management by showing positive images of the future, or 'compliance based', changing behaviours by imperatives.

Coaching for executives started to develop in the USA and in Europe during the 1980s. Team coaching began to be a reality at the beginning of the 1990s. Logically, organizational coaching should have emerged early in the millennium. In fact, its development has been slowed down by the existence of several strong 'compliance based' methodologies like, for instance, business process reengineering (BPR) (Stewart 1993) and performance management. These methodologies assume a top-down approach with an 'external expert' or 'guru' role for highly paid consultants. Very often the resistance of the system is such that the mission fails (Millward 2005: 243–92).

Organizational coaching has been conceptualized recently (Moral and Henrichfreise 2008, 2009) and its development in France is very encouraging. The basic principles are as follows.

If we consider the many theories of organization, from the very beginning, with Frederick Taylor (1911) and Henri Fayol (1918), up to the most recent ones, we eventually come to represent an organization as a system interacting with its environment. Within this system, four subsystems are possible entry points when one wants to trigger a change. Our experience in France is that the first two are those on which coaches are working and the last two are beloved of consultants:

1  *Corporate culture:* many authors have considered changing the organization by changing its culture: Edgar Schein (1985), of course, but also Ronald Burt (1999), John Kotter and James Heskett (1992), Gareth Morgan (1989), Millward (2003), Weick and Quinn (1999), Giroux and Marroquin (2005), etc.;
2  *Corporate structure,* which is more or less represented by a combination of the organization chart and the corporate processes, both being implicit or explicit depending on the country and the activity;
3  *Information technology,* which provides new opportunities not only in terms of communication between people but also in terms of managing data, information and knowledge. Recent technology development makes it possible to have organization patterns that were beyond our imagination a few years ago. Enterprises are more and more like cyborgs, half human, and half cybernetics;
4  *The decision system,* which carries objectives to execution, usually from top to bottom.

There are tight interactions between the four subsystems. Acting on one of them usually strongly impacts on the other three. Experience shows that while there are four potential entry points, it is necessary to traverse all four subsystems to facilitate sustainable change.

At the levels of executive and management teams, coaches are now familiar with techniques that can be embedded in an organizational coaching mission (Moral and Henrichfreise 2009). For instance, Open Space Technology (Owen 1997) and World Café (Brown et al. 2005) are appropriate to working with large groups.

# A 'several to several' coaching approach

The definitions of coaching now include multiple to multiple as a category of coaching process. For instance the European Mentoring and Coaching Council (EMCC, www.emccouncil.org) states: 'Within organizational contexts coaching and mentoring may include "one-to-several" or "several-to-several" coaching or mentoring activities/interactions. The coaches and mentors may be internal or external.'

An organizational coaching request can be expressed throughout the organization in terms of its different forms – training, individual coaching, team coaching, leadership seminars, reorganization projects, and so on. Therefore the coaching process needs to combine various competencies, such as consulting, facilitation, coaching, creativity and intercultural sensitivity. Coaching an organization means managing different interventions, at different places, at the same time, through different people in more than one language. Hence it follows that the coaches have to create a 'mirror image' of the client organization by creating a community of coaches able to connect to all levels of the client system.

Assembling several individual coaches who act independently will not be effective. They will focus only on the individual or team coaching missions with limited communication with their colleagues. What is needed is a community of coaches who are individually able to let go of their personal approaches in order to give way to some sort of collective and creative wisdom. The community has to be capable of using their system as a 'mirror image' of the client's system so as to sense the emergent opportunities and risks, to co-create appropriate interventions and to explore collective coaching and leadership and all questions which may arise during the coaching process.

Finally, these coaches have to be willing to take the risk of being excluded at any time, not because they are not good enough but because the client system rejects a specific coach symbolizing its own scapegoat. There will inevitably be 'victims along the way' in organizational coaching carried out through this kind of engagement. Incidentally, with respect to financial remuneration, innovative ways of 'getting fairly paid' are needed. This question has been addressed in detail (Moral and Henrichfreise 2008) but there is still room for improvement: clearly, organizations are quite brutal and unfair when excluding a coach.

In this approach the coaching process follows a very classical logic which was first mentioned by Lewin (1951): unfreezing-changing-refreezing. The difficulty is to pass the 'wall of resistance' shown in Figure 5.1 which schematizes the fact that a system in a stable state moving to another stable state has to come upon an unstable position. This figure summarizes some of the notions of the First Systems Theory initiated by Ludwig Von Bertalanffy (1947). Since then new concepts have been developed to address the issue of the 'wall of resistance' in a team.

One of these concepts is the 'triple point metaphor'. In physics there is a combination of temperature and pressure where matter is at the same time a gas, a liquid and a solid. A very small variation of the conditions drives to one of the three states. The idea in organizational coaching is to enable the client team to

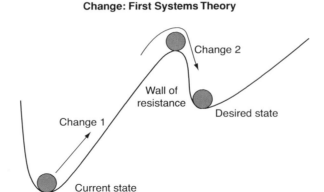

**Figure 5.1**  Systemic approach of change

reach a state where they can collectively appreciate the value of the past, sense the emergence of the new, and feel the freedom of choice. Then they can experience simultaneously the world of chaos, protection and emergence. At this point, minimal interventions like encouragement, a speech from a member of the board of directors (or an outside speaker) or a specific language can cause a group to 'collapse' to one of the three possible states: remaining in the past, embracing the future or getting stuck in the process of choice.

Identifying what is the resistance and when it appears is quite central in the organizational coaching process. In the case illustration described later, the resistance emerged when the triple point was attained: seminars with the client team were more and more intense and the objective of the coaching mission became visible. At the beginning of the most critical seminar, the CFO replaced the CEO who decided to give priority to a customer call. In the previous seminars the opening speech of the CEO was always encouraging the participants to think long term and to forget about their current business difficulties. This time, the opening speech given by the CFO was abruptly short term achievement oriented. This broke the momentum but the coaches were hopefully able to identify this as a major resistance and use the negative energy to push the participants into a 'Change 2'. Temptation was high to cope with the CFO request and use the seminar to set short-term action plans.

## Supervising a team of coaches: concepts

As a consequence of the above, supervising a team of coaches involved in an organizational coaching mission is not like supervising a person or a group. Technically speaking, attention given by the supervisor to what is variously called 'parallel process', 'systemic reflection' or 'isomorphism' has to increase. As we have put in place a team of coaches that mirrors the organization, we can expect this mechanism to occur intensively and extensively.

The mechanism under these names was first identified by Searles (1955: 135) who called it 'reflection process' and gave the following definition: 'Processes at work currently in the relationship between patient and therapist are often reflected in the relationship between therapist and supervisor'.

A lot of attempts have been made to give an explanation of this mechanism. The fact that something is replicated from a system to another was the source of several theories combining identification and projection (Miller and Twomey 1999).

In France we often use the term 'systemic reflection' to identify this phenomenon. Isaac Tylim (1999) described it as enactments that occur during group supervision. These enactments differ from counter-transference where the therapist or supervisor is given the role of an actor from the past. Typically, contradictions, missing elements in what is reported, symbolic interactions, unexpected emotions and unusual behaviours should be considered as signs of the systemic reflection.

The members of the group of coaches are receiving the representations and affects embodied in the group of clients. Due to the coaching relationship, events taking place in the client groups are shared and the enactments within the supervision process may be regarded as metaphors of what is happening in the organization. The supervisor's tactic is to anchor their interventions in those metaphors. Such metaphors are sometimes extreme: at some point of the mission described later, the three coaches suffered intestinal disorders which were not medically explainable. The supervisor gave attention to what was reflected from the client organization to the group of coaches and the symptoms 'magically' disappeared at the end of the supervision session.

This is the principle. We can imagine that everything will depend entirely upon the subjectivity of the supervisor if nothing else is done to provide some reliability to the process. A frame has to be set.

## Supervising a team of coaches: some practicalities

First, the supervisor is not the leader of the team of coaches, neither are any of the coaches. This is congruent with an important systemic concept which can be summarized with the analogy, 'it is difficult to make your bed without getting out of it'.

Second, in order for the supervisor to be fully available for the detection of the systemic reflection, he delegates to the members of the group of coaches the facilitation, the time management and the meta roles (Cardon 2003: 173–205).

Third, there should be a high degree of regression within the supervision group. The frame is set in such a way that the reflection process is amplified as much as possible, but also controlled as much as possible. This is done by enforcing a combination of functioning rules based on an interesting contribution made by Altfeld (1999). He had the idea of creating a supervision frame favouring the emergence of the systemic reflection: one of the participants presents their own view of what is happening with the client, and the other participants can react to what is presented or to the comments of anyone else, but only at the emotional level. Altfeld's hypothesis is that all the reactions of the participants can then be interpreted as systemic reflections. This layout helps to make the difficult affects explicit, but its key value is to help the supervisor to understand the core issues of the client.

Fourth, Tylim, like Altfeld, considers that a solid frame (including for instance a code of conduct) is also a factor amplifying the systemic reflection. Therefore they both recommend interpreting the interactions within the frame to regulate regression and allow progress.

## Case illustration

Company X is facing a declining market trend and its Marketing and Sales division is anticipating difficulties within its senior executive group of roughly sixty high level directors. In particular, it is expected that motivation will drop and that key executives will leave. A well-known coach is called in to propose a preventive intervention, in the form of team coaching. The objective of the team coaching is to develop some sense of solidarity within the top executives of this division. The current situation is as follows: six sales executives have responsibility for the income in their respective geographical areas (Europe, North America, Eastern Europe, Middle East, Asia, Africa and South America). A second group of executives also have marketing responsibility but it cuts across geographical boundaries. For instance, one of them is in charge of worldwide development of maintenance, technical support and parts. Another one manages the so-called 'global accounts'. The third category of executives in the team is made up of those in charge of support functions such as the financial controller, the chief lawyer or the communications director. An assessment of the current culture in this division is carried out with the CTT (Cultural Transformation Tools) tool (Barrett 2006). It shows that the current values describe a very individualistic corporate culture.

Consequently, in addition to the split between professions, there are splits between young and old, men and women, westerners and easterners, etc. These splits generate unstable alliances and chaotic conflicts.

In order to transform this team coaching into an organizational coaching programme, it is decided with the client to include the *change agents* and *influencers* who can be identified within the division. The 'High Potential Managers' succession plan is used to select these people.

As the client group is a large and international one, it is decided to create a coaching community by grouping together three different coaches who represent three very different profiles: two men and one woman, with different educational backgrounds, each speaking two languages and presenting various types of expertise facilitation and coaching skills. A previous, successful common coaching experience is an additional criterion. Furthermore, the leading coach who was contacted by the client decided to experience the role of the 'meta' coach, meaning to stay in the meta-position, interconnecting the different interventions and acting as the client's contact point.

The coaching community meets via telephone conference calls and regular face-to-face meetings in order to ensure more thought-provoking conversations, to clarify possible interrelational cultural difficulties, and allow space for co-creation, learning and exploration. In addition, the group of coaches is supervised in a monthly three-hour session by a specialist in this kind of supervision.

The organizational coaching strategy was set up as follows: to respect the client's search for a cohesive culture and to help their leaders abandon their current 'silo behaviour'; the option of creative chaos based upon the idea of 'letting go of control' was proposed, as well as a series of interviews throughout the organization with the intention of finding the unifying source for organizational coaching. The coaches were assigned randomly across the organization to conduct the interviews. The idea was that self-organization could emerge.

During the third supervision session, the supervisor notices that the relationship between the three coaches starts to look like the relationship between the three groups of executives in the client's team. The same patterns slowly but surely develop, as the coaching journey proceeds. The supervisor is then able to recognize the signs of systemic reflection and help the coaches to understand the client issues. Once the systemic reflection is identified and made explicit, the supervisor can work with the team of coaches on the future actions.

## Evaluation of the model

The model is quite demanding and requires the closest attention from the supervisor. Of course, for a given mission and team of coaches the supervision starts with the usual process of helping the coaches to structure the sequence of workshops with the client. Also, at the beginning some interpersonal and personal issues within the coaching team need to be cleared up. The first two supervision sessions usually address these questions. It is when the mission is really underway, when coaches and customers are stretching their legs, that the model is fully deployed. At the end of the mission the normal process of assessing the journey is done. Therefore the tense period is hopefully limited to the middle part of the supervision journey, say from the third to the seventh session.

Organizational coaching is a growing market segment in France. A small number of coaches have developed methodologies and are training more and more coaches in applying this approach. The response is very enthusiastic because it appears to be very effective. Supervision is an essential element of the process. At the beginning, pioneers have been supervisors but currently, a coach who has a combined experience of organizational coaching and supervision can act as a supervisor for a team of coaches involved in coaching an organization.

## Key points for further reflection

Organizational coaching is in its infancy. We now have an idea of what to do if the situation matches the first systems theory (see Figure 5.1) where there is a 'wall of resistance'. But the enterprise's development could follow one of a number of paths, such as the two illustrated in Figure 5.2.

We do not see many of the 'revolution models' in industry and commerce. Such changes have been seen during the French revolution in 1789 or the Russian revolution in 1917. This model is part of the second Systems Theory initiated by Heiz Von Foerster (1973/1995) and specifically addressed by René Thom (1972) in his theory of catastrophe. Instead a lot of companies correspond to the 'evolution model' because the challenge is to adapt to a continuously changing market. When change is permanent, the issue is to change faster than the environment and there is no 'wall of resistance'. 'Change 2' occurs during a 'pause' where key decisions are made. For instance, in an environment where the price/performance of the technology is sharply declining, IBM and Hewlett-Packard followed this

**Change: Evolution Model**

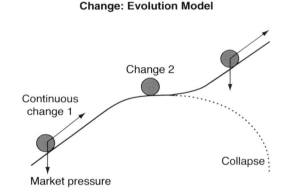

**Change: Revolution Model**

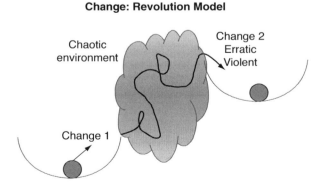

**Figure 5.2**  Change in the second and third systems theories

pattern when they moved from hardware and software to services. At the same time Control Data and Univac collapsed and a possible hypothesis is that they were unable to cope with such a model. There is still a lot of research to be done on organizational coaching and an enduring key question is how resistance to change occurs and how to help the client to go beyond it.

Identifying the 'wall of resistance' of coaches during supervision helps client teams and organizations to pass their own walls of resistance. The proposed approach invites us as coaches and supervisors to be more focused on the systemic aspects of work. We have to develop new reference frames to address properly the current evolutionary environment and to find ways to coach very advanced companies like Google. Theoretical studies (Kaneko and Suzuki 1994) suggest that evolution, itself driven by a changing environment, leads the system to this 'edge of chaos'. It is our ambition, as organizational coaches and supervisors of organizational coaches, to help locate this exact point and work from there with the client.

With our current knowledge, the role of coaches and supervisors is to find the most appropriate entry to a tunnel through the 'wall of resistance'. The first step consists in analysing the four subsystems (culture, structure, technology, decision process) and encouraging clients to consider all of them – instead of focusing only on the one familiar to the HR community (culture) or management (decision process). Rather similar is the Ken Wilber (2000) Integral Model of four quadrants, or the Bolman and Deal (1997) Four Frames Model (structural/systemic, cultural/symbolic, psychosocial and political).

The second step is to use the team of coaches as a replica of the organization and analyse this replica during supervision. The third step is to co-create a coaching programme which precisely addresses, at the client level, the difficulties identified during the second step.

This approach, compared to other approaches, is not a rigid frame like a methodology. On a sailing boat, the skipper uses the rudder as much to understand what the boat wants, as to maintain a direction.

## Learning more

Organizational coaching, team and group coaching and their supervision are new areas in the coaching industry. Readers who would like to invest in these topics can begin with:

Hawkins, P. and Smith, N. (2007) *Coaching, Mentoring and Organizational Consultancy: Supervision and Development*. Maidenhead: Open University Press.

Thornton, C. (2010) *Group and Team Coaching: The Essential Guide*. London: Routledge.

Bianco-Mathis, V., Roman, C. and Nabors, L. (2008) *Organizational Coaching: Building Relationships and Programs That Drive Results*. New York: Astd Press.

## References

Altfeld, D. (1999) An experiential group model for psychotherapy supervision, *International Journal of Group Psychotherapy*, 49: 237–54.

Barrett, R. (2006) *Building a Values-Driven Organization: A Whole System Approach to Cultural Transformation*. Oxford: Butterworth-Heinemann.

Bolman, L.G. and Deal, T.E. (1997) *Reframing Organizations: Artistry, Choice, and Leadership*. San Francisco, CA: Jossey-Bass.

Brown, J., Isaacs, D. and the World Café Community (2005) *The World Café*. San Francisco, CA: Berrett-Koehler.

Burt, R. (1999) *Quand La Culture D'entreprise Est-Elle Un Atout Stratégique?* [Is the Corporate Culture a Strategic Asset?]. Paris: Echos.

Cardon, A. (2003) *Coaching d'équipe* [Team Coaching]. Paris: Editions d'Organisation.

Darmouni, D. and Hadjadj, R. (2010) *La supervision des coachs. Enjeux, pratique et méthode* [Coaching Supervision: Methodology and Practice]. Paris: Eyrolles.

Delourme, A. and Marc, E. (2008) *La supervision en psychanalyse et en psychothérapie* [Supervision in Psychoanalysis and in Psychotherapy]. Paris: Dunod.

Devienne, E. (ed.) (2010) *Le grand livre de la supervision* [The Reference book of Supervision]. Paris: Eyrolles.

Fayol, H. (1918) *Administration Industrielle et Générale* [Administration in Industry]. Paris: Dunod.

Giroux, N. and Marroquin, L. (2005) L'approche narrative des organisations, *Revue Française De Gestion*, 159: 15–42.

Kaneko, K. and Suzuki, J. (1994) Imitation games, *Physica D*, 75: 328–42.

Kotter, J. and Heskett, J. (1992) *Corporate Culture and Performance*. New York: Free Press.

Lewin, K. (1951) *Field Theory in Social Science*. London: Tavistock.

Malarewicz, M.A. (1999) *Supervision en thérapie systémique* [Supervision in Systemic Therapy]. ESF.

McGregor, D. (1971) Theory X and theory Y, in D.S. Pugh (ed.) *Organization Theory*. New York: Penguin.

Miller, L. and Twomey, J.E. (1999) A parallel without a process: a relational view of a supervisory experience, *Contemporary Psychoanalysis*, 35: 557–80.

Millward, L. (2003) *Managing Diversity In Multinational Teams* (report under contract). Farnborough: Quinatec.

Millward, L. (2005) *Understanding Occupational and Organizational Psychology*. London: Sage.

Moral, M. and Henrichfreise, S. (2008) *Coaching d'organisation: Outils et Pratiques* [Organizational Coaching: Tools and Practice]. Paris: Armand Colin.

Moral, M. and Henrichfreise, S. (2009) Considerations on the emergence of organizational coaching, international perspectives, in M. Moral and G. Abbott (eds) *The Routledge Companion to International Business Coaching*. London: Routledge, pp. 15–33.

Morgan, G. (1989) *Images of Organization*, Thousand Oaks, CA: Sage.

Owen, H. (1997) *Open Space Technology: A User's Guide*. San Francisco, CA: Berrett-Koehler.

Schein, E. (1985) *Organisational Culture and Leadership*. New York: Jossey-Bass.

Searles, H.F. (1955) The informational value of the supervisor's emotional experiences, *Psychiatry*, 18: 135–46.

Stewart, T. (1993) Re-engineering: the hot new management tool, *Fortune*, 127(23): 41–8.

Taylor, F. (1911) *Principles of Scientific Management*. New York: Harper & brothers.

Thom, R. (1972) *Structural Stability and Morphogenesis, trans*. D.H. Fowler. Reading: Benjamin.

Tylim, I. (1999) Group supervision and the psychoanalytic process, *International Journal of Group Psychotherapy*, 49: 181–95.

Von Bertalanffy, L. (1947) The history and status of general systems theory, *Academy of Management Journal*, 15(4): 407–26.

Von Foerster, H. (1973/1995) *Cybernetics of Cybernetics*, 2nd edn. Minneapolis, MN: Future Systems.

Weick, K. and Quinn, R. (1999) Organisational change and development, *Annual Review of Psychology*, 50: 361–86.

Wilber, K. (2000) *Integral Psychology: Consciousness, Spirit, Psychology, Therapy*. Boston: Shambhala.

# 6 The self in supervision

*Katherine Long*

## Introduction

Most coaches and supervisors intuitively understand that *who* they are has a fundamental bearing on *how* they practise, and yet the coaching literature has on the whole tended to bypass this area, focusing on the principles and methodologies of coaching, rather than on the person of the coach. For many novice, and indeed more experienced coaches, it is easy to feel swamped by the vast array of techniques and processes that compete within this multidisciplinary field.

Exactly why our profession has largely overlooked the significance of the self-evident – the fact that every coach is unique – is open to debate. Occupying ourselves with definitions, methods and techniques of coaching, we have placed greater emphasis on performance and process than on person and purpose.

There is, however, within the growing literature regarding the coaching relationship (De Haan 2008), mindfulness in coaching (Silsbee 2008) and gestalt coaching psychology (Bluckert 2006, 2010; Allan and Whybrow 2007), a greater emphasis on the person and presence of the coach. Bluckert (2006: 125) argues that 'Being able to connect with more aspects of yourself and to bring them authentically into the coaching relationship can make a profound difference to the quality and depth of your work.' This suggests that a key focus of supervision should be on the 'self as instrument' and further implies exploration of a deeper awareness of the common themes running through our interactions and relationships, approaches and principles, identity and development.

This chapter introduces the diamond model as a way of viewing the relationships between facets of our practice and person, the connection between who we are and what we do, as a means to achieving a more authentic and congruent whole. The use of 'we' and 'our' is deliberate; if we choose to adopt the self as a primary focus of supervision, it follows that as supervisors, we must apply the same focus to ourselves.

The diamond model is the result of personal heuristic enquiry gained through hundreds of hours of supervision to independent and internal coaches, to candidates on coach-mentoring qualifications and as assessor to their portfolios of evidence, as well as research into my own practice. The model draws from a range of influences introduced throughout this chapter, and has been shaped by two key questions:

- What does the coach bring into the room?
- How do different coaching competences interact as a whole, as embodied by the person of the coach?

## The diamond model

To explore this model we need to begin with the first question, 'What does the coach bring into the room?' If we were to take a field theory perspective, we would need to look with an expanded focus on 'not just one particular map, but to a whole section of the atlas' (Parlett 1991). Whilst it is important not to lose sight of a wider, systemic perspective of the coach, a more immediate and experiential way of engaging with the question might be to imagine ourselves as onlookers to a coaching session, noticing:

1  what is happening in the moment, the coach's presence, interactions and interventions in response to their client;
2  the relationship, trust and rapport which has been created, the patterns of communication, perhaps what has been contracted for, e.g. purely personal or organizational objectives, or a mix of both;
3  a sense of some of the core principles the coach is operating from, how they bring these into the session (whether expressed and applied overtly, or more subtly in the background);
4  our intuitions and guesses about aspects of the person of the coach, a sense of their life experiences, their personality, beliefs and values, groups and systems to which they belong.

Furthermore, we may even have formed an opinion regarding the extent to which the coach reflects in and on their practice, how much they invest in the development of each of the levels mentioned above, including work on themselves. When we translate this into a model, we get something like we see in Figure 6.1.
   The diamond model is based on two premises which have a logical outcome:

That who I am as a coach is connected to who I am as an individual
That gaining congruence and authenticity brings greater effectiveness to my practice.
   Therefore . . .
to be more effective to my clients there needs to be congruence between who I am as a person and who I am as a coach.

If we accept the equation, and recognize that both coach and client work with their intuition about each other, then there are implications for how holistic the scope of supervision may need to be.
   The model provides a framework for looking at multiple dimensions of the coach, suggesting a relationship or hierarchy between the different levels. It is *not* intended to replace a coach's own model of coaching, or prescribe what should

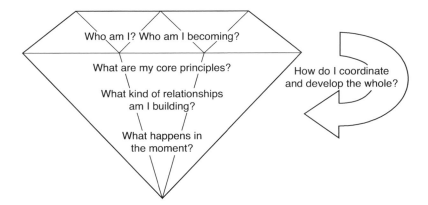

**Figure 6.1** The diamond model

populate the different levels, or pretend to fully explore the interface between the coach and client, but it can provide a starting point for coaches and supervisors to think about their own 'identikit', their essence, and how this communicates within their practice.

## Levels within the diamond model

### 'Who am I? Who am I becoming?'

There seems to be a tendency within Western cultures to define self in static and objectified terms such as through role, experience and achievements (Handy 2002: 92–9). Yet our identities are based on a complex mesh of elements which include life experiences and our interpretation of them, accumulated values and beliefs, sense of purpose, cultural, sexual and spiritual identities, the different systems and relationships of which we are a part, as well as personality traits and physicality. At any given time some aspects will be relatively stable, whilst others are in a state of flux. As supervisors attending to the whole person of the coach, it behoves us to attune to the coach's process of becoming, transitioning and meaning-making in this regard.

> If I accept the other person as something fixed, already diagnosed and classified, already shaped by his past, then I am doing my part to confirm this limited hypothesis. If I can accept him as a process of becoming, then I am doing what I can to confirm or make real his potentialities.
>
> (Rogers 1958/1967: 55)

Each of the facets of our identity has the potential to impact, whether directly or indirectly, on the coaching relationship and building awareness of 'being and becoming' must be an important part of a coach's self-development (Bachkirova and Cox 2007).

### 'What are my core principles as a coach?'

Flaherty (2005: 12) asserts that coaching is a 'principle shaped ontological stance' and 'not a series of techniques', yet much popular coach training (as opposed to coach development) has focused on teaching tools and processes than in developing an understanding of underpinning principles (Palmer and Whybrow 2007). The supervisor can play an important role in supporting a deeper understanding of the foundations of the coach's practice, yet whilst it may be useful to gain a theoretical knowledge of a range of methodologies, it is vital, according to De Haan's research, that the coach develops approaches to which they can commit wholeheartedly:

> Commitment to a coaching ideology and a coaching approach, to which you gear your interventions, will contribute towards your effectiveness, provided that commitment is genuine, and focussed on helping the client. In other words, commit yourself heart and soul to your approach, but resist the temptation to believe that it is truly superior.
>
> (De Haan 2008: 49)

The skill of the supervisor is to support the coach in gaining clarity regarding the principles and supporting methodologies to which they most align and commit themselves, building a principle shaped stance which is congruent with other aspects of their person, which they can embody through their practice.

### 'What kinds of relationships am I building?'

The relationship with the client encompasses a complex range of factors, including an inevitable interplay with the relationships with sponsors and stakeholders, and the systems of each. The primary coach–client relationship is furthermore influenced by factors including the coach's engagement and contracting with the client, their management of expectations and boundaries, contribution to structure and flow within the conversation, and building of trust and rapport.

The need for the coach to work empathically from the client's perspective, as well as to operate from a place of deep self-knowledge is particularly apparent within the relationship (De Haan 2008: 39–46), which is a fruitful and important focus within supervision.

### 'What happens in the moment?'

Whilst the use of recordings or notes from coaching sessions can add great value in helping coaches review and learn from the more obvious interactions with their clients, it is much harder to capture the subtle shift of states within a meeting, or moments of presence—'a state of awareness, in the moment, characterised by the felt experience of timelessness, connectedness, and a larger truth' (Silsbee 2008: 20–1), or indeed the depth of empathic resonance achieved (Reitz 2007). In exploring interventions and interactions, the supervisor needs to help the coach attune to and identify the subtle energy levels of the moment from which they generated, and to notice their impact on ways of responding to the client.

Research from neuroscience (Lewis et al. 2000) shows that owing to the open-loop system of the limbic brain, individuals are in constant subconscious dialogue, impacting both physiology and emotions as they tune into each other's inner states. Observable interactions in the moment can be understood as arising from less observable yet powerful forces, so supporting the coach in understanding what they bring to bear in the moment must also include a focus on their thoughts, emotions and felt sensations in relating to the client.

### 'How do I coordinate and develop the whole person?'

The final element of the model refers to the coach's ability to continuously coordinate and develop themselves and their practice. If there is any part of the diamond model in which the internal supervisor (Carroll and Gilbert 2005: 36) resides, it is here. Supervision has the potential to play an important role in supporting the coach's self-generative facility, 'the capacity to be present and a learner in all of life in order to make choices from the inner state of greatest possible awareness and resourcefulness' (Silsbee 2008: 50), and it is my belief that supporting the coach in developing their own self-generative capabilities is the ultimate goal of supervision.

Working in this area of the diamond model will include a focus on how the coach reflects in and on the different facets of their practice and being, and how they develop abilities in accessing the wealth of strengths at their disposal in the service of their client. It will also include a focus on the coach's self-development, whether through personal practices for self-care and restoration, continuing professional development (CPD) and supervision activities, use of feedback processes, reflecting or journaling. By developing awareness of their self-generative facility, the coach's choices regarding self-development become less like random, unprocessed events, and more of a coordinated strategy to challenge, support, augment and enhance himself/herself as the whole person.

## Interaction of the different levels within the model

It may be helpful to think of the two upper levels of the diamond model as being a coach's accumulated store of wealth, which is available to access whilst working with the client. The two lower levels describe the capital the coach is constantly building – what happens in the moment is 'banked' in the relationship with the client. The self-generative facility supports the flow between each of the different levels so that they inform each other and allow the coach constant access between them.

Using the levels in the diamond model as a set of lenses can also help us explore the second question posed in the introduction to this chapter, regarding the way in which the coach embodies different coaching competences. If we take, for example, EMCC's competence category 'Action and Outcome Orientation' we might look at how this plays out within the coach's own identity (e.g. what is the coach's approach to achieving action and outcomes in their own life?); how may this may be connected (or not) to the core principles and methodologies to which they hold in their practice; how the coach's personal and espoused beliefs impact within the relationship and contracting; and how this manifests in the moment with different clients at different times. Finally, we might look at how the coach reflects on, reviews and develops this competence within themselves and their practice.

## Approaches underpinning use of the diamond model

There are many different pathways to exploring the self, and the diamond model can be used to complement a range of psychological, philosophical or metaphysical paradigms. My personal experience indicates that there are several key perspectives which support effective use of this model.

### Holistic and person-centred

The supervisor needs to hold a perspective of the whole person in the coach's being and becoming, including the temporal aspect of their journey of growth and development. This does not imply that supervisors are invited, or indeed equipped to support the coach to fully explore each of the levels in the model, but does suggest that they adopt an approach that takes into account the unique ways in which these interact and impact within an individual's practice.

Tudor and Worrell (2004: 20) contend that 'a supervisee's willingness to explore those areas of his work about which he feels most unsure is in direct proportion to his perception of his supervisor's unconditional acceptance of him'. A person-centred approach, with its core conditions of unconditional positive regard, empathy and congruence is a vital underpinning to helping the coach explore the different levels within the model.

### Appreciative, non-attached and non-judgemental

It is relatively easy to conceive that a supervisor's tendency to focus on *deficiency* can create a very different kind of relationship to one where the default position is one of *sufficiency*. Yet maintaining an appreciative and non-judgemental stance can be tested, especially when the topics presented within supervision are framed as problems. This can draw the supervisor into a diagnostic, deficiency oriented mindset, which may be at the expense of helping the coach to access their own awareness and resourcefulness. Hawkins and Smith (2006: 148) warn against the dangers within the emerging field of coach-mentoring supervision of applying mindsets directly from therapeutic traditions, which tend to focus 'more on pathology than on health'.

The supervisor needs to support a non-judgemental environment where the coach can observe their practice without unhelpful interference from the 'inner critic as supervisor' (Carroll and Gilbert 2005). By relinquishing their own attachments and judgements regarding outcomes for the supervision, and in respecting diverse coaching methodologies and approaches (which may run counter to their own beliefs), the supervisor co-creates conditions for transformation. In the language of Scharmer's Theory U (2009), this supports the coach to 'let go' and 'let come', enabling them to try out new perspectives and act from an undefended position with an open mind, heart and will, thus allowing the future to emerge within themselves and their practice.

### The need for safety

Paradoxically, creating a non-judgemental space can surface what may have become incongruent or intolerable for the coach either in themselves or in their work, and can be experienced as cathartic, liberating and sometimes painful. It is *not* the role of the coaching supervisor to try and root out these issues, but to allow the freedom and safety for them to emerge as they will, and to support the coach in deciding what, if any, course of action is needed. Frequently the fact of surfacing an issue is sufficient for it to start to diminish, whilst counselling or other sources of help may be appropriate in other instances.

### Supervisor's own integrity

The integrity of the supervisor is essential for any successful supervision relationship, and in this context, the nuance of 'wholeness' is especially important. The supervisor needs to be in touch with their own process of being and becoming, committed to self-care and restoration, and attuned to what they 'bring into the room'.

## Case illustrations

There are no prescribed processes or stages for using the diamond model, which can be used effectively both in the foreground and background of a supervision conversation.

### 'Foreground' examples

Use of the model in the foreground can have the impact of grounding a coach's practice very powerfully.

In the early contracting stages:

> *I introduced the model at the beginning of a supervision relationship with P, an independent coach and trainer. This created an openness to explore her signature presence as a unifying theme throughout our sessions, as opposed to just focusing on snapshots of her practice. This created a common language and means of navigating the different elements of P's practice ('oh, that's part of my diamond'), helping her to see the relationship between her strongly activist learning style and tendency to set high expectations for her own performance, and her focused, goal driven approaches to coaching. This created an awareness of her own offering in relation to other coaches, as well as how to adapt and flex her approaches to different clients and contexts, and allow herself adequate self-care and restoration to balance her highly dynamic ways of working.*

As a mapping exercise at the start of a new supervision relationship (which can be adapted to include a strongly appreciative focus, look at a coach's development through time, or highlight degrees of congruence between the different levels):

> *With the CEO of a coaching consultancy, we worked through the mapping exercise very rapidly, allowing for more intuitive rather than overly deliberated answers to emerge. On reflecting on the exercise afterwards, this highlighted to her how fundamental her own values are to her work and how they underpin everything she does, identifying these as a deep respect for other people, a love of diversity and transparency and openness about 'who we are and what we do'.*

And just reading about the model in its original articulation (Long 2009) supported a coach in developing her own model:

> *'Something clicked when I came across Katherine's article on the Diamond Model . . . all of which begged the question of the "who of me" in coach-mentoring. I was inspired to start building a "Dynamic Model-of-Me" as a coach as it led to a fundamental acceptance that "who I am, is how I coach". Reflecting on "who I really am, and what I believe in" helped me then to find congruent coaching approaches to add to my professional tool kit.'*

## 'Background' examples

Keeping the model in the background is perhaps more usual, and is especially appropriate in the following instances.

With novice coaches, who might experience overt use of the model as overwhelming, or irrelevant to their immediate needs:

> *With N, an internal coach in health management, it acted as a mental framework (for the supervisor) to support him in making connections between different parts of his practice. N frequently worried about getting his interventions 'right', and worried that the client didn't seem as motivated as he would like within the sessions. In exploring his practice at the relationship level, it helped him understand the impact of the way the coaching relationship had been set up, both on himself and the client, and take actions to address potential misunderstandings that were hindering effective coaching. Looking at both 'in the moment' and 'relationship' levels drew out greater understanding of himself and his own drivers and preferences within coaching.*

In group supervision, examples of working creatively to deepen understanding of the self as instrument include:

> *Inviting coaches to find on their person an item or piece of clothing which they feel says something particular about themselves as individuals, and explain why to the group. Then invite them to say what this item says about their coaching practice. In most cases, coaches can readily find strong links, though not always obvious ones; in one case it revealed to one coach that she invests a lot of energy in keeping part of herself out of her coaching relationships. In another case a coach complained that he didn't have any items that were indicative of his personality, but in exploring further it turned out that he tends to travel light, both as a person and as a coach!*

Or:

> *Invite coaches to sit silently in pairs, asking themselves, as they observe each other, 'I wonder what wonderful qualities this person brings to their work as a coach?', taking time afterwards to observe the impact of this question on the attitude towards the individual (curiosity, anticipation). The second stage of the exercise involved working in pairs again, asking each other 'What are the key qualities you bring as a coach?' and writing the responses on each other's hands (in washable coloured pens), paying special attention to what colour, which hand or part of the hand those elements*

*should be written. The following discussion was very rich – some coaches were very clear regarding on which hands certain attributes were located, and what colour they needed to be. In one case, what the coach brought was so encompassing of their whole self that their qualities needed to be written across both hands, i.e. what I bring requires all of me to deliver it.*

In both cases, what emerges from the exercises can then be explored through the different levels of the model, by asking, for example, 'How are you nurturing or developing this aspect of yourself?'; or, 'How might your clients experience this aspect within the relationship?', etc.

As a mental checklist of areas of focus and awareness in any supervision conversation, and to help the coach to notice when they are aligned or unaligned, borrowing this analogy from a very different field is helpful: 'Running with your posture out of alignment can create tension, fatigue, discomfort, and even pain. When your posture is aligned properly, your structure is supporting the weight of your body instead of your muscles having to do it' (Dreyer 2004: 63). By supporting awareness of what good alignment in the coach's practice looks and feels like, the supervisor can enable coaches to access the qualities of their own person to support the weight of their practice, rather than strain to conform to internal or external expectations or restrictions.

*F had undergone a coach training programme where a rigid view of 'right and wrong' coaching behaviours was taught. He was unwilling or nervous to access his own wisdom and judgement, even when the methods taught created tension within his practice. He directed stress and frustration at himself (for feeling inadequate to coach in the way he was taught), his coachees (for not fitting into the model) and with me (for not immediately fixing the problem)! Using the Diamond model in this context required greater sensitivity to support F in shedding his rigid views whilst showing respect for his methodology. This approach elevated his sense of self as instrument, dissolving unhelpful constraints which were manifesting as lack of congruence in his practice, enabling him to serve his clients with greater ease and flexibility.*

*N presented frustrations in working with a number of clients from the same organization. In looking at his relationship with the sponsor it became clear that he felt restricted in dealing with a number of unhelpful patterns within the organization which were compromising the effectiveness of the coaching. As we discussed this, it emerged that he was holding himself back from bringing more of a systems thinking and consulting role to his coaching, due to a lack of confidence in articulating his own perspective and intuitions. We reframed the issue from 'How to manage the relationship with the client and sponsor' to 'How to access and make use of my strengths'. When we looked at how he might make shifts within himself and future relationships with new sponsors, it resulted over time in N being able to utilize his consulting and leadership skills with far greater congruence and authenticity, adding value to his own experience and to the client's.*

## Evaluation of the model

As with any model, there are constraints and strengths, some of which are introduced below.

### Only half the picture?

Given the model focuses entirely on the person of the coach, one might question the apparent lack of emphasis on the client and their system. However, the model does not preclude a supervisor from offering other interventions, and can be complementary to other models such as Hawkins and Shohet's (2006) seven-eyed supervision model which more explicitly expands the frame to focus on relationships within the wider system, or feedback tools such as The Coaching Working Alliance Questionnaire (De Haan and Duckworth 2010) based on Horvath's Working Alliance Inventory.

Whilst these interventions are entirely congruent with working with the diamond model, it is important to remember that the supervisor (in most cases) can only work with the coach they supervise and not with their client. There is a danger that, based on descriptions from the coach, the supervisor builds assumptions regarding the client and their system and forms what Hawkins and Shohet (2006: 96) call the 'fantasy relationship between the client and the supervisor'.

### Too rosy?

The diamond model and approaches outlined in this chapter appear to be highly geared towards the developmental and resourcing functions rather than the qualitative or managerial modes of supervision (Hawkins and Smith 2006: 151), and may appear too accepting of the coach and their practice, uncritical enough to provide challenge and stimulus.

The diamond model *is* underpinned by an attitude of sufficiency, not in a blindly optimistic sense, but in the recognition that in the end, as supervisors or as coaches, all we have to bring to the service of our clients is ourselves, and must necessarily become effective in accessing our inner resources. Often the greatest stretch is to connect with our own greatness, humility and compassion, an experience which can be profound and deeply challenging.

In addition, experience suggests that the rigour of exploring self and practice through the different lenses has proved a very effective means of surfacing potential ethical and safety issues in the coach's work, and subsequently in supporting the coach to identify appropriate strategies or resources.

## Learning more

Whilst many coaches aspire to work in ways which feel true to themselves, there is an equal desire to be responsive to a wide range of clients and contexts. Using the diamond model in the ways described here has, I believe, the advantage of supporting both aspirations. The more readily a coach can access their wealth of inner resources, the greater the authenticity and flexibility that can be brought to bear in their coaching. I believe we have much to gain from a deeper understanding of the relationship between authenticity and flexibility, one which is perhaps analogous to that of a tree which has the capacity to bend more easily and without damage *because* it is well rooted and watered.

Two titles which address this area are *Let Your Life Speak* by Quaker teacher and activist Parker J. Palmer (2000), writing on themes of wholeness and purpose. He presents a compelling narrative of his own experience and learning through engaging with vocation, and a life lived authentically. *The Ecology of Coaching* by Simon P. Walker (2009) proposes that coaching, at its best, is 'an act of hospitality, opening up the space within ourselves for the other', and introduces eight key postures which enable the coach to serve their clients flexibly and responsively.

Finally, a writer who compassionately and comprehensively addresses the growth of the person and presence of the coach, is Doug Silsbee (2008), author of *Presence-based Coaching*. His work expands on some of the themes within this chapter, addressing how we as coaches and supervisors create conditions within ourselves to enable qualities such as compassion, gratitude, mindfulness and non-judgement.

## References

Allan, J. and Whybrow, A. (2007) Gestalt coaching, in S. Palmer and A. Whybrow (eds), *Handbook of Coaching Psychology: A Guide for Practitioners*. Hove: Routledge.

Bachkirova, T. and Cox, E. (2007) A cognitive-developmental approach for coach development, in S. Palmer and P. Whybrow (eds), *Handbook of Coaching Psychology: A Guide for Practitioners*. Hove: Routledge, pp. 325–50.

Bluckert, P. (2006) *Psychological Dimensions of Executive Coaching*. Maidenhead: Open University Press.

Bluckert, P. (2010) The Gestalt approach to coaching, in E. Cox, T. Bachkirova and D. Clutterbuck (eds), *The Complete Handbook of Coaching*. London: Sage, pp. 87–8.

Carroll, M. and Gilbert, M. (2005) *On Becoming a Supervisee*. London: Vulkani Publishing.

De Haan, E. (2008) *Relational Coaching – Journeys Towards Mastering One to One Learning*. Chichester: Wiley.

De Haan, E. and Duckworth, A. (2010) *The Coaching Working Alliance Questionnaire©*. http://www.ashridge.org.uk/Website/Content.nsf/wFARACC/Developing+psychometric+tools+for+coaches?opendocument (accessed 15 February 2011).

Dreyer, D. (2004) *Chi Running: A Revolutionary Approach to Effortless, Injury-Free Running*. London: Simon & Schuster UK Ltd.

Flaherty, J. (2005) *Coaching: Evoking Excellence in Others*. Oxford: Elsevier Butterworth-Heinemann.

Handy, C. (2002) *The Hungry Spirit: New Thinking for a New World*. London: Arrow.

Hawkins, P. and Shohet, R. (2006) *Supervision in the Helping Professions*, 3rd edn. Maidenhead: Open University Press.

Hawkins, P. and Smith, N. (2006) *Coaching, Mentoring and Organisational Consultancy: Supervision and Development*. Maidenhead: Open University Press.

Lewis, T., Amini, F. and Lannon, R. (2000) *A General Theory of Love*. New York: Random House.

Long, K. (2009) Greater than the sum of our parts, *The OCM Journal*, 9, Spring: 26–8.

Palmer, S. and Whybrow, A. (2007) Coaching psychology; an introduction, in S. Palmer and A. Whybrow (eds), *Handbook of Coaching Psychology: A Guide for Practitioners*. Hove: Routledge, Ch. 1, pp. 1–20.

Palmer, P.J. (2000) *Let Your Life Speak: Listening for the Voice of Vocation*. San Francisco, CA: Jossey-Bass.

Parlett, M. (1991) Reflections on field theory, *The British Gestalt Journal*, 1: 68–91.

Reitz, M. (2007) Leading in the moment, *The Ashridge Journal*, Spring: 24–9.

Rogers, C. (1958/1967) *On Becoming a Person*. London: Constable.

Scharmer, O. (2009) *Theory U: Leading from the Future as it Emerges*. San Francisco, CA: Berrett-Koehler.

Silsbee, D. (2008) *Presence-based Coaching: Cultivating Self-Generative Leaders Through Mind, Body and Heart*. San Francisco, CA: Jossey-Bass.

Tudor, K. and Worrall, M. (2004) *Freedom to Practice: Person-centred Approaches to Supervision*. Ross-on-Wye: PCCS Books.

Walker, S.P. (2009) *The Ecology of Coaching: A New Approach to Transformational Coaching*. Oxford: Simon P. Walker.

# 7 Ethics and professional standards in supervision

*David Lane*

## Introduction

This chapter considers the development of coaching and the emergence of supervision as a component of practice. It will argue that this area builds on principles of ethics which have universal applicability. The universality of ethical codes raises the question of the need, or not, for a code for coaching supervision. As supervision develops in coaching (and a number of professional bodies now endorse it) questions arise over the difference between that and other forms of supervision. Is there, in practice, a profession of supervisor applicable across a range of professional areas? The chapter considers the work that has been done on this so far. The increasing use of separate and formalized structures or 'registers' of supervisors in psychology, other professions and coaching will be explored.

The chapter argues that supervision is occupying different professional spaces. In its traditional role as an activity between the experienced expert and the student learning their craft it operates in an apprenticeship mode and codified and linear principles apply. However, as a field of activity between experienced practitioners it is operating in more emergent spaces to deal with complex issues. In this space expertise in supervision appears to operate in a new cross-disciplinary framework for which knowledge of the specific field is less important than competence in supervision processes.

## The emergence of coaching and demand for professionalism

An increasing number of training programmes and newly emerging bodies have developed to provide credentials and regulate the field. Coaching research has blossomed and there is now little difficulty finding accredited coaches to offer their services in what previously had been an open arena. Yet buyers of coaching services continue to express concern about standards and the availability of qualified and certified practitioners. Within the business and executive coaching field, companies employing coaches have responded, even given a number of clear guidelines (Jarvis for CIPD 2006), by establishing their own selection processes, of varying validity (Jarvis et al. 2006). There remains uncertainty and no institution (including professional bodies) has yet gained sufficient credibility to allay the anxiety that results. These processes often ask the coach to identify their supervision arrangements – there is a belief in its value. Yet evidence for its influence on coaching outcomes has been difficult to ascertain with authority. This has resulted in confusion between providers and buyers. This has in turn led to increased interest in finding shared approaches within the coaching community (Global Coaching Community 2008) but as yet shared guidelines have not been adopted.[1]

## Does coaching supervision meet the criteria for a profession?

Generally accepted core features of a profession include the requirement for members to have formal academic qualifications; adherence to an enforceable code of ethics; practice licensed only to qualified members; compliance with applicable state-sanctioned regulation; and a common body of knowledge and skills (Spence 2007: 261).

There is a way to go before coaching can be defined as a profession in the narrowest sense yet professionalism is increasing (Lane et al. 2010b). This certainly raises doubts about coaching supervision as a professional area (in spite of a number of high level and well regarded courses in this area) yet maybe supervision as a profession separate from the specific application in coaching has made progress. In the following sections we consider developments within the wider professions, and argue for a different approach before specifically considering coaching supervision.

## Professions are increasingly fragile – do we need a new approach?

The role of professions in society is long established but has increasingly been challenged. A number of authors from within the sociology of the professions have pointed to factors that have undermined the traditional respect with which they were held (see Lane and Corrie 2006, for a review).

A number of factors are seen as undermining this traditional respect. The challenge to the idea that professionals in training need to complete a certain number of hours to be accredited has been under assault from the move to competence models, which themselves have been criticized and present their own problems. If someone can show that they are competent why should they have to serve an artificial number of hours in an apprenticeship model? The speed of change of knowledge has directed professions to consider the implications of the position that once qualified you can be seen as for ever competent – hence the need for a serious evaluated approach to CPD (rather than merely a log of hours completed) and renewal of licence to practise through re-accreditation every five years as suggested in some fields such as medicine and psychology at the European level.

The demand for consumer voice and client autonomy has changed the basis for commissioning of services and the state and insurers are demanding a say in standards and service model rather than this being a matter of professional control. The move to employee rather than self-employed relationships has also altered the factors influencing professional service standards and the definition of the client relationship (Corrie and Lane 2010).

This is affecting many professions. A recent review of 50 professions (Lane et al. 2010a) across several countries found that many were seeking to renew their licence to practise based on:

- position of client;
- autonomy of client;
- profession as social contributor.

So what has happened to professions to cause this? Increasingly the challenges we face require rapid, cross-disciplinary responses. The concept of the profession has itself become fragile. Professionals have been losing their monopoly of knowledge. Knowledge has become something that evolves in specific communities of practice. It is no longer a list of facts that is stable, but is contextualized and relational. The body of knowledge is growing and knowledge is democratized by being accessible through channels open to everybody, mainly through the Internet. In that sense there is no profession that has exclusive ownership over the knowledge base in specific areas of expertise. So the professions of the future may look very different from those of the past.

## If professions are changing what might they look like in future?

Cavanagh and Lane (2010) have argued that to deal with an increasingly complex world different models of professional practice are likely to emerge. Drawing on Stacey's work on complexity (1996) they present three possible stories for professional practice (see Figure 7.1).

### The traditional profession

In a world in which there are high levels or agreement about what to do and high predictability that we can achieve defined outcomes, we can, perhaps, work within the traditional rational models of the professions. It assumes we can agree its basis and conform to our own professional body or state regulated codes. It assumes a clear relationship with the client that works for the client's benefit. Sanctions for breeches for that client relationship can be defined in terms of a prescribed code because practice can be codified accordingly to rational criteria that are stable and predictable. Our identity as professionals is generated by membership of a defined body. We are, for example, psychologists because the British Psychological Society (BPS) or the Health Professions Council says so. This is also the framework that

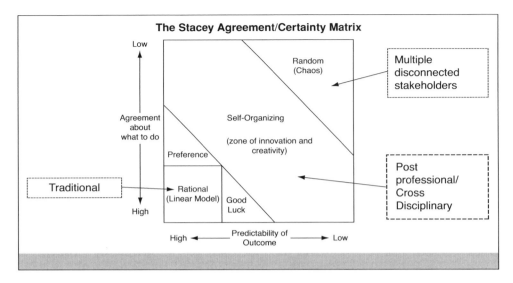

**Figure 7.1**  Matching profession to context
*Source:* Adapted from Zimmerman et al. (1998).

has informed much of the debate about the role of supervision in developing future practitioners – the expert/apprentice model. It is all codified, predictable and rational and proceeds through a linear process. In coaching the International Coach Federation (ICF) adopt a similar position – you need as a student to be supervised by an ICF-recognized practitioner.

### The post-professional cross disciplinary

What happens in the more complex world that faces many professions and certainly professional coaches and those who supervise experienced practitioners? They are often confronted with limited levels of agreement about what to do, and limited predictability of outcome. We do not know what to do and even if we did we could not be sure of achieving it. Rather than relying on codified knowledge from within one professional sphere we often are facing unique issues that require cross-disciplinary knowledge or an unusual synthesis of ideas and therefore we have to practise outside of the prescribed codes that define the traditional profession. We look to communities of practice to explore standards and quality creatively. In operating in these new spaces our identity is more diffuse and we are faced with complex patterns of client relationships not the linear model as traditionally defined. We might indeed be negotiating the relationship client by client (Lo 2004) that is 'identity generated in practice'. This leads us away from a traditional model of professions towards a more emergent framework that is post-professional (Drake 2010) and cross-disciplinary.

## Profession as multiple disconnected stakeholders

What happens is a more chaotic space in which there are multiple ideas and little agreement about what we might do and low predictability of outcome. In a professional world populated by diverse and disconnected stakeholders each operating for their own ends it is difficult to prescribe any frameworks – all is contestable. Is this perhaps the world we currently inhabit as coaches and supervisors of coaches? There are many organizations contesting the space and a very diverse practice and client base. What is the professional stance? One possibility here are universal features of practice that have consistently emerged across time, space and cultures. In a chaotic situation there is a tendency to revert to previous and potentially unhelpful patterns of behaviour. Whereas, using universal features such as ethics provides possible nodes around which conversations can happen. Some of these universal features are considered.

# Do we look at ethics as drawing on universal principles?

A key question we might ask is whether we look at ethics as drawing on universal principles applied to all professional practice or as arising from the specific content of defined disciplines?

Many bodies define a code of conduct (or ethics) which they expect members to uphold and for some it is the starting point towards a journey of defining the professional standards. Certain features are shared across many professional bodies and therefore appear to be context independent.

Common features, increasingly, have been noted in the ethical frameworks used by the professions which are seen as underpinned by universal principles shared across a range of disciplines. As argued elsewhere (Lane and Corrie 2006; Corrie and Lane 2010) a profession may be defined in terms of a minimum of three areas and these can form the basis for examining professional ethics and standards:

The **purpose** defines the profession in terms of who we are and what we are for in serving clients, a social good and the profession itself. It therefore includes the belief systems, values and ethics which define the profession identified by its governing bodies, stakeholders and local, national and global influences which impact how the profession is able to define its purpose.

This is the fundamental building block to any profession – its purpose. The purpose defines the profession: what it shares with other professions as well as what differentiates it. All else follows from this.

The **perspective** includes the knowledge base of the profession and in coaching this implies the theories of human nature which are influential within the profession, and in the case of coaching supervision, theories within a range of disciplines which are influential in understanding the way individuals function and learn in the context of their professional practice and its enhancement through a supervisory relationship. It incorporates our theories of change for individuals and organizations as well as beliefs about the nature of evidence and how that should be incorporated within practice (in this case as a coach supervisor). For some professions (which include coaching and supervision) it often includes a sense of self – the person of the professional is considered relevant as is the relationship between their personal philosophy and practice.

The content of these, of course, changes as the evidence base changes – but the principle that a profession is built upon core knowledge remains constant.

The **process** defines what happens when a professional works with a client. In coaching supervision this includes the process by which the agenda for the work emerges; the process by which the encounter between supervisor and coach develops to include responsibilities towards client, sponsor and other key players; the formulation of any understanding of the concerns that supervisor and coach reach and their use to inform the work, interventions undertaken and evaluation of outcomes sought.

This is the area that probably changes the most as new frameworks for practice are developed and the competence required to carry out those processes is adapted. What remains constant is the concept that the professional can enact the processes judged appropriate to competent practice. So the professional can be judged by their performance even if the competences that are deemed to underlie that change as understanding of practice morphs (Corrie and Lane 2010).

In the study noted above the Worldwide Association of Business Coaches (Lane et al. 2010a) reviewed some 50 professions and the wider literature. They found that the definitions of purpose and perspective are usually clearly incorporated within professional standards. The definitions of process that mark how professionals work with clients are less so and are sometimes implied rather than defined and often emerge as increasingly shared assumptions about what happens between clients and professions in the process of the engagement between them. There are those matters which sit outside of the boundaries of acceptable process defined in the code of conduct and sometimes those codes are positively crafted to state what good practice looks like, but what happens day to day is often discretionary. However, in more recent years and with increasing moves towards evidence-based practice in many professions the process by which the service is offered to clients has been more often the subject of debate in defining professional standards.

However, what also emerged in the Worldwide Association of Business Coaches (WABC) study was the considerable overlap between diverse professions on core underpinning principles – the ethical stance which defines being a professional rather than simply being paid to undertake an occupational role. For example, Gardner and colleagues have looked at traditional and newer professions and distinguish those that have at the centre the idea of doing 'Good Works' that follows from a 'calling' to the profession. This is explored in various examples at a dedicated website (www.goodworkproject.org): 'This project (The GoodWork™) Project is a large scale effort to identify individuals and institutions that exemplify good work – work that is excellent in quality, socially responsible, and meaningful to its practitioners – and to determine how best to increase the incidence of good work in our society.'

This universality has been marked in a number of projects considering the possibility of universal codes for professions. For example: the Universal Declaration of Ethical Principles for Psychologists was adopted in Berlin in 2008 (IUPsyS 2008). This was the culmination of a global collaboration and research into codes governing professional practice across cultures and the ages. For as long as groups have combined together to form associations to deliver service to others codes appear to have emerged. The studies for this project cover codes going back millennia. These include the codes of Hammurabi to Hippocrates and on to modern codes such as the Declaration of Helsinki on Medical Research and the Universal Declaration of Human Rights. (See ethical codes in the References; also debates in Gauthier 2004; Attia et al. 2009).

As we begin to think about ethics and professional standards for coaching supervision (either as part of coaching or a separate profession) it is perhaps important to have a dialogue on building these from universal precepts.

The preamble to the 'Universal Declaration' speaks to the fundamental purpose in what we do – (it is beyond ticking the boxes of an ethics release form or signing up to follow a code) and makes a plea for ethics as the core of our calling. It boldly asserts that ethics is at the core of every professional discipline. Psychologists, it contends, recognize that they carry out their activities within a larger social context which is connected across generations, and natural and social environments. It has as a purpose its contribution to a stable society that enhances the quality of life for all human beings. Thus it ties our profession to a wider purpose and our practice to the greater good.

While it talks to psychologists would coaches say otherwise? It argues that there are four principles covering all professional work. These are:

- respect for the dignity of persons and peoples;
- competent caring for the well-being of persons and peoples;
- integrity;
- professional and scientific responsibilities to society.

So as coaches and supervisors how do these (or should these) principles show up in our work?

- Do I regard my purpose as coach and supervisor to act with respect, competence, integrity and responsibility? If so what do I say and do that embodies these principles in my purpose?
- What perspectives do I hold that inform my beliefs and understanding of these principles? How do these perspectives inform my journey as a practitioner and enable the client's journey?
- How does my process of working demonstrate these principles (as central, or not, to my practice) to myself, my client, my supervisor and my profession? How does my process help and hinder the client in their attempts to follow their principles?

## What are the coaching bodies saying about ethics and supervision?

For this chapter a number of coaching bodies were asked to provide details of their stance on ethics and supervision. The following bodies cooperated with the request: Association of Coaching (AC); Association of Executive Coaches and Supervisors (APECS); Coaches and Mentors of South Africa (COMENSA); European Mentoring and Coaching Council (EMCC); International Coach Federation (ICF); Worldwide Association of Business Coaches (WABC). Additionally the BPS provided details in relation to supervision. Information was also provided by the British Association of Counselling and Psychotherapy (BACP), and Association of National Organizations for Supervision in Europe (ANSE).

Each of the organizations listed has a code of ethics (not ANSE which is in development and is discussed below), which members are required to support. While they differ in detail the four principles above are traceable in each of them. Explicit statements to support these are not always present. The codes vary in their specificity and some contain elements related to their specialism. For example, the WABC is intended for business coaches and APECS for executive coaches whereas the others have a broader range of coaches as members and therefore are less specific on certain points. The BPS has a general code and one related to research with human participants which contains considerable detail. Hence the purpose of the organization and the breath of its membership does influence the codes. This becomes important as we begin to consider supervision. There have been attempts within coaching bodies to establish general principles that might cover more than one body. Key examples of this, both initiated in 2008, are the UK Roundtable for Coaching which produced a set of 'shared professional values' and the Global Convention on Coaching (Dublin Declaration 2008).

The principle of a meta code signed by all is exemplified by the European Federation of Psychologists Associations. Their meta code is used as a guidance document for national associations in framing local codes. All psychologists who appear on the European level register which is being implemented have to endorse both the meta code and their own local code. ANSE as a body representing national organizations of supervisors is also currently considering the development of a meta code and, it too (in preliminary documents generously shared with this author) is looking at universal principles.

However, none of the coaching bodies currently have a separate code of ethics for supervisors although they are subject to the main ethical code. The development of supervision is a matter of current lively debate within a number of the bodies. EMCC has participated in a project to establish a framework for supervision and APECS has a separate supervision register. COMENSA has developed guidelines for supervision. The WABC is currently undertaking a survey of members to develop an approach to supervision. The matter is the subject of a review in the ICF (who currently use the term 'mentor coach' for activities that others would call supervision). The Association of Coaching is also currently discussing developments in this area.

Outside of the coaching arena there are long established frameworks for supervision practice in the BACP. It has a register of supervisors, a competence model for supervision and requires its members both trainees and practising to use supervision regularly. It is currently the only body which has all of this in place for its practitioners (of those listed here) although APECS (for example) does require annual reports from supervisors to maintain accreditation of members.

In 2010 the BPS replaced its lists of supervisors (available to those in training) which were specific to defined areas of practice (clinical, counselling, etc.) with a Generic Supervision Register. The development of this new register followed detailed work over a five year period which investigated supervision – its evidence base and competences. This resulted in a detailed competence list. This runs to 51 competences covering knowledge, skills, values, social context, training and assessment.[2]

The list is very context non-specific (apart from the first item asking for knowledge of the area of practice). This raises a question, 'Is supervision a separate activity, perhaps even a separate profession?'

## Is supervision an expert/apprenticeship model or a separate specialism?

Supervision is claimed to provide 'a formal, independent process of reflection and review which enables practitioners to increase individual self-awareness, develop their competence and critique their work' (Lane and Corrie 2006: 192). So we can view supervision as one form of CPD – taken as such there is little to debate. There is less agreement, however, about what exactly constitutes 'supervision', whether it can be precisely defined (see the interesting account by Milne and James 2000) and whether it is necessary throughout a career or just while training. It is this later point that is critical to determining if supervision requires a separate code of ethics and professional standards or is simply an additional skill base for senior practitioners to pass on expertise to those in training or junior colleagues. Thus we can consider supervision models based on the need for content and/or process knowledge. Depending on the answer to this question we have four different approaches to supervision and choice of ethical code available to us (see Figure 7.2).

Some fields of practice take a much stronger line on supervision than others (Lawton and Feltham 2000). Hawkins (2010) argues that it is a fundamental aspect for the continuing development of coaches but also argues that coaching needs to develop its own frameworks for this – thus coaches supervise coaches. However, in a survey for CIPD Hawkins and Schwenck (2006) found less than half of coaches were receiving supervision and many of these were using counsellors or psychotherapists to provide it.

Stoltenberg and Delworth (1987) have argued for a developmental approach in which supervision is modified according to stage of professional development and this comes closest to presenting a framework for supervision as a lifelong process

|  | Process Model | CPD Model |
|---|---|---|
| **Y** **E** **S** **S U P E R V I S E E** | Supervisee has the content expertise and supervisor does not have that expertise but provides process expertise in supervision. Supervisor can work outside of own area of practice. This will require at the least an agreement on the code to govern their work but is more likely to lead to the demand for a new separate code for supervisors. | Both supervisor and supervisee have content and process expertise. This could include refining practice or fundamental challenges to practice. Both may work together across practice model or disciplinary boundaries. This may require a new framework for agreeing the ethical code which they choose to govern their work. |
|  | Peer Mentoring Model | Expert/Apprentice Model |
|  | Neither has the content or process expertise and work together as thinking partners to explore their newly emerging practice. Both should peer-mentor within their area of practice. They work to the code of their respective governing body. | Supervisor has the content and process expertise and mentors a junior partner to develop their practice in an apprenticeship model. Supervisor must work within area of own practice. No new ethical code is needed as both work to the agreed code of their governing body. |
| **N** **O** | **NO**    SUPERVISOR | **YES** |

**Figure 7.2** Types of supervision based on the question: Does the supervisor need to have content expertise in the area of the supervisee's practice?

for all practitioners. They identify how practitioners' capacity for autonomy and self-awareness, their degree of anxiety and confidence, need to be accommodated by the style of supervision and supervisory methods. This also feeds into the argument above on three modes or stories of professional practice from the traditional, post professional and diverse, thus, didactic supervisory input early on in individuals' careers offers structured advice in a way that is helpful and containing – logical and predictable. Later stages are increasingly focused on the less tangible aspects such as case formulation, the working relationship and process-oriented variables but also include the more complex and less agreed and predictable and maybe even the chaotic.

Lane and Corrie (2006) have pointed out that some have warned against applying stage models too rigidly (see Hawkins and Shohet 1989), and that developmental approaches can be mapped on to theories of the stages of professional development more broadly (Skovholt and Rønnestad 1995; Eraut 2000) and thus, foster practitioner progression more systematically. Stage models tend to imply that only certain forms of development are appropriate in the early stages of a career and these generally are seen as based on structured processes or even manuals laying out the steps required. Broader models raise the question of the difficulty in enabling practitioners to move from structured to less structured models and call for early training in decision making to choose approaches rather than following a given text.

If the argument of Cavanagh and Lane (2010) has any merit, supervision provides a key mechanism for promoting a culture which transcends relying on the traditional one-to-one mentor figure to a junior colleague. It can take its place in dealing with the more fragile world of professional practice as it increasingly exists.

If supervision is an additional skill base for senior practitioners in a mentoring role then there is no requirement for a code of ethics outside of existing professional codes. There is a need to define the competencies required for that role – but this has been done and has an increasingly extensive evidence base for it (at least as evidence derived from sister disciplines). It also implies that supervision has to take place within defined professional contexts – thus as Hawkins argues (2010) we should look to coaches to supervise coaches. However, interestingly the professional body with the longest experience of this – counselling – through the BACP do not make it a requirement that supervisors must be counsellors for counsellors – rather they must have relevant competence in supervision.

However, if supervision is to add value beyond students and junior practitioners and deal with the complex and chaotic then it will cross discipline boundaries and require broader communities of practice and multiple and diverse groups. This points to the need for supervision to develop as a separate field with its own ethics, competencies, training and eventually professional standards. If it were to emerge as such it would look very different from existing traditional professions and the supervisory role they currently promote. The fundamental difference would be that supervisors would not be content experts in the supervisee's field and therefore would be unable to comment 'as experts' but rather would rely on process frameworks.

## What are the concerns and questions still present?

This is a fascinating time to consider supervision. All the coaching bodies are engaged in internal discussions of the issue – some are cooperating with others within the field of coaching although not outside of it. There is little evidence of an emerging cross-disciplinary debate even though there is much to share.

The next few years will see if supervision is to remain within the expert/apprentice model or truly reach out as a field in its own space contributing to a more creative approach to professional practice. It is too soon to say but if coaching supervision is to move beyond traditional apprenticeship towards truly being a practice that can deal with the complexity then it will have to move across traditional boundaries. This creates the potential for a separate professional grouping of supervisors who can work with a range of professions, not just coaches.

These are interesting times for coaching but for supervision fundamental choices are about to be made by several of the coaching bodies. Will these choices be made in silos or through dialogue between interested stakeholders?

## Learning more

Readers interested in issues raised in this chapter may find it useful to look at:

Milne, D. and I. James (2000) A systematic review of effective cognitive-behavioural supervision, *British Journal of Clinical Psychology*, 39(Pt 2): 111–27. This is a systematic review of studies that have assessed objectively the impact of supervision and consultancy that gauges the effectiveness and methodological rigour of the studies. An important source.

UK Roundtable for Coaching (2008) *Shared Professional Values*. http://www.google.co.uk/#hl=en&sa=X&ei=4xlATdfPHsqGhQegt8m9CA&sqi=2&ved=0CB UQBSgA&q (accessed 25 January 2011). This is a very useful starting point for discussing shared values.

## Notes

1   The research for this paper included more than 200 sources including detailed responses from several bodies in the field and the review of existing and emerging codes. Many professional bodies provided detailed accounts of their work and I am grateful to them. It is only possible to report trends in the space available but I acknowledge the openness of the organizations to engage with the questions and their generosity in sharing.
2   The referenced table is from the supervision workgroup of the 2002 APPIC Competencies Conference. The article discussing that workgroup's activities and elaborating on this table are available in the following:

Falender, C.A., Cornish, J.A.E., Goodyear, R.K. et al. (2004) Defining competencies in psychology supervision: a consensus statement, *Journal of Clinical Psychology*, 60: 771–85.

## References

Attia, A., Buisson, G. and Geller, M.J. (eds) (2009) *Advances in Mesopotamian Medicine from Hammurabi to Hippocrates, Proceedings of the International Conference* 'Oeil malade et mauvais oeil', Collège de France, Paris, 23 June 2006, Cuneiform Monographs, vol. 37, Leiden and Boston, Brill.
Cavanagh, M. and Lane, D.A. (2010) Coaching psychology: coming of age? Keynote at 1st International Coaching Psychology Conference, City University, London, December.

Corrie, S. and Lane, D.A. (2010) *Constructing Stories, Telling Tales: Case Formulation in Psychology*. London: Karnac Books.

Drake, D.B. (2010) What story are you in? – four elements of a narrative approach to formulation in coaching, in D. Corrie and D.A. Lane (eds), *Constructing Stories, Telling Tales: Case Formulation in Psychology*. London: Karnac Books.

Eraut, M. (2000) Non-formal learning and tacit knowledge in professional work, *Journal of Educational Psychology*, 70(1): 113–36.

Falender, C.A., Cornish, J.A.E., Goodyear, R.K. et al. (2004) Defining competencies in psychology supervision: a consensus statement, *Journal of Clinical Psychology*, 60: 771–85.

Gauthier, J. (2004) *Toward a Universal Declaration of Ethical Principles for Psychologists: A Progress Report*. http://www.am.org/iupsys/resources/ethics/ethic-wg-2004-report.pdf (accessed 25 January 2011).

Global Coaching Community (GCC) (2008) *Dublin Declaration on Coaching: Including Appendices*, Global Convention on Coaching, September, Dublin: GCC.

Hawkins, P. (2010) Coaching supervision, in E. Cox, T. Bachkirova and D. Clutterbuck (eds), *The Complete Handbook of Coaching*. London: Sage, pp. 381–93.

Hawkins, P. and Schweck, G. (2006) Coaching supervision – a paper prepared for the CIPD coaching conference. http://www.cipd.co.uk/NR/rdonlyres/C76BD1C9-317C-4A2C-B0D3-708F3ED2EC81/0/coachsupevrp.pdf (accessed 25 January 2011).

Hawkins, P. and Shohet, R. (1989) *Supervision in the Helping Professions*. Maidenhead: Open University Press.

IUPsyS (2008) *The Universal Declaration of Ethical Principles for Psychologists*. www.iupsys.net/index.php/policy/113-universal-declaration-of-ethical-principles-for-psychologists (accessed 25 January 2011).

Jarvis, J. (2006) *Coaching and Buying Coaching Services: a CIPD Guide*. http://www.cipd.co.uk/NR/rdonlyres/C31A728E-7411-4754-9644-46A84EC9CFEE/0/2995coachbuyingservs.pdf (accessed 25 January 2011).

Jarvis, J., Lane, D.A. and Fillery-Travis, A. (2006) *The Case for Coaching: Making Evidence Based Decisions on Coaching*. Wimbledon: Chartered Institute of Personnel and Development.

Lane, D.A. and Corrie, S. (2006) *The Modern Scientist-practitioner: A Guide to Practice in Psychology*. Hove, East Sussex: Routledge.

Lane, D.A., Hurton, N., Stelter, R. and Stout-Rostron, S. (2010a) *An Inquiry into Professional Standards for Business Coaching*. British Colombia: Worldwide Association of Business Coaches.

Lane, D.A., Stelter, R. and Stout-Rostron, S. (2010b) The future of coaching as a profession, in E. Cox, T. Bachkirova and D. Clutterbuck (eds), *The Complete Handbook of Coaching*. London: Sage, pp. 357–68.

Lawton, B. and Feltham, C. (2000) *Taking Supervision Forward: Enquiries and Trends in Counselling and Psychotherapy*. London: Sage.

Lo, M.-C.M. (2004) The professions: prodigal daughters of modernity, in J. Adams, E.S. Clemens and A.S. Orloff (eds), *Remaking Modernity: Politics, History, and Sociology*. Durham, NC: Duke University Press, pp. 381–406.

Milne, D. and I. James (2000). A systematic review of effective cognitive-behavioural supervision, *British Journal of Clinical Psychology*, 39(Pt 2): 111–27.

Skovholt, T.M. and Rønnestad, M.H. (1995) *The Evolving Professional Self: Stages and Themes in Therapist and Counselor Development*. Chichester, West Sussex: Wiley.

Spence, G.B. (2007) Further development of evidence-based coaching: lessons from the rise and fall of the human potential movement, *Australian Psychologist*, 42(4): 255–65.

Stacey, R.D. (1996) *Strategic Management & Organisational Dynamics*. London: Pitman Publishing.

Stoltenberg, C.D. and Delworth, U. (1987) *Supervising Counsellors and Therapists: A Developmental Approach*. San Francisco, CA: Jossey-Bass.

UK Roundtable for Coaching (2008) *Shared Professional Values*. http://www.google.co.uk/#hl=en&sa=X&ei=4xlATdfPHsqGhQegt8m9CA&sqi=2&ved=0CBUQBSgA&q (accessed 25 January 2011).

Zimmerman, B., Lindberg, C. and Plsek, P. (1998) *Edgeware: Insights from Complexity Science for Health Care Leaders*. Irving, TX: VHA, Inc.

# Part II

# The use of theoretical approaches in coaching supervision

# 8 The use of psychodynamic theory in coaching supervision

*Catherine Sandler*

## Introduction

The psychodynamic model of the mind offers a fascinating contribution to coaching supervision practice. As an executive coach, I find that psychodynamic concepts enable me to work both at pace and in depth with my clients. They direct my focus towards the emotions that lie 'below the surface' of conscious awareness. They can unlock the door to helping clients address longstanding behavioural patterns that hinder their effectiveness yet have proved resistant to change. This frequently results in significant and sustainable improvements in their leadership capacities and clear benefits for their organizations.

As a coaching supervisor, I have found that sharing this perspective with other coaches can transform the way they work, helping them to gain new insights into their clients and into themselves. It also illuminates the powerful links that can emerge between the coach–client and the supervisor–supervisee relationships in the form of *parallel process* (Martindale et al. 1997; Hawkins and Shohet 2007).

In this chapter, I aim to bring the application of the psychodynamic model alive by highlighting:

- the key tenets of psychodynamic theory;
- those concepts most relevant to coaching supervision;
- how they can be applied – illustrated with case examples;
- the risks and advantages of this approach;
- suggestions for further reading.

## The origins of the psychodynamic approach

The psychodynamic model has its origin in the revolutionary theory of the human mind developed by Sigmund Freud (1856–1939), the founder of psychoanalysis (Strachey 1953–74; Freud 1991, 2006; Gay 1995). Freud continually revisited and refined his ideas during his lifetime, while disciples such as Jung broke away to develop their own variations of the model. Since Freud's death, this process of evolution has continued as thinkers and practitioners have modified their theories as a

result of experience and research. Within today's psychoanalytic and psychotherapeutic organizations there are many groups and standpoints. These range from
traditional Freudian psychoanalysts to those who combine psychodynamic ideas
with the latest thinking from the fields of child development and neuroscience
to produce new forms of treatment such as Intensive Short-term Psycho-Dynamic
Therapy (ISPDT) (Sandler et al. 1992; Neborsky and Ten Have-De Labije 2011).

Therefore, given the long, complex and multi-stranded history of this field, it is
important to remember that current adherents of the psychodynamic approach are
likely to have varied theoretical perspectives and different ways of applying their
ideas. For those readers interested in knowing more, there is a wealth of literature
in this field so I shall confine myself here to outlining those key psychodynamic
concepts that I believe are most relevant to coaching and coaching supervision.

## Key psychodynamic concepts

At the heart of the psychodynamic model is the belief that human beings have
an *unconscious* as well as a conscious mind and that there is a constantly-shifting
(dynamic) interaction between the two. In part this reflects the inevitable tension,
as we grow, between our biological aggressive and sexual urges and our emerging
moral and social conscience. Yet it is not only what Freud called our *instinctual
drives* that are pushed into the unconscious part of our mind. Psychodynamic
theory also places great emphasis on the role of *emotion* in our lives, underlining
the extent to which feelings such as fear, anger, resentment, envy, shame or guilt
are present in all of us. The model argues that, at times, we experience such
feelings as too painful, threatening or uncomfortable to be admitted into conscious
awareness. Instead they are consigned to the unconscious parts of our minds
through a range of psychological *defences* that we are not even aware of using.
These defences are designed to give us a sense of *psychological safety* – a feeling of
physical, psychological and emotional security that we are programmed to seek
from birth.

The most important point I would like to make here is that the psychodynamic
model places our emotions, and how we handle them, at the centre of human
functioning. It suggests that our emotions play a much more significant role in our
lives – including our working lives – than is generally acknowledged or understood.
Anxiety, for example, is a common response to new or threatening situations. Yet
this often goes unrecognized as the unconscious defences used to deal with it –
such as *denial, rationalization, idealization* or *projection* – lead to behaviour that does
not appear to have any link with anxiety at all. This insight alone is invaluable for
both coach and supervisor (Sandler 2010).

The psychodynamic model regards unconscious defences against anxiety and
other uncomfortable emotions as a normal part of mental functioning. They prevent us from being overwhelmed and help us to deal with life's difficulties. However, they can also become the obstacles that prevent us from fulfilling our potential and performing at our best. If defences are used in an excessive or rigid way,

they can distort our perceptions of ourselves and other people and lead to unskilful or dysfunctional behaviour and the development of psychological symptoms.

The psychodynamic model views childhood experiences, and particularly our relationships with key carers and role models, as having a central influence on the adults we become. They mould the emotional and behavioural patterns that individuals develop early in life. One of psychodynamic theory's most useful insights is that we find it extremely difficult to change these patterns, *even when they have outgrown their usefulness or are not serving us well.*

The final psychodynamic concepts I shall highlight here are those of *transference* and *counter-transference*. These refer to the tendency we all have to transfer aspects of past relationships with parents, siblings and others, to relationships with significant figures in the present. This idea has great relevance to any practitioner–client relationship. It means that the way a client or supervisee relates to their coach or supervisor (the transference) reflects and provides valuable information about their inner world. The same applies to the way that the coach or supervisor relates to the client or supervisee (the counter-transference) (Sandler et al. 1992; Howard 2009).

# The use of psychodynamic theory in coaching supervision

As a supervisor, I hold myself accountable to four different entities: the coaching client, their organization, the coach/supervisee and the coaching profession. My main focus is on helping the supervisee deliver maximum benefit to each coaching client and their organization and on helping the supervisee improve their practice over time. On occasion, my primary function is to provide a safety mechanism for the client who is not receiving safe or competent coaching or for the coach who is overwhelmed by a challenging or ethically complex client situation. These activities are also designed to raise professional standards within the field.

However, these goals are shared by supervisors with different theoretical perspectives so what is the particular contribution of the psychodynamic approach?

### 1 Helping the coach to understand aspects of their clients' internal world which they might otherwise misinterpret or miss altogether

First and foremost, the psychodynamic perspective enables me to help supervisees understand their clients in greater depth and, in particular, to make sense of puzzling, contradictory or hard-to-shift attitudes and behaviour. I encourage the supervisee to listen carefully to their client's words but not to take them at face value, to observe the client's non-verbal communications and to monitor their own mental, emotional and physical reactions. I invite them to draw on these sources of information so that we can explore the hidden thoughts and feelings that the client may be experiencing around a particular issue. Some of these may simply be withheld from the coach while others may be outside the client's conscious awareness. I shall illustrate this with an example from my practice.

*At his third monthly supervision session, **Liam,** an experienced coach, presented a new client called **Natasha**. He introduced her with a sigh, saying that she was proving very difficult to engage. Natasha was a 35-year-old marketing executive in a multinational retail group who had entered coaching in preparation for possible promotion. At the brief 'chemistry check', she had expressed enthusiasm for learning new skills. Liam and she then met her boss who pinpointed some development areas. However, at the first coaching session, Natasha had spent most of it 'showing-off' – recounting the praise she had received from various senior colleagues and listing her achievements. Liam's attempts to explore her development needs were consistently blocked by Natasha who seemed to have all the answers to each of the issues he raised. Liam was left feeling frustrated and discouraged.*

*Having listened to Liam's account of this session, I invited him to consider Natasha's behaviour with the concept of unconscious defences against anxiety in mind. This helped him to shift focus from his 'failure' to engage the client to what was really going on for her. On reflection, Liam felt that the client's showing-off and name-dropping felt a bit desperate as if she had to impress him at all costs. When he re-examined his own feelings during the session, he realized that he had felt irritated and controlled by Natasha. He also remembered the fleeting sense of anxiety he had picked up when she joked on arrival about the radio programme 'In the Psychiatrist's Chair'.*

*Through these observations, Liam began to see Natasha's apparent confidence and resistance to engaging in a different light – as forms of unconscious psychological defence against the feelings of anxiety and threat that the coaching had evoked. She seemed to be using denial to handle her fear of being exposed or criticized in the coaching, and rationalization in the form of apparently logical arguments about why none of the issues Liam raised needed to be discussed. This hypothesis helped Liam regain his confidence and feel less stuck.*

*I also directed Liam's attention to what else this session had taught us about Natasha. The nature and strength of her defences suggested that her underlying self-esteem and confidence were quite fragile, that she depended heavily on external praise and recognition to feel good about herself and that she was probably vulnerable to feeling easily shamed. Her response to coaching was likely to reflect a characteristic pattern which would show up – equally unhelpfully – in other situations at work. Therefore an important developmental objective would be to strengthen Natasha's capacity to tolerate her weaknesses so that her sense of self became less dependent on maintaining a continually successful image.*

## 2 Helping the coach to intervene in a way that promotes learning in the client without triggering defensive behaviour

The psychodynamic approach also highlights the importance of *how* the coach communicates with the client. It underlines how easily human beings can feel threatened and the need for coaches to find skilful ways of engaging the client in learning without triggering their defences. So Liam and I discussed how he could use his new understanding of Natasha's behaviour to reduce her anxiety and help her feel safe enough to open up.

> *The first point we clarified is that he must not share his insights explicitly. This would almost certainly trigger a defensive reaction as Natasha would feel attacked and shamed in just the way she feared. We focused instead on how he could contain and reduce her anxiety as simply pushing her to focus on her development needs was clearly counterproductive. Instead, Liam decided to engage more fully with Natasha's success stories – affirming her achievements and empathizing with the pride and satisfaction they gave her. Through recognizing her successes, he hoped to build trust and give her a sufficient sense of safety to begin showing some vulnerability and exploring her development areas. He reported back that this strategy had worked well.*

Liam also went on to use a psychodynamically-influenced technique that I often share in supervision. It is designed to raise the client's self-awareness without triggering their defences. It involves suggesting to the client that they would naturally have *mixed feelings* about an issue or situation and then describing both sets of feelings in *sympathetic terms* to make it as easy as possible for them to identify with both sides. This also 'normalizes' the idea of having conflicting views and emotions and points to the benefit of exploring them.

> *Thus Liam commented lightly to Natasha that many leaders who came into coaching had mixed feelings about the process. On one hand, they wanted to learn new skills but on the other they already had a successful formula and felt hesitant about tampering with it. Natasha responded thoughtfully and acknowledged for the first time that part of her was unsure about coaching. Liam's comment also acknowledged, and thus reinforced, the part of her that did want to engage.*

### 3 Exploring the coach–client and supervisor–supervisee relationships to help the coach become more self aware and to gain insight into the client

This is an area in which psychodynamic concepts are particularly useful in helping coaches to:

- use the way the client relates to them (the transference) as a valuable source of information;
- become more self-aware through exploring their own response to the client (the counter-transference);
- learn from the dynamics of the supervisor–supervisee relationship.

### Learning from the client's transference to the coach

When I supervise, I encourage the coach to explore how the client perceives and experiences them, consciously and unconsciously. This is based on two psycho-dynamic assumptions. First, clients transfer to the coach some of the attributes of significant figures from their past, and relate to them accordingly, which illuminates their internal world. Second, how the client relates to the coach provides insight into how they relate to others at work.

> *In the case of Natasha, her behaviour at the outset of the coaching indicated her perception of the coach as a potential threat who she must impress at all costs. This enabled Liam to understand more about her 'inner landscape' and specifically her relationship with her boss. It emerged that she found him critical and unsupportive, giving her insufficient recognition of her efforts and achievements.*
>
> *In supervision, I helped Liam see the link between Natasha's transference to him and her behaviour with an unaffirming boss. It seemed likely that the anxiety (and anger) this evoked would unconsciously prompt similar attempts to impress the boss and distance herself from him. This appeared to be so and our discussion enabled Liam to explore these dynamics with Natasha which proved very helpful.*
>
> *I must emphasize that at no point did Liam use the terms 'transference' or 'unconscious defences'. Instead, he empathized with Natasha's wish for her boss's overt approval and then used another model about individual differences to explore the boss's leadership style in greater depth. This helped Natasha reluctantly accept that she had to adjust her expectations and learn to 'manage upwards' more skilfully. She gained at two levels: her relationship with her boss improved significantly and her underlying capacity to remain confident without constant external praise was also strengthened.*

### Building the coach's self-awareness through their counter-transference to the client

Just as with the client's transference to the coach, the coach's experience of the client – the counter-transference – will partly reflect their own past and their inner world. It is important that the coach can identify and acknowledge these aspects of their response, rather than attributing them to the client. This needs a high level of self-awareness. Even then, we *all* have our 'blind-spots' and supervision can be crucial in this context.

> *Returning to our case, we saw that Liam's reactions to Natasha in the first session provided valuable clues to her anxiety and defences. However, as I knew Liam quite well, I felt the intensity of his frustration reflected something about his own emotions.*

*When we explored this, he realized that his response to Natasha had been coloured by his experience of a younger brother whose 'showing off' had always been a source of irritation. On reflection, he realized that unconsciously he had subtly withheld the acknowledgement and recognition that Natasha wanted, though consciously he had simply been attempting to focus her on the coaching agenda.*

*We also explored Liam's sense of discouragement and failure when Natasha had proved difficult to engage. I linked this with his general tendency to put a great deal of pressure on himself to make the coaching a success. This was especially marked when starting work with a new client – he was vulnerable to losing confidence if things did not go well at the outset. While this is common with novice coaches, Liam was quite experienced. Rather than simply reassure him about his competence, I felt it was important to raise his awareness of this dynamic so that he could recognize and manage it more effectively in the future.*

### Learning from the coach's transference to the supervisor

Much can also be learned from the coach's transference to the supervisor. In my experience, many of the dynamics that we find between coach and client are also present here. Opening oneself to learning always involves a degree of vulnerability and most supervisees will feel some anxiety about exposing their practice to the scrutiny of a more experienced colleague (though the degree and awareness of this varies). How the coach deals with this anxiety and relates to the supervisor can provide useful insight into their characteristic emotional and behavioural patterns which will of course influence the way they work with clients.

Therefore in supervision I am always alert to the conscious, unacknowledged or unconscious feelings that the coach may have about me and the process. There are three common examples of supervisee transference:

**Idealization:** This is when a supervisee brings a quality of hero-worship to the relationship with the supervisor, endowing them with exceptional qualities while playing down their own. This can lead to a position of dependency whereby the supervisor is looked to for all the answers and their comments are swallowed whole rather than being considered and explored. Idealization unconsciously serves to reassure the supervisee that they are in the best possible hands and protects them against the anger or disappointment that perceiving the supervisor in a more realistic way might evoke.

**Projection:** Another common transference dynamic involves the supervisee experiencing the supervisor as a critical authority figure. This usually reflects the supervisee's acute anxiety about their own performance. They use the defence of *projection* whereby an aspect of themselves that they find too painful or uncomfortable to admit to conscious awareness is unconsciously 'exported' on to the supervisor who is then seen in a negative light. These supervisees invariably suffer from a strong *superego* – or highly critical inner voice – and it is this which is projected onto the supervisor, who is then experienced as taking an attacking or shaming approach to supervision.

**Competition:** A final example of transference involves feelings of competitiveness towards the supervisor. Again, this usually reflects insecurity on the supervisee's part which is expressed in envy and resentment of the supervisor's perceived superior knowledge, experience and expertise. This can be well hidden and is often unconscious, typically emerging as subtle resistance to the supervisor's interventions and sensitivity about any comments that could be taken as criticism.

In group supervision, some competition between members is almost inevitable. This is most likely to take the form of 'sibling rivalry' though sometimes a member will behave as if they were an alternative supervisor, competing for the leadership of the group.

## Addressing the transference in supervision

As a supervisor, how I address these dynamics depends on the nature of the transference and the self-awareness and maturity of the individual concerned.

When a supervisee idealizes, it can feel very flattering so I must resist the temptation to play the guru and ensure that I engage the supervisee in mobilizing their own thinking. Over time, as trust grows, I will usually share my sense that they have exaggerated the difference between my wisdom, confidence and skill and their own in order to raise their awareness of this tendency.

When a supervisee's transference includes projection of a critical part of themselves onto the supervisor, there is a high risk that the supervision will fail if it is not addressed. This is because the supervisee will resent a supervisor they experience as negative and attacking. The supervisor needs first to ensure that they are resisting the supervisee's unconscious invitation to behave in a more critical way than usual. Second, they must share their observation of what is going on as unthreateningly as possible in the hope that the supervisee will gain insight and the projection will lessen.

In the case of a competitive supervisee, it is the degree of rivalrous feeling that determines the supervision's chance of success. This is a difficult dynamic to raise with a supervisee as it is often unconscious and is typically met with denial. However, if the supervisor is able to feed back their experience of competition skilfully enough, and the supervisee has the maturity and self-awareness to acknowledge these feelings, this can provide a positive 'breakthrough moment' in the supervision process.

I would like to make two general points about *how* I address transference issues in supervision. The first is the need to raise them with great care and sensitivity so as to avoid the supervisee feeling shamed or attacked and triggering a defensive reaction. Second, as I am in a supervisory rather than coaching role, I do not undertake in-depth exploration of their transference behaviour but focus on *raising their awareness* of this aspect of their transference (Martindale et al. 1997). This is vital – if the supervisee remains unaware that they tend to project or compete, they are likely to repeat this behaviour when coaching and of course to miss the same tendencies in their clients.

## Learning from 'parallel process'

The final area of psychodynamically-influenced supervision I shall address relates to the supervisor's experience of the supervisee and in particular to the phenomenon known as *parallel process*. This refers to the unconscious links between the supervisor–supervisee relationship and the coach–client relationship, which can be used to gain insight into the client's inner world.

Parallel process involves the psychodynamic concept of *projective identification*. This is closely linked to the defence of projection, described above, but it goes further. Not only is the intolerable aspect of the self projected onto another person but the emotions involved are subtly evoked in the recipient who unconsciously accepts (identifies with) and experiences them. Parallel process takes place when the supervisor is the recipient of projective identification from the supervisee, who has themselves been the recipient of projective identification from the client. It is best explained through illustration.

*Parallel process took place when I supervised a coach called **Bridget**. A talented but relatively inexperienced coach, she presented her first three sessions with a client called **Henry**. A finance manager in a large manufacturing business, he had entered coaching at the insistence of his line-manager who was concerned about his excessively task-focused style and its impact on his team's performance. Though his intentions were good, Henry annoyed his colleagues by continually reminding them of deadlines, micro-managing their work and being critical and abrasive, especially when under pressure.*

*Bridget started by saying that she was really keen to explore some practical ideas about how to help this client change his behaviour as only five coaching sessions remained. As she described her work with Henry, I found myself losing the thread of her narrative and stopping to ask for clarification. I knew Bridget well and she seemed less relaxed than usual; it felt as if she was rushing through her account. The thought then occurred to me that perhaps I was slowing down and needed to make more effort to concentrate.*

*Bridget explained that she was organizing a 360 degree feedback survey for Henry. The questionnaires had just gone out to his colleagues and she told me with a grimace that he was already emailing her to ask how many had been returned. Apparently Henry had also asked her at the last session if she thought they were making fast enough progress. As she recounted this, Bridget suddenly saw the link between his behaviour towards her and his tendency to chase up his colleagues. We agreed that this was very helpful first-hand data.*

*At this point, my mind turned to what lay behind Henry's behaviour. Despite acknowledging the need for change, Henry was clearly struggling to do so. I felt we needed to gain more insight into what was driving him to pressurize and control others so relentlessly. Bridget's wish to focus on practical techniques seemed a little premature and I felt hurried along by her . . . Yet I also found myself feeling anxious at the thought of time running out and wondering whether giving Henry some behavioural models might be the best thing to do after all. It was when I noticed that Bridget was sitting upright on the edge of her chair rather than sitting back in it as usual – and then noticed my own stiff shoulders and neck – that I realized something significant had happened to the way we were working.*

*I sat back and suggested that we review how we were both feeling about this client. Bridget looked surprised but also sat back. I remembered how thoughtful and measured she usually was and became more convinced that Henry's dynamics had somehow been internalized, first by her and then by me. As we identified our shared sense of anxiety and tension, it became clear that we had both felt there was little time or space to stop and think about this client; instead we had felt pressurized to come up with quick solutions. These insights enabled us to have a very fruitful conversation. Bridget left the session having regained her capacity to reflect. She had more understanding of the hidden fears and frustrations that Henry might be experiencing and some ideas about how gently to explore them. She was clear that raising his self-awareness was a necessary prerequisite to helping him change his behaviour.*

*When I reflected on the session, I hypothesized that Henry had unconsciously used projective identification to push the part of himself that felt intolerably anxious about failing to deliver on time onto Bridget – and had then evoked these feelings in her. As a newish coach, her own anxiety about delivering good results for this client (her first with this company) facilitated this process. She in turn had unconsciously used projective identification to evoke these same feelings in me during supervision.*

This example illustrates the fascinating way in which the client's dynamics can be revealed through the unconscious dynamics of both coach and supervisor and how the concept of projective identification can help to surface and explain what is taking place. That said, I shall end with an important caveat. There is a risk of parallel process becoming such an attractive idea to some supervisors that *all* their responses to the supervisee are interpreted in this light. In fact, the supervisor's reactions will often simply reflect their own counter-transference, namely the aspects of their *own emotional landscape* that colour their response to the supervisee. Given this potential for confusion, a high level of self-awareness on the part of the supervisor is crucial. Over the years I have learned what attributes or behaviours in supervisees are liable to 'press my buttons'. Nevertheless, in common with all supervisors, I must remain vigilant to the intrusion of my own material into the coaching session and work hard to recognize when this occurs (Martindale et al. 1997).

# Evaluation of the approach

In evaluating the role of psychodynamic theory in coaching supervision I hope to dispel some of the myths surrounding the psychodynamic approach while setting out its potential strengths and weaknesses. This highlights some of the issues that prospective supervisees or supervisors-in-training might usefully consider when choosing a theoretical orientation.

## The organizational dimension

Although psychodynamic concepts can be fruitfully applied to group and organizational dynamics, its main use in coaching supervision is to help the coach understand the client's inner world and relate it to their behaviour at work. This emphasis on developing the individual can be seen as both a strength and a possible limitation. On the one hand, it enables the coach to gain a depth of insight into human psychology that other perspectives do not provide. On the other hand, there is a risk that the organizational dimension of coaching may be insufficiently explored or addressed, particularly if the supervisor's background is solely in psychotherapy or counselling.

This does not have to be the case, however. In my supervision practice, I encourage the coach to take into account the role and task of the client, the structure, culture and history of their organization and the views of key stakeholders, particularly their line-manager. Helping the coach to manage dual accountability – to deliver benefits to the individual and to the organization – is a significant part of the supervision process. That said, if your main interest lies in the dynamics of the organizational world, you may prefer supervision that places the organization at the centre of the coaching process and takes a more systemic perspective (Hirschhorn 1993; Obholzer and Roberts 1994; Kilburg 2000; Huffington et al. 2004; Hawkins and Smith 2006).

## Coaching or therapy

Given the origins of the psychodynamic approach – and popular notions of psychoanalysis – some people assume that psychodynamically-influenced supervision will routinely involve in-depth investigation of the client's early life. Linked to this is a fear that the boundary between coaching and therapy may become blurred.

These perceptions are understandable and, if true, would constitute valid concerns. However, in supervision I help the coach recognize and explore the client's *current patterns of functioning at work* rather than analyse their family background. If aspects of the client's history or personal life do arise, they are briefly explored and the implications related to the workplace. For instance, if a supervisee's client talks about needing her father's approval, I shall ensure the coach links back this discussion to the relevant coaching issue – in this case her relationship with her boss.

Ensuring that psychodynamically-influenced supervision and coaching do not become forms of unofficial therapy is very important indeed. The different aims and methods of coaching and therapy must be clarified by the supervisor who should play an important part in ensuring that this crucial distinction is well understood and carefully observed by the coach. When it emerges that a client (or supervisee) would benefit from therapy or counselling, careful referral to the appropriate professional should be made (Buckley and Buckley 2006).

### Only for the trained?

Psychodynamic theory is complex and multi-faceted. In unskilful or careless hands it can lead to poor practice that can be ineffective at best and damaging at worst. Generally, supervisors using this approach will have had some training in psychodynamic thinking and practice to ensure that they have the necessary skills, experience and self-awareness to guide coaches to use it safely.

In assessing a potential supervisor, do explore their approach to *how* psychodynamic insights are shared with the client. Coaches who are new to the psychodynamic approach may become enthused by the concepts but share them with clients in too bald and explicit a way. Clumsy interventions and technical jargon will trigger the client's defences and leave them feeling exposed or attacked. So the supervisor must ensure that the coach who uses psychodynamic concepts to guide their thinking, uses everyday language to communicate this to the client with care and sensitivity.

### The evidence base

One of the criticisms levelled at psychodynamic theory is that there is no evidence for its claims about unconscious processes. Some see its ideas as fanciful, unprovable assertions unsuited to the world of executive coaching. Clearly, the psychodynamic model will not appeal to everyone and those for whom it lacks all plausibility will select supervisors with alternative perspectives.

That said, it is vital that psychodynamically-oriented supervisors take a rigorous and systematic approach to basing their views on specific observations or experiences. They should encourage the coach not to rely on theory alone. They should develop *working hypotheses* about clients based on identifiable evidence and then seek further evidence to confirm or disprove them as the work progresses. For instance, a coach might plausibly sense that a client who fears conflict is in denial about their unconscious anger with a colleague. In supervision, I would seek to explore what *exactly* they had learned, perceived or experienced in working with this client that gave rise to this hypothesis.

### Who does this kind of supervision suit best?

Psychodynamically-oriented coaching supervision suits those who are open to the essential premises of the psychodynamic model and have a deep curiosity about individual psychology. As coaches, they should aspire to work at depth with their clients and to help them change at an emotional as well as behavioural level.

In my view, coaches do not have to be trained in psychodynamic theory or practice. A good degree of self-awareness is crucial, however, preferably developed through some form of experiential learning, along with genuine interest in developing this further. To benefit from this perspective, the supervisee needs to explore *themselves as well as their clients*. They must be open to learning about their own patterns, defences and blind-spots if they are to understand those of the client.

Therefore psychodynamically-oriented supervision is emotionally as well as intellectually stretching and will lead coaches to revise assumptions about themselves, as well as about their clients. For some, this may feel too personal or intrusive. For those who have the necessary capacities and interest, it can provide a powerful and transformative experience.

## Learning more

No chapter can do full justice to the complexity and subtlety of psychodynamic theory and its application to coaching supervision. From the longer list below, here are three contrasting books that will contribute to further exploration:

Susan Howard (2009) *Skills in Psychodynamic Counselling and Psychotherapy*. This is a really well-written introduction to the psychodynamic model and, despite the title, many of the points can be applied in the coaching or supervision context.

Catherine Sandler (2011) *Executive Coaching: A Psychodynamic Approach*. This provides a clear, concise explanation of how I apply psychodynamic ideas to executive coaching, linking theory with practice through numerous case examples.

Brian Martindale et al. (editors) (1997) *Supervision and Its Vicissitudes*. This thought-provoking collection of writings by psychoanalysts is an advanced read, offering a deeper understanding of theory and practice in this area.

## References

Buckley, A. and Buckley, C. (2006) *A Guide to Coaching and Mental Health: The Recognition and Management of Psychological Issues*. Hove: Routledge.

Freud, S. (1991) *The Essentials of Psycho-Analysis: The Definitive Collection of Sigmund Freud's Writing*. London: Penguin.

Freud, S. (2006) *The Penguin Freud Reader*. London: Penguin.

Gay, P. (1995) *The Freud Reader*. New York: W.W. Norton & Co.

Hawkins, P. and Shohet, R. (2007) *Supervision in the Helping Professions*. Maidenhead: Open University Press.

Hawkins, P. and Smith, N. (2006) *Coaching, Mentoring and Organizational Consultancy: Supervision and Development*. Maidenhead: Open University Press.

Hirschhorn, L. (1993) *The Workplace Within: Psychodynamics of Organizational Life*. Cambridge, MA: MIT Press.

Howard, S. (2009) *Skills in Psychodynamic Counselling and Psychotherapy*. London: Sage.

Huffington, C., Armstrong, D., Hatton, W., Hoyle, L. and Pooley, J. (eds) (2004) *Working Below the Surface: The Emotional Life of Contemporary Organisations*. London: Karnac Books.

Kilburg, R.R. (2000) *Executive Coaching: Developing Managerial Wisdom in a World of Chaos*. Washington: American Psychological Association.

Martindale, B., Morner, M., Cid Rodriguez, M.E. and Vidit, J.P. (eds) (1997) *Supervision and Its Vicissitudes*. London: Karnac.

Neborsky, R.J. and Ten Have-De Labije, J. (2011) *Mastering Intensive Short-term Dynamic Psychotherapy: Roadmap to the Unconscious*. London: Karnac Books.

Obholzer, A. and Zagier Roberts, V. (eds) (1994) *The Unconscious at Work: Individual and Organisational Stress in the Human Services*. London: Routledge.

Sandler, C. (2010) How to manage leaders' anxiety, *People Management*, 8 April: 33.

Sandler, J., Dare, C. and Holder, A. (1992) *The Patient and the Analyst*. London: Karnac Books.

Strachey, J. (ed.) (1953–74) *The Standard Edition of the Complete Works of Sigmund Freud* (24 volumes). London: The Hogarth Press & the Institute of Psychoanalysis.

# 9 The use of a Gestalt approach in supervision

*Sue Congram*

## Introduction

This chapter outlines a model for Gestalt supervision illustrating three major components of Gestalt: dialogic process, phenomenological method and the holistic field (Perls et al. 1951; Mackewn 1997; Brownell 2008). These three components distinguish Gestalt as a *process* methodology, with a focus on psychological patterns, or forces that influence the way people interact with each other and their environment. Characteristic of Gestalt, and building on these three components, is a creative means of inquiry (Spagnuolo Lobb and Amendt-Lyon 2003), working with what is embodied, the emotional field and language. What this means in Gestalt supervision is that the holistic nature of being human is central to the work; body responses are as important as the way that we think about and perceive our world; emotions emerging between the coach and the supervisor inform the supervision; and the language used to talk about the coaching, offers structure, metaphor and focal points.

What does Gestalt supervision look like? From this holistic view the supervisor and coach explore emerging themes in the coach's professional practice. I will use one of my own case studies to illustrate how this works:

> My client comes for regular supervision on her coaching. On one occasion she tells me about a difficulty that she is having coaching a woman who is stressed by what she describes as emotional bullying at work. She narrates in detail how her coaching proceeded.

It is worth mentioning at this point that as Gestalt is informed by the phenomenological method, the content of what a coach brings to supervision is of less concern than *how* they present their case material, *how* they do their coaching and *how* the coach and supervisor relate to each other in the here-and-now. The bullying case story therefore briefly describes observations of *how* the coach was presenting her client work and my response to that, rather than the story itself:

> *I noticed as the coach was telling me about the client that she became more animated and descriptive when she talked about the bullying. When I shared my observation of this she sidestepped it and drew attention to another issue of concern. I became even more curious. I referred back to her description of the bully, sharing my curiosity and inviting her to tell me again. This time she paid attention, eventually revealing a past experience of hers where she had been bullied at work and realizing that the issue had not been fully resolved.*

My client had not made the connection between her own past experience and the client situation during her coaching. Her embodied emotional bruising had been forgotten or ignored. Through these reflections the coach was able to recognize how her own emotional reactions had become confused with the client work. With new awareness of this she was able to see the client situation in new light.

The dialogic aspect of supervision is continuous; it is demonstrated in this illustration through the sharing of my curiosity about the coach's animated behaviour, typically for a Gestalt-informed approach, that is reflected back without interpretation. The phenomenological method involved focusing on the here-and-now process of observation, whilst attending to the holistic field meant recognizing how something outside of the present situation could be entering and affecting the work. As such, the supervisor is in service to the coach, and the coach is in charge of sculpting their own learning. The following sections describe these components in more detail.

## The use of Gestalt theory in supervision

In this section I will briefly describe and illustrate the three main components of Gestalt in the context of coaching supervision. These interconnecting components of *dialogic process*, *phenomenological method* and attending to the *holistic field*, together provide an imaginative and creative process for reflection and transformative learning.

A commonly accepted view of supervision in the helping professions is that it is a reflective activity (Hawkins and Shohet 2000; Lahad 2000; Carroll and Tholstrup 2001; Carroll and Gilbert 2005; Hawkins and Smith 2006; Shohet 2008), a process where learning and evaluation of professional work takes place. Gestalt too, is a reflective practice. In Gestalt supervision the supervisor and coach reflect on the professional practice and case studies of the coach through a holistic lens. What that means is that the client's concerns (now situated in the past) and the current reality of supervision are considered to be connected through the work; through the narrative of case studies told by the coach, the way that they bring their work to supervision and the interrelational dynamics between the supervisor and coach.

The impact of this can be more fully understood through the holistic field, which I describe below (see page 126).

It is worth mentioning that I supervise both Gestalt and non-Gestalt coaches. What I notice is that I use a different language in supervision according to the coach's focus, but the supervision process for both is otherwise similar.

## Dialogic process

A dialogic attitude means being aware of, and making choices on how the 'other' is perceived in the process of relating. This idea stems from the work of Buber (1937) who differentiated between 'I-it' and 'I-thou', where 'it' refers to a role, position, thing, profession, guru or a stereotype, where the other person is seen through the screen of 'it' (manager, teacher, leader, boss). 'I-it' usually implies that the relationship is hierarchical in some way. Whereas 'I-thou' is about seeing the other as a human being on mutual terms. Referring to the work of Buber and 'genuine dialogue', Jacobs (1989) describes three important elements: (1) presence, (2) genuine and unreserved communication and (3) inclusion, offering some indications of the richness of a dialogic process.

In Gestalt-informed supervision the supervisor and coach will likely achieve moments of exceptional 'I-thou' contact where something changes, as well as 'I-thou' dips in the relationship where contact seems more distant. The dips interest me in supervision, for in these dips may exist interruptions within the dialogue in the form of *confluence*, *projection* and *transference*. In Gestalt terms these are phenomena that naturally occur at the contact boundary between self and the environment (Mackewn 1997; Woldt and Toman 2005), which I discuss more fully in the next sections. The task in Gestalt supervision is to bring into awareness patterns that do not serve the coaching well but occur through habit rather than awareness. This may require the coach attending to their own fixed patterns that become interruptive to their coaching.

Many professional relationships interweave between 'I-it' and 'I-thou'; the art of effective Gestalt supervision is to engage in genuine dialogue, pay attention to the moments when the dynamics of the relationship change, to be aware of such shifts and to make choices that can fulfil healthy and effective supervision.

## *Confluence*

'Confluence' in Gestalt terms is a 'contact style'; it means merging together, where difference is not apparent and there is 'no appreciation of boundary' (Perls et al. 1951: 118) nor 'sense of differentiation' (Mackewn 1997: 27). Often detected by the use of the word 'we', there are times when confluence is appropriate and enjoyable, such as in meditation or when two people are in love. It can also interrupt dialogue when used to avoid difference or conflict.

When someone seeks coaching they are looking for a different voice, a new perspective, a way of expanding their own way of thinking in order to learn or change. If a coach becomes habitually confluent with their clients, their coaching ability will become limited, raising a number of ethical questions around their professional capabilities. Confluence in coaching lacks confrontation and there is an agreeable rather than challenging air about the work: wanting to 'be nice' or 'be good' for the client, acting in a way that keeps the dialogue safe, regularly engaging in a conversational style, being what the client expects, avoiding conflict or a difference of opinion. When I am supervising I am constantly on the look-out for signs of confluence, to bring awareness of habitual patterns to the coach so that the coach can become more professionally competent, more integrated in the way they work.

### Projection and transference

'Projection' in traditional Gestalt terms means denying or repressing a quality or feeling and attributing it to another person (Perls et al. 1951). As Joyce and Sills (2001) point out, there is today some confusion about this concept because the word is used in at least two other different ways: (1) to imagine what is not there, to anticipate a future; (2) and as transference, when projected material is historical and inappropriate. I would add two further usages: (3) where people make assumptions and expectations about others and the world around them, then act as though that is true; (4) as embedded in many forms of feedback.

Projection sits within a wide body of knowledge rooted in both Freudian (Gay 1995) and Jungian ideas (Samuels et al. 1986), and today has found its way into coaching (Rogers 2004) and supervision (Hawkins and Shohet 2000; Schaverien and Case 2007). In Gestalt supervision, the supervisor attends to what the coach may be projecting onto the client. For instance, when interpretation and meaning-making is narrow and rigid, a coach may be acting from a fixed projection. Other projective scenarios in coaching might be linked to role, gender, age, race, where attention is drawn to the role or stereotype, rather than the person. The link between 'I-it' and projection becomes more apparent when a client is better qualified and more experienced in their particular field of work than the coach, and the coach is intimidated or unconsciously affected by this. If the coach projects onto the client 'better than me', then the coaching is unlikely to work well.

This leads to *transference* and *counter-transference*, which are forms of projection rooted in the history of a person. A Gestalt perspective of transference is the way that a person organizes their *perceptual field* (Mackewn 1997); that is, they organize their thoughts through the lens of their history, key figures from the past, habitual behaviours and unfinished business, rather than through the current reality.

Transference and counter-transference are part of life and social interaction. However, out of awareness it can become disruptive, or create co-dependence in relationships. Awareness of a transference brings choice and consideration for dealing with the current reality in a different way. In supervision, when the coach is troubled or seems confused about the work, I inquire into the transferential dynamics, inviting the coach to reflect on their relationship with the client. This may also involve explaining to the coach what transference is, what is happening, the value of transference and how to manage it. It has to be said that when coaching training does not include awareness of transference and counter-transference, the coach may well fall into difficulties somewhere along the line and become perplexed by it. Complex as it may be, I consider this to be critical as well as ethical learning in coaching, and an essential part of supervision.

## Phenomenological method

'Phenomenological method' in Gestalt is directly related to the holistic field (discussed in the next section), where attention is given to what comes into awareness within the flow of the here-and-now, described in Gestalt terms as 'figure/ground', where figure is the focus of attention and ground is the context (Burley and Bloom 2008). According to Spinelli (1989) the Gestalt approach of awareness-raising and methods of investigation are essentially the same as phenomenological therapies.

Phenomenology is one of the strengths of the Gestalt method, taking the perspective that you can only really explore what is emerging and revealed in the present moment. There are three skills to phenomenological inquiry that have developed in the world of therapy and counselling (Mackewn 1997; Joyce and Sills 2001), which are particularly relevant in coaching supervision. These skills are *bracketing*, *describing* and *equalization*.

First, the supervisor is able to 'bracket off' their interpretations, judgements, concerns, ideas, and so on, in order to fully meet the coach. Working from a phenomenological frame-of-reference this is essential, but as Joyce and Sills (2001) point out, it is not so easy because we unconsciously interpret and judge the world as we meet it all the time. We have to become aware of our interpretations before we can begin to put them to one side.

The second skill, 'describing', is saying 'what is', that is, what is noticed and observed as it is happening. Typically this would be stated in language such as 'I notice that...(your voice has softened)'; 'You look...(flushed)'. What can happen in supervision is that both supervisor and coach fall into doing this together, noticing 'what is', is not just the responsibility of the supervisor; it is a skill that both supervisor and coach can develop.

The third skill is a process of 'equalizing', where emerging observations are treated with equal importance and tiny or big shifts are given equal consideration. It is worth noting that 'noticing the obvious', an aspect of equalizing, is really what a phenomenological method is interested in, yet the obvious can easily be obscured by the content of issues being discussed. What becomes obvious in supervision might not have been so obvious to the coach when working with their client, or treated with equal value alongside other concerns.

The phenomenological method is not so much a technique but an attitude, which particularly draws on the curiosity and open-mindedness of the supervisor.

Joyce and Sills (2001) include *active curiosity* as one of the facets of phenomeno-logical method. What it means is that the supervisor holds a position of interest and curiosity in situations arising in the room, as well as in the case stories told by the coach, 'being curious about all that the [client] experiences' (Joyce and Sills 2001: 21). So rather than giving answers or solutions, what brings supervision alive is the exploration of possibilities, bringing in questions and offering observations of gestures, voice tone, shifts in dialogue or body language, as well as the use of language.

## Holistic fields

The concept of *field theory* is rooted in the work of Kurt Lewin (1946, 1947) who described a field as 'the totality of coexisting facts, which are conceived of as mutually interdependent' (Cartwright 1951: 240). What he meant by this was that in order to understand people's behaviour it is necessary to look at the whole psychological, emotional or experiential field within which people act, behave and respond. This view has been more explicitly interpreted and defined by Parlett (1991, 1997), Staemmler (2006), and O'Neill and Gaffney (2008), describing how people are influenced by and are also influencers of the field.

In a supervision group that I run, the holistic field became evident from the way the group members were behaving. A group member talked about a client who was struggling to achieve recognition in her work. As we explored this, examples of 'feeling invisible' and 'lack of recognition' began to get voiced between members of the group. This is a situation that is referred to as 'parallel process' in Gestalt, where a supervision group exhibits characteristics that exist in a client not present in the room (Gaffney 2008). Gaffney asks a series of questions to bring awareness to this: how is that which is happening around us now entering the room? How have we brought it here with us? How are we playing it out?

Gestalt supervision takes into account multiple *fields*. What this means is that unless the supervision is direct, the coach's client is always absent – in Gestalt terms, *the absent presence in the room*, where all aspects of the field are inter-connected and potentially significant. This brings with it a very particular sce-nario where the coach is talking about events that are not in the here-and-now. Whether supervision is face-to-face, on the phone or in a group, this is always the case.

Supervision by its nature brings with it multiple fields as illustrated in Figure 9.1. First there is the supervisor–coach field. Second is the coach–client field which is not physically present but in focus in supervision. Third there is the client-context field, not present in coaching or supervision but in focus from time to time in both the coaching and the supervision.

The field perspective is in some ways similar to the seven-eyed model of super-vision described by Hawkins and Smith (2006), in that it takes into consideration the contextual field beyond the immediate work of the client in the room. Gestalt is different in the way that it attends to the wider processes: where the seven-eyed model helicopters over the different fields, dropping into each mode (pp. 171–2)

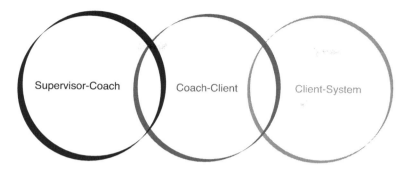

**Figure 9.1** Interconnecting fields

to gain understanding, the holistic field perspective assumes an interconnection between them in which change in one field will have an effect on the other fields (Parlett 1991; O'Neill and Gaffney 2008). As such, the supervisor pays attention to field dynamics that otherwise might go unnoticed.

When we look deeply into the holistic field, what we begin to see is that the interactive and psychological world of coaching and supervision is incredibly rich in information, connecting what's in the room with what isn't in the room but exists as part of the unfolding work.

## Case illustration

*Sara is an experienced coach. She coaches people at work, as well as offering in-depth coaching for people who meet difficulties in their lives, which she calls 'life coaching'.*

*Some time after we had started working together Sara brought to supervision a case story about a client who is the managing director of a family business, a role that he took over from his father three years ago. His father is now fully retired and yet makes his views clear about the way the business should be run. The client's sister also works in the business in a management role. The brother and sister do not get on particularly well. The situation is complex and often difficult. The client has asked for some coaching to try to deal with some staff issues. He wants to grow the business and believes that the current situation is not supporting growth. The sister has refused to take part in any intervention of this kind.*

*Sara is Gestalt trained. She is aware of overlapping boundaries between family life and business in the client situation. In supervision she was able to map out the multiple fields at the client's workplace and consider some of the themes being played out within each different field. Sara mapped them as 'emotional fields' (see Figure 9.2). In the client system a number of themes stood out, such as sibling*

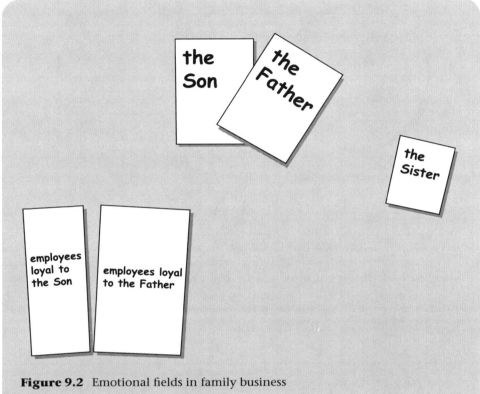

**Figure 9.2**  Emotional fields in family business

*rivalry, which was carried through splits within the organization; old and new staff, which brought tensions between traditional ways of doing things against modern practices; and loyalty to the retired father, which showed up as resistance to the son. These dynamics were getting in the way of business growth.*

*Sara then amplified this emotional map by using objects in my room to symbolize characters in the business, describing each one in colourful and descriptive ways. This narrative process amplified her understanding of power oppositions at play in the client system. Seeing this gave a much clearer perspective to Sara who, until then had concentrated on emerging themes from her direct relationship with the client.*

The phenomenological method discussed earlier (see page 125), maintains an approach where the clues for learning and growth are in the emerging process rather than the content of what is being said. So the mapping was held within a phenomenological frame as well as providing some insight into the holistic field. My attention was on the coach, her relationship with her client, how she maintained her attention, and what was happening in the here-and-now that might be relevant to the coaching work. This was not so much about what was evident, but what might be out of awareness yet influencing the holistic field. One aim in Gestalt is to bring into awareness what is otherwise unknown, on the basis that without awareness change cannot happen. The next step in this case illustration shows this, and how an experience from the past in the coach's own life was affecting the holistic field of coaching:

*In a later supervision Sara raised questions about her work with this same client. Although progress was being made, and her client had started to see the extent to which family dynamics were impeding business growth, relationships remained difficult and obstructive. Sara said that 'he was becoming hard work' and she didn't know what to do next. I invited her to recall the last coaching session – to tell the story of her experience with her client. As she described her client's relationship with his sister she appeared angry; this part of the story seemed to carry more vitality in it compared to the other difficult relationship between the client and his father, which she seemed to be focusing on. I commented on this.*

*Sara looked at me puzzled. I asked her what the puzzled look was and the following exchange took place:*

*Sara*    *It was only when you spoke that I realized my reaction. My feeling is that I want R to settle his differences with his sister.*

*Sue*    *What do you notice as you hear yourself say that?*

*Sara*    *I feel hooked in (touching her stomach), I feel a knot in my stomach. His sister avoids him (in an exasperated and questioning tone).*

*Sue*    *What are you avoiding with R . . . ?*
*[Long silence]*

*Sara*    *I think that I've diminished myself. I've put him in the role as Managing Director, as better than me and lost sight of him as a person.*

My intervention of 'commenting' on Sara's shift in energy, was a moment of describing and equalizing, both of which I explained earlier (see page 125). This simple intervention led to a moment's reflection in which the exasperated comment 'his sister avoids him' suggested to me that there might be a projection around avoidance of R in the comment. I could have asked a number of questions at this point that would have raised awareness of this as a possible projection, or even questioned my own assumptions. But I felt that Sara had already sidestepped some issues regarding her client, so I decided to trust my intuition and ask the question with some directness.

Sara went on to tell me how she had often felt intimidated by men in senior roles when she was employed full time. She had never managed to overcome that fully, nor the discomforts that came with feeling belittled. This is an example of an 'I-it' shift described at page 123, putting the client in an 'it' role of Managing

Director with a further possible transference on the authority that the role carried. From a Gestalt perspective the coach will be less effective from this position. We agreed that Sara would take some time in supervision to explore her own projections and transferential patterns more fully – outlined earlier (see pages 124). She had a choice: she could have taken that issue and worked with it in therapy or coaching elsewhere.

## Evaluation of the model

One of the greatest challenges for Gestalt-informed practice in today's coaching world is the predominant culture that favours short-term rather than the longer-term, in-depth learning that is favoured by Gestalt. For example, corporate coaching is frequently on a budget and therefore time limited to around six to eight sessions. That is not to say that Gestalt cannot provide time-limited coaching or supervision: it means that research has not yet taken place in these professions to show how effective or relevant Gestalt can be. Houston (2003) offers a very useful critique of Gestalt as an approach for brief therapy, where she argues that the relational qualities of Gestalt, along with an inquiring and inventive methodology make *brief* work possible. Her text provides many useful hints and tips that equally apply to supervision.

Research is also absent on remote supervision, that is, Gestalt-informed telephone and video conferencing. Although my own preference is face-to-face, experience has shown me that these other forms of supervision can work well when face-to-face is not possible.

Strengthened by its holistic and phenomenological methods, Gestalt supervision works well for individual work and supervision groups (Gaffney 2008). Attuned with a variety of different coaching approaches, a Gestalt supervisor could support a coach where their practice has roots in existential ideas (Spinelli 2010), has concern for *ways of being* (Sieler 2010), and positive psychology (Zinker 1994; Kauffman et al. 2010). It is not so aligned with cognitive and transactional methods and yet will complement these approaches well. I particularly wish to add, that where coaching training programmes do not include psychological competence, Gestalt-informed supervision is able to compensate for that, providing a psychological perspective that need not be difficult to grasp. In my view as a supervisor, coaching is strengthened when the coach has an ability to understand and work with psychological processes, as some of the concerns raised here will inevitably present themselves in coaching at some stage.

What Gestalt does not do is to provide professional knowledge and experience of different contexts, such as corporate work, educational experience, life coaching, executive coaching, groups and teams. It only provides a method that can be applied in these contexts. The supervisor's contextual experience is part of the skills, knowledge and wisdom that they bring to the work and to which they have applied their Gestalt knowledge. In other words, Gestalt alone is not the whole.

## Learning more

Although literature on Gestalt supervision for coaches is sparse, Gaffney (2008) illuminates a Gestalt approach for group supervision which provides insight where cross-cultural differences were present in the group. It is a fine example of working with the holistic field and bringing into awareness an aspect of the field – culture – that is often not considered.

For anyone keen to read more about Gestalt, Mackewn (1997) *Developing Gestalt Counselling* and Joyce and Sills' (2001) *Skills in Gestalt Counselling and Psychotherapy*, provide comprehensive texts of Gestalt in practice (in counselling and psychotherapy), which are easily digestible and translatable into coaching supervision.

A brief and introductory text on the basics of Gestalt, called *Gestalt a Philosophy for Change*, was originally published as a series in the Training Journal, and is now available as a free downloadable e-booklet from my website (www.thespace between.com).

## References

Brownell, P. (ed.) (2008) *Handbook for Theory, Research, and Practice In Gestalt Therapy*. Newcastle: Cambridge Scholars Publishing.

Buber, M. (1937) *I and thou* (trans. R.G. Smith). London and New York: Continuum (original work published 1923).

Burley, T. and Bloom, D. (2008) Phenomenological method, in P. Brownell (ed.) *Handbook for Theory, Research and Practice in Gestalt Therapy*. Cambridge: Cambridge Scholars Publishing, pp. 151–83.

Carroll, M. and Tholstrup, M. (2001) *Integrative Approaches to Supervision*. London: Jessica Kingsley Publishers.

Carroll, M. and Gilbert, M. (2005) *On Being a Supervisee: Creating Learning Partnerships*. London: Vukani.

Cartwright, D. (ed.) (1951) *Kurt Lewin: Field Theory in the Social Sciences, Selected Theoretical Papers*. London: Harper-Torchbooks.

Gaffney, S. (2008) Gestalt group supervision in a divided society: theory, practice, perspectives and reflections, *British Gestalt Journal*, 17(1): 27–39.

Gay, P. (ed.) (1995) *The Freud Reader*. London: W. W. Norton & Company (originally published 1989).

Hawkins, P. and Shohet, R. (2000) *Supervision in the Helping Professions: An Individual, Group and Organizational Approach* (3rd edn). Maidenhead: Open University Press.

Hawkins, P. and Smith, P. (2006) *Coaching, Mentoring and Organizational Consultancy*. Maidenhead: McGraw-Hill.

Houston, G. (2003) *Brief Gestalt Therapy*. London: Sage.

Jacobs, L. (1989) Dialogue in Gestalt theory and therapy, *Gestalt Journal*, 12(1): 25–67.

Joyce, P. and Sills, C. (2001) *Skills in Gestalt Counselling and Psychotherapy*. London: Sage.

Kauffman, C., Boniwell, I. and Silberman, J. (2010) The positive psychology approach to coaching, in E. Cox, T. Bachkirova and D. Clutterbuck (eds) *The Complete Handbook of Coaching*. London: Sage, 158–71.

Lahad, M. (2000) *Creative Supervision: The Use of Expressive Arts in Supervision and Self-supervision*. London and Philadelphia: Jessica Kingsley.

Lewin, K. (1946) Behaviour and development as a function of the total situation, in D. Cartwright (ed.) *Kurt Lewin: Field Theory in the Social Sciences, Selected Theoretical Papers*. New York, Evanston and London: Harper Torchbooks, pp. 238–97.

Lewin, K. (1947) Frontiers in group dynamics, in D. Cartwright (ed.) *Kurt Lewin: Field Theory in the Social Sciences, Selected Theoretical Papers*. London: HarperTorchbooks, pp. 188–237.

Mackewn, J. (1997) *Developing Gestalt Counselling*. London: Sage.

O'Neill, B. and Gaffney, S. (2008) Field theoretical strategy, in P. Brownell (ed.) *Handbook for Theory, Research, and Practice in Gestalt Therapy*. Newcastle: Cambridge Scholars Publishing, pp. 228–56.

Parlett, M. (1991) Reflections on field theory, *British Gestalt Journal*, 1(2): 63–81.

Parlett, M. (1997) The unified field in practice, *Gestalt Review*, 1(1): 16–33.

Perls, F., Hefferline, R.F. and Goodman, P. (1951) *Gestalt Therapy: Excitement and Growth in the Human Personality*. London: Souvenir Press (re-issued 1984).

Rogers, J. (2004) *Coaching Skills: A Handbook*. Maidenhead: Open University Press.

Samuels, A., Shorter, B. and Plaut, F. (1986) *A Critical Dictionary of Jungian Analysis*. Hove: Brunner-Routledge.

Schaverien, J. and Case, C. (2007) *Supervision of Art Psychotherapy*. London: Routledge.

Shohet, R. (2008) *Passionate Supervision*. London: Jessica Kingsley.

Sieler, A. (2010) Ontological coaching, in E. Cox, T. Bachkirova and D. Clutterbuck (eds) *The Complete Handbook of Coaching*. London: Sage, pp. 107–19.

Spagnuolo Lobb, M. and Amendt-Lyon, N. (eds) (2003) *Creative Licence: The Art of Gestalt Therapy*. New York: SpringerWien.

Spinelli, E. (1989) *The Interpreted World: An Introduction to Phenomenological Psychology*. London: Sage.

Spinelli, E. (2010) Existential coaching, in E. Cox, T. Bachkirova and D. Clutterbuck (eds) *The Complete Handbook of Coaching*. London: Sage.

Staemmler, F. M. (2006) A Babylonian confusion?: on the uses and meanings of the term 'field', *British Gestalt Journal*, 15(2): 64–83.

Woldt, A. and Toman, S. (2005) *Gestalt Therapy*. London: Sage.

Zinker, J.C. (1994) *In Search of Good Form*. San Francisco, CA: Jossey-Bass.

# 10 The person-centred approach in coaching supervision

*Bernard Cooke*

## Introduction

Like many other methodologies that underpin coaching supervision, the person-centred approach has its roots in therapy, but has grown and adapted to the demands of coaching and coaching supervision. The manner of this adaptation, the value that it might add and the extent to which it has been true to the original theory are the topics for this chapter. Many coaches and supervisors maintain that they adhere to the principles of person-centred coaching by regarding their clients as resourceful and capable of finding their own solutions. But a warm, generalized intent is not quite the same as a conscious application of a theory, so it is always valuable to dig a little deeper and examine our practice to see exactly how we are incorporating its principles and to what effect. To date there is very little written about how these principles are adopted by supervisors in a coaching context, so this chapter is offered as a starting point for this examination. We will start by examining the principles of the person-centred approach and explore, with the help of a short case illustration, how the theory has been interpreted and applied in the practice of supervision. Just how one does relate the underlying theory to practice can vary considerably, but I will argue that it is a clear and conscious application of the approach that can add a rewarding dimension to one's supervision.

## Key principles of the person-centred approach

The fundamental assumption that underpins person-centred therapy is that people are intrinsically motivated to grow and develop into optimally functioning human beings. The approach was originally developed by the psychologist Carl Rogers (1961) as a form of psychotherapy but the principles are now widely incorporated in coaching and coaching supervision. The *actualizing tendency* was viewed by Rogers as the central driving force of an individual to develop all of their capacities in the direction of maintaining and enhancing itself. This fundamental belief of Rogers, that every individual can grow and develop into their 'optimal form', is central to the person-centred approach. However this *self-actualization* can only occur in an environment where the individual feels understood, valued and accepted for who they are, and without conditions. If this is not the case, then the individual may actualize their personality in a way that is *incongruent* with their natural actualizing tendency and develop a *self-concept* that is more related to meeting the needs and expectations of others. This incongruence results in distress and dysfunction for the individual, as would be the case, for example, if someone's self-concept is based more upon some external evaluation of their worth ('you ought to be like this . . .') than their real, underlying 'organismic' self which is in line with their own experience ('I want to be like this . . .').

## Rogers' necessary and sufficient conditions

For any therapeutic change to take place in individuals, Rogers maintained that six conditions have to be met within the relationship between client and therapist, in order to facilitate the individual's tendency to actualize.

1   *Psychological contact.* A minimal awareness of each other's presence, with the behaviour of one impacting upon the other, would have to be present in any therapeutic relationship. Without this, then the following five conditions would be redundant.
2   *Client incongruence.* The client should be experiencing some discrepancy between their actual feelings and either the expression of those feelings or the external perception of them. This will occur, for example, when a person feels some inner pain which their self-concept finds unacceptable to display.
3   *Congruence of the therapist.* The feelings of the therapist must be available to him and he must be able to live with these and communicate them, if appropriate, within the therapeutic relationship.
4   *Unconditional positive regard.* The therapist accepts the client as they are, without imposing any conditions of worth.
5   *Empathic understanding.* The therapist should take on board the client's perceptions, experiences and concerns, as though they were his own.
6   *Perception.* The client should perceive the therapist's unconditional regard and empathy.

## The use of person-centred theory in supervision

How might these principles, grounded in therapy, be incorporated into coaching supervision, where the needs of the supervisee may be less about therapeutic change but more about requests for direction and support? First, let's examine how they might enable the key functions of supervision, as defined by Hawkins and Smith (2006).

The *developmental* function is facilitating the coach to reflect upon their work with their clients and to develop new skills, understanding and insight on their coaching practice. Clearly the person-centred supervisor would work from an assumption that their supervisee has an innate capacity to develop, both as a person and as a professional coach, and they would place their trust in them to take their own learning from the thoughts and reflections arising during the session. However, explicit in some and implicit in most models of development, is the existence of different stages, where the coach moves through a number of levels from novice to master. Some difficulties with this model are outlined by Tudor and Worral (2004), who maintain that most developmental models are based upon theories of child development and, therefore, are inherently infantilizing. Instead they advocate the use of *process* theories (Casement 1985) which view development as an ongoing and unfolding phenomenon, with the supervisor and supervisee in a constant state of 'becoming'. Whether a 'stage' or 'process' perspective is adopted, a purely person-centred approach may present challenges for the supervisor who is expected to provide some guidance or share some experience. As coaches are more usually working with clients to identify and realize some defined goal, it would be expected for them to bring to supervision, issues relating to the learning and growth of their clients and of themselves as coaches. In fact, the increasing 'professionalization' of the coaching community positively reinforces the notion that there are incremental levels of coaching capability, and the supervisor will inevitably be a part of that system.

The *resourcing* function is concerned with helping coaches to face and remain working with difficult and often emotionally charged situations. As coaches will inevitably be affected by their work, the supervisor will help them to understand their responses better, sometimes surfacing feelings that relate to issues belonging to the coach rather than the coachee. With its emphasis on empathy, unconditional regard and congruency, the person-centred approach to supervision is highly compatible with this function. However, many supervisors also draw upon other theories, such as psychodynamic, to provide this function, so raising the issue of compatibility with other approaches. We will return to this issue in the evaluation of the approach.

The *qualitative* function is concerned with the reinforcing of the quality and ethical standards that the coach should be maintaining in their practice. This raises the issue of who is taking responsibility for the quality of work carried out, as the purely person-centred approach would rule out the possibility of the supervisor taking any of this responsibility. However, there may be situations where the supervisor is contracted to ensure that the quality of coaching offered meets certain standards and that the coach and coachees are suitably protected. In these cases the person-centred approach would place more emphasis on the coach and supervisor jointly exploring any external frameworks of standards and values.

From this brief review of how a person-centred approach fits with the tasks of coaching supervision, we have immediately run into some challenges around the interpretation of Rogers' theory in a context which is different from the one for which it was intended. Should we adopt a fundamentalist approach and stick to the literal definitions of Rogers' conditions, or are we advocating some interpretation, where the underlying beliefs may inform a variety of methods? Can the person-centred approach sit alongside others that are underpinned by different theoretical models? Indeed, these points are frequently debated within the community that comprises person-centred practitioners.

## Interpretation of the person-centred theory

Hitchings (2004) outlines some of the disputes between the 'tribes' of the person-centred community, principally between the 'literalists' and the 'experimentalists'. Whilst the literalists maintain that Rogers' six conditions and the non-directive attitude of the therapist are non-negotiable, the experimentalists claim to remain true to the core theory, but view it as permissible to be more directive about the emerging processes within and between the therapist and client. For Hitchings this raises the issue of where the expertise is located or whose perception of reality is most valid. It could be argued that the psychoanalytic school would place the expertise with the therapist, whilst the literalist person-centred school would view it as residing solely with the client. By contrast, the experimentalists would take an 'inter-subjective' perspective, seeing the client's reality as something that is co-created between the two. Worsley (2002), in support of this inter-subjective stance, acknowledges that the therapists can never be the experts in their clients, but questions the notion that the clients can always be experts on themselves!

So would the process of supervision look different between a literalist and an experimentalist person-centred supervisor? The devout literalist would see their role purely as facilitating the coach's awareness of their relationship with their client. Expertise would be viewed as residing only with the supervisee and the six conditions above should be strictly adhered to. By contrast, the experimentalist may take a more flexible approach, depending upon the personalities of the two people involved, the needs of the coach and issues arising from the session. A model of supervision outlined by Merry (1999), for example, regards the process as 'collaborative inquiry', where both people are self directed and can contribute equally to the process. The experimentalists may also question as to whether the six conditions need to be so strictly adhered to. For example, Tudor and Worall (2004) argue that the first two conditions are not strictly necessary for the process of supervision. Supervision that is carried out through the exchange of emails for example, where the sender may be engaged in a completely different activity when the receiver is reading the message, means that the kind of psychological contact that Rogers described, cannot be achieved. If we accept this as a form of supervision, then we cannot assert that such psychological contact is a *necessary* condition. Also the supervisee may not need to feel incongruent in some way to benefit from a supervision session, should they simply want to share and explore their case work. Of course some may experience a great deal of incongruence between their organismic self and their self-concept of themselves as a professional coach. But for others, supervision can still be valuable even when, despite the inevitability of its potential existence, the level of incongruence may not have developed to such a level.

Supervision may, therefore, look different between these two schools of practitioner groups. This would certainly underline the importance for both supervisor and coach to be clear in their contracting about what it is they offer and need. Part of this process could be an exchange of the principles and theories that underpin their respective practices and an exploration of how these might complement or conflict with one another. Having agreed their positions on what constitutes a person-centred approach and established a framework for their ongoing collaboration, they might also ask how other theories might be integrated into the supervision. For the supervisor, questions could also arise as to how the various models of supervision might fit with the person-centred theory.

The seven-eyed model of supervision (Hawkins and Smith 2006) for example, poses some challenges for the person-centred supervisor. For instance, in mode 2, the focus is on the *interventions* that the supervisee has made with their client. Is this encouraging the coach to adopt a mindset of *doing things to* their client, as opposed to facilitating a resourceful client to find their own approach? In mode 3, the focus is on the relationship between the coach and client, including the way that the client may experience the supervisee. This discussion may include possible transference, by the client towards the supervisee, of attitudes developed from earlier relationships. In mode 4, counter-transference is explored, that is possible unconscious reactions by the supervisee towards the client, and in mode 5 the supervisor focuses on their own unconscious reactions and potential parallel processes occurring in the supervisory relationship. In Rogers' views, dealing with transference was a 'grave mistake' (Rogers 1990) which could lead to dependency and lengthen the therapeutic process. To him, the creation of the therapeutic relationship using unconditional positive regard, empathy and congruence were all that are required, and far more important than specific therapeutic techniques. Whilst the use of psychodynamic theory in supervision is not a problem per se, as seen from a person-centred perspective it may place too much emphasis on the technique of the supervisor, at the expense of the relationship between supervisor and supervisee.

These challenges of interpretation of the necessary conditions and compatibility with supervision models are not, however, impediments that prevent the beneficial application of the person-centred approach in practice, as the following example will illustrate.

## Case illustration

*Liz (not her real name) was an experienced coaching psychologist who I was supervising during a time when she was experiencing some significant doubts and questions about her own effectiveness as a coach. She described how, with certain* clients, her confidence in her own ability as a coach seemed to dissipate and her skills and knowledge felt 'like a jigsaw that had broken into 3000 pieces. I don't know where I am – I can't get a sense of whether my coaching is working or not!' Having worked with Liz as a colleague in the past, I knew her well and had a high degree of respect for her professional capabilities. She had approached me for supervision support at a time when she was undergoing a formal accreditation process and managing a demanding caseload of coaching. As a supervisor who integrates the person-centred with other approaches and models, in line with the 'experimentalist' school described above, Liz and I shared a common set of philosophies and practices in coaching. Our previous sessions had focused on issues related to specific clients, but now I was being presented with a generalized and overwhelming sense of anxiety – what was going on?

Liz described her anxiety in terms of her apparent inability to find and utilize the 'appropriate coaching technique' when working with a client. I was curious about this reference to 'technique', partly because it was unusual for her to focus on this but also because Liz had always impressed me with the degree of empathy that she appeared to show towards her clients and the focus she placed upon the relationship that she held with them. Using the Hawkins seven-eyed model as a framework, I encouraged Liz to talk more about the client, her impressions of him and the interventions that she had made (modes 1 and 2). Liz described how this particular client had, at one point, 'appeared quite manic and confused about his own identity and place within the organization'. This had appeared to trigger a reaction in Liz that made her feel that her coaching was 'not working' and that she ought to have some technique available to put it right! In describing her relationship with this client, Liz said that she found it difficult to show him unconditional positive regard. So here was a coach who would usually describe her approach as person centred, seeking supervision on a breakdown in this methodology. So what is the person-centred supervisor supposed to do?

Initially I picked up on Liz's jigsaw metaphor, reflecting that '3000 pieces is an awful lot! I'm wondering how you ever kept all of them together?' Liz smiled in response, perhaps recognizing that she had been expecting quite a lot of herself. At this stage I was unclear about where Liz wanted to take our session and I allowed her space to reflect. She soon began to talk about her feelings on her relationship with this client and I asked her about what she believed that she was providing for him, even if she felt that she wasn't coaching effectively. As Liz spoke about this, she visibly relaxed, become more energized and talked more positively about instances where she had felt empathy and positive regard for the client. Feeling that I was being re-acquainted with an old friend, I shared this with Liz and she acknowledged that something different was emerging for her. The discussion then opened up new insights for Liz on what might be happening in their coaching relationship and some areas that she was curious about exploring further. Her concern for finding the 'right technique' for this situation subsided, as did her anxiety about her efficacy as a coach.

Whilst this short vignette of a supervision session is not intended as a complete demonstration of the person-centred approach, it provides sufficient material to review the application of the theory. First of all, we might ask whether the six conditions considered necessary were present in this scenario? The psychological contact between Liz and myself was present, although it would be presumptuous to assume so, simply on the basis of our familiarity with each other, as there could be many forms of interference preventing such contact. Liz was in a state of incongruence – experiencing a feeling of anxiety about meeting expectations as a coach and confusion about her relationship with this client. With regard to my own state of congruence, it is difficult to answer with a simple yes or no. What I did feel at that time was empathy for Liz, as I could recognize the anxiety that arises when one questions one's own abilities. Equally, I did not have any 'answers' to Liz's dilemma but felt a calmness and belief that something positive would emerge from our session together. The positive regard that I held for Liz was not compromised in any way by expectations that I held of her as a person or professional and I hoped that my empathy for her situation was perceived by her, to at least the 'minimal degree' that Rogers described.

In person-centred fashion I placed my trust in Liz to find some resolution to her manifest anxiety, without trying to impose models or frameworks. My sense is that the presence of the trusting relationship between Liz and myself allowed Liz's focus to be drawn towards her own relationship with her client and then for new insights to emerge. Rogers' initial term for his approach was in fact 'relationship therapy', and it is this that is key to the process. Liz's initial presentation of a concern for techniques and capabilities could so easily have prompted, on my part, a guided tour of tools and techniques and some discussion on what might be 'missing'. In one sense I was being invited to re-build Liz, arming her with the appropriate equipment, but in another I was simply being invited to listen and provide some of the positive regard for herself that she had lost. As a result, Liz began to view her own challenge of finding positive regard for her client as a relationship issue, rather than one of technical competence.

Of course there were alternative approaches that could have taken us to a similar or different place. The interference that Liz was experiencing, which prevented her experiencing positive regard for her client, could have been explored from a gestalt or psychodynamic perspective. Perhaps this was a case of 'parallel processing', where the Liz's fragmented sense of identity had been a reflection of her client's 'manic behaviour'? Perhaps this client had triggered some association in Liz with some anxiety-provoking situation or individual? Perhaps a systems perspective of Liz and her client would yield some insights on the emerging processes? These are all reasonable possibilities which could have formed the basis of an equally valid and effective supervisory session. The choices presented to a supervisor are not necessarily on *whether* to adopt a person-centred approach or not, but *how* to apply the principles of the theory and how they might integrate into other dimensions of their practice. The reward of such integration is the deepening of the working relationship between the supervisor and their client.

## Evaluation of the approach

Having examined the interpretation of person-centred theory to supervision and illustrated a practical application, the challenges of 'when' and 'how' to apply it will be discussed. First, where would the person-centred approach to supervision be of most benefit? The short case illustration above provided an example of the coach feeling some anxiety, in this case about her own performance and the relationship with her client. This would seem to be both a relevant and commonly occurring supervision topic, as indicated by the following research.

In research by De Haan et al. (2008) experienced coaches were asked to identify 'critical moments' that they encounter when coaching. These moments were de-scribed as 'exciting, tense or significant moments . . . when you did not quite know what to do'. They were characterized by intense emotions and anxieties within the coaching relationship and could often be seen as turning points in their work. Example topics of the coach's anxieties included: the boundaries of coaching (for example between coaching and psychotherapy); satisfying client outcomes; the coach's own role (what did the client want from them; what were they getting into and were they doing enough?). Many of the coaches took these experiences to supervision in order to make sense of their reactions and to gain reassurance that they had handled the moment competently. De Haan et al. found that coaches tend to 'internalize' the responsibility for any tensions or difficulties in their work, seeing the problems as their own, rather than as problems with the management of the coaching relationship as a whole.

How coaches deal with difficult emotions, both their own and those of their clients, was researched by Cox and Bachkirova (2007). In looking at difficult sit-uations arising from the coach's emotions, they found that coaches tend to see these as testing their understanding of the boundaries of their profession, partic-ularly that between coaching and counselling or psychotherapy. It also appeared that some coaches may be identifying with their client's emotions, thus making them less able to adopt a person-centred, empathic approach. They concluded that there is a significant role for supervision in helping coaches to build their awareness and understanding of emotions in coaching and building their capacity to work with these.

The person-centred supervisor would seem to be well suited to responding to issues of the type which this research suggests are important and frequently oc-curring in coaching. When the coach is presenting with anxiety and emotion, the supervisor with congruence, empathy and positive regard is very likely to be perceived as supportive and restorative. Supervision provides the coach with the opportunity to explore doubts and concerns, where emotions and anxieties can be 'contained'. The term containment was used by Bion (1963) to describe a calming, receptive and authentic approach, even in situations that involve emotion and tension. This allows the coach to reflect upon their anxiety and to find new op-tions in going forward with the relationship. Just as the coach needs to stay in the coaching relationship with their coachee when confronted with difficult emotions and anxieties, so must the supervisor provide such containment with the coach.

Are there any situations where the person-centred approach to supervision might be less useful? It would be true to the spirit of the person-centred approach to be led by the needs of the client. If the client is seeking a psychodynamic perspective to explore transference issues or if they were concerned about mental health issues of their clients, then a person-centred approach would not be appropriate. The level of experience of the coach may also be a factor, with the novice requiring and asking for more direction and guidance – something that the purist person-centred coach may feel compromises their principles. Some critics of person-centred therapy point to the need for an articulate, self-aware client and sufficient time to allow for them to work through their issues. However, in the context of coaching supervision, the presenting issues are very different from the intractable ones requiring therapy, and supervisees are hopefully more likely to have greater than average levels of self-awareness. This supervision contract may not always simply be between the supervisor and coach; in some cases the supervision may be contracted for as a part of a large coaching initiative with a sponsoring organization, with the supervisor having some explicit obligation to review standards of coaching and to oversee the quality of service provided. Such situations require the supervisor to show a flexibility of style and responsiveness to multiple clients and stakeholders. Person-centred supervision in this context would have to accommodate the legitimacy of needs and concerns of stakeholders outside of the coach–coachee relationship.

To suggest that the choice of supervision approach generally, and person-centred specifically, is an either/or question is confusing and unhelpful. The selection of a person-centred approach is not necessarily at the expense of other methodologies, such as cognitive-behavioural, solutions-focused, psychodynamic and positive psychology. For Joseph (2006) the person-centred approach does not prescribe techniques of practice, but allows a multidisciplinary approach that is grounded on the principles of the theory. Important for Joseph is that the techniques are an expression of the meta-theoretical assumptions of person-centred theory; it is not what the supervisor *does* that is important, but how they *think* about their relationship with the coach and how their actions relate to the underlying assumption that they are there to facilitate the coach to self-actualize. This 'thinking about the relationship' and consciously attending to Rogers' conditions is what distinguishes the person-centred approach. Incorporating other methodologies into this framework without compromising these principles is possible, as long as they are purposefully translated rather than casually imported.

## Learning more

The person-centred approach to coaching supervision is something that few would argue against in principle. In practice, what actually is offered in the name of a person-centred methodology may look very different from one supervisor to another. The underlying principles of a non-directive style, empathy and positive regard appear so deceptively simple that many coaches and supervisors espouse them as constant guiding values. But these principles may become compromised and challenged when applied in a different context from the one in which they were originally formulated. The field of coaching supervision, as opposed to the grounds of therapy in which the theory took root, presents a range of challenges to the aspiring person-centred practitioner – the differing functions of supervision and the multi-faceted needs of the supervisee for example, will demand compromises and flexibility on the part of the supervisor. But if we passively assume the necessary conditions to be in place, rather than actively reviewing them, then we run the risk of playing deceptive lip service to the theory, whilst practising something else.

### Questions for reflection

- Where do I stand on the 'literalist' versus 'experimentalist' school of person-centred coaching?
- To what extent do I see the six necessary conditions evident in my own supervision practice?
- Are these other approaches fundamentally compatible with the person-centred theory?
- How can they be utilized in such a way that the client can remain directive of the content, even if the supervisor is being directive on the process?

### Recommended reading

- For an overview of person-centred therapy and its origins, see *Theory and Practice of Counselling and Therapy* (2006) by Richard Nelson-Jones.
- For the application of the person-centred theory to coaching, see *Person-centred Coaching Psychology* by Joseph and Bryant-Jefferies, pp. 211–28.
- For useful texts on the use of person-centred theory in supervision see *Freedom to Practise – Person-centred Approaches to Supervision* (Tudor and Worrall 2004)

Above all, Rogers' own writing gives a very human insight into the motivation and values underlying his development of the person-centred approach. *On Becoming a Person* (2004, originally published in 1961) is a collection of Rogers' papers, some of them lectures, which provide an accessible insight into his reflections on his own experience.

## References

Bion, W. (1963) *Elements of Psychoanalysis*. London: William Heinemann.

Casement, P. (1985) *On Learning from the Patient*. London: Tavistock.

Cox, E. and Bachkirova, T. (2007) Coaching with emotion: how coaches deal with difficult emotional situations, *International Coaching Psychology Review*, 2(2): 178–89.

De Haan, E., Day, A., Blass, E., Stills, C. and Bertie, C. (2008) Coaches have their say: how to handle critical moments? in E. De Haan, *Relational Coaching*. Chichester: Wiley, pp. 131–53.

Hawkins, P. and Smith, N. (2006) *Coaching, Mentoring and Organizational Consultancy: Supervsion and Development*. Maidenhead: Open University Press.

Hitchings, P. (2004) On supervision across theoretical orientations, in K. Tudor and M. Worrall. *Freedom to Practise: Person-centred Approaches to Supervsion*. Ross-on-Wye: PCCS Books, pp. 203–25.

Joseph, S. (2006) Person-centred coaching psychology: a meta-theoretical perspective, *International Coaching Psychology Review*, 1: 47–54.

Joseph, S. and Bryant-Jefferies, R. (2007) Person-centred coaching psychology, in S. Palmer and A. Whybrow, *Handbook of Coaching Psychology*. Hove: Routledge, pp. 211–28.

Merry, T. (1999) *Learning and Being in Person-Centred Counselling*. Ross-on-Wye: PCCS Books.

Nelson-Jones, R. (2006) *Theory and Practice of Counselling and Therapy*. London: Sage.

Rogers, C.R. (1961) *On Becoming a Person*. Boston, MA: Houghton Mifflin.

Rogers, C. (1990) *The Carl Rogers Reader*. London: Constable.

Rogers, C. (2004) *On Becoming a Person: A Therapist's View of Psychotherapy*. London: Constable.

Tudor, K. and Worrall, M. (2004) *Freedom to Practise: Person-centred Approaches to Supervision*. Ross-on-Wye, Heredfordshire, UK: PCCS Books.

Worsley, R. (2002) *Process Work in Person-Centred Therapy*. Hampshire: Palgrave.

# 11 Using transactional analysis in coaching supervision

*Julie Hay*

## Introduction

Transactional analysis (TA) is an approach to understanding why people behave as they do, and of helping them achieve more autonomy. It is also an established psychotherapy modality, practised worldwide and with internationally-agreed professional qualifications, with university accreditation of masters programmes in several countries, and registration for graduates with the UK Council for Psychotherapy. Developmental TA (DTA) is when the original psychotherapeutic focus on cure shifts to an emphasis on development and growth, as when the practitioner is working within an organizational, educational or coaching context.

This chapter sets out to introduce you to some key elements of TA, mainly with a DTA perspective, and how these can enhance the supervisory process. Hopefully it will also tempt you to find out more. Learning aims for the chapter are that:

- you will acquire two or three new perspectives of the supervision process;
- you will be able to apply TA concepts interwoven with any of the models described elsewhere in this book;
- you will be interested to share TA concepts with supervisees in order to increase their self-awareness and professional competence.

TA originated in the 1960s (Berne 1961), and has become a robust and comprehensive approach, with varying schools (Barnes 1977) that focus on elements such as regression – the cathexis school (Schiff 1975); TA combined with Gestalt (Goulding and Goulding 1979); constructionism (Allen and Allen 1977); and co-creativity (Summers and Tudor 2000). The classical school initiated by Berne has been likened to cognitive behavioural therapy (English 2007). More recent approaches include relational TA (Hargaden and Sills 2002) which returns to a focus on the role of the unconscious within the therapeutic relationship, and Schmid (2008) who writes of systemic TA and the nature of roles.

In the 1990s (Hay 1992/2009, 1993/2009) I began to adapt many of the therapeutically-aligned TA constructs so that the emphasis shifted from pathology to health. I also introduced apparent simplifications which allow us to share complex ideas in ways that coaches can readily understand and apply for themselves.

Each of the TA schools have contributed theoretical constructs of particular value in the coaching process, and hence for supervision also. My selection here, to fit the constraints of one chapter, covers the following: contracting from the classical school; discounting from the cathexis school; and the impact of the unconscious from the relational school. I also give a very brief description of some key TA concepts that may have been encountered elsewhere as a way of raising the reader's awareness of their source.

## Relating the theory to supervision

The term transactional analysis originally referred to analysing the transactions, or interactions, between people, using Berne's (1961) concept of ego states. This analytical process is now referred to as 'TA proper' because TA has come to represent a wide ranging set of interlinking concepts, many introduced by Berne. We develop *ego states* that interact with others to get our needs met; these interactions can also be thought of as exchanges of *strokes* which are the units of human recognition we all need to survive; we interact in *time structuring* clusters of increasing intensity in order to form relationships; we engage in unhelpful *psychological games* when we fail to achieve the closeness, or *intimacy*, we seek; and all of this often serves to reinforce a life *script* we adopted when we were too little to interpret our circumstances as a grown-up would. Internally, we may view the world through distorting *windows* (Hay 1993/2009) that allocate *OK/not OK* to us and others, we may *discount* (Mellor and Schiff 1975) evidence that conflicts with our preconceptions, run self-fulfilling prophecies (*racket systems*; Erskine and Zalcman 1979) that influence how others react to us, and have internal processes (*miniscripts*; Kahler 1974) that repeat our script patterns in micro format. As if all that were not enough, we also operate within patterns that reinforce our *drivers* (Kahler 1975), or compulsive ways of behaving that are linked to our *process script* (Kahler 1978), although when these patterns are under conscious choice they are seen as *working styles* (Hay 1992/2009) and hence as strengths.

Any of the wide range of interlocking TA constructs can shed light on the supervision process and many are relatively easy to apply. For instance, we can analyse ego states to identify, and avoid, potential parent–child co-dependent relationships between supervisor and supervisee. Or we can review stroking patterns to take account of the risks of supervisees with inadequate support networks relying on these units of recognition from clients or their supervisor – or the same problem for supervisors who need 'admiration strokes' from supervisees.

### Functions of supervision

If we think of the functions of supervision as being some variant of Proctor's (1986) normative, formative and restorative, TA will be most relevant for the formative element. It will also prompt a style of supervision that might better be labelled super-vision (Hay 1992/2007), where the hyphen is to emphasize that the objective is to develop a super vision, or meta perspective, of the practice of the supervisee. The TA principle of autonomy also means that it is the supervisee who needs to develop this super-vision, so the main task of the supervisor is to facilitate this.

The supervisory normative function may be needed if a supervisee is failing to meet professional norms but hopefully this will occur only occasionally and may be better addressed with training. The restorative function will usually also be reduced because clients (should) bring less severe problems to coaching than to therapy; I have re-labelled this supportive (Hay 1992/2009) and have found that the need is reduced for coaching compared to therapeutic counselling.

## Unconscious processes

It hardly needs saying that there will be unconscious processes within the supervisory dynamic. This is where the contrast between classical and relational TA can be so helpful. The principles of classical TA are that: we all have *physis* (Berne 1957), which is the urge to develop to our potential (like plants growing from under concrete to be in the sun); we all made decisions when small and can therefore change these now we know more about the world; and we are all OK and need to function in ways that allow us to connect genuinely with others. These principles lead to a supervisory style that is focused on developing the awareness and decision-making abilities of the supervisee.

At the same time, relational TA prompts us to keep in mind that much of significance will be occurring at the unspoken psychological level of the interaction. Stark (2000) identifies one, one and a half, and two person forms of therapy, meaning respectively that the therapist facilitates the client to do the work, that the therapist provides a reparative experience for the client, or that the therapist uses their counter-transference to shed light on the dynamics of said client. If we apply this to supervision, we may opt to facilitate the supervisee in applying TA concepts, we may act like a reassuring or challenging parent they lacked in childhood, or we may invite the supervisee to pay conscious attention to hitherto unconscious processes between us and consider how these may illuminate their processes with clients.

Berne (1961) identified the psychological level, or ulterior transaction, as where the real power of any interaction resides. English (1975) extended this into consideration of the three-cornered contract, where she noted that training programme participants often arrive with negative fantasies about what the presenter might be about to 'do to them' on behalf of the wicked organization. Micholt (1992) added the notion of how the psychological distances might vary, with the practitioner too close psychologically to either participant or organization. These are classical TA school explanations of what might otherwise be referred to as transference/counter-transference. A quick sketch of a triangle allows us to illustrate the dynamics and prompt the supervisee to consider whether all sides are equal – or does the supervisee feel closer to the client than to the supervisor, or vice versa, or might it be that they feel the supervisor is psychologically aligning with the client?

We can add other parties if appropriate, although the triangles may need to be imagined in multidimensional space! We might need to add a professional body that supervisor and/or supervisee subscribe to, whose norms must also be taken into account. Perhaps this turns the supervisor into a 'police officer' in the view of the supervisee. There may be an organization paying for the supervision; if so, we may need to take into account what expectations they have of the supervisory process, and how these may impact on aspects such as confidentiality and the openness of the supervisee.

## Contracting

Having considered unconscious processes, the next TA concept I describe is contracting. This is regarded as a key element of TA and is how we invite the supervisee to be autonomous. Autonomy is another key TA concept, being the notion that each of us can function in the here-and-now; being aware of who we and other people are right now instead of engaging in regression, projection and/or transference; being open so no ulterior transactions occur; being aware that we have options for how to behave instead of being stuck in familiar unhelpful patterns; and knowing that we and others are OK even when our behaviour sometimes is not.

Contracting needs to be achieved on three levels: in addition to the unconscious, or psychological, level described above, we need to have clear agreements with all relevant parties about the administrative and professional aspects. When, where, for how long will sessions last; what happens about cancellations; what are the fees and how and when will they be paid; what documentation needs to be kept and who is allowed to see this; what actions by a client would justify breaching confidentiality? Professionally, what are we here to do; what coaching style is expected; is the practitioner appropriately qualified; where are the boundaries of coaching versus therapy or consulting; how is the coaching linked to the client's professional role?

The above are just sample questions to show what a supervisor might ask a supervisee. Often, exploring the coaching contract will result in a coach realizing what was missed that led to any current problems. Contracting needs similar rigour between supervisor and supervisee, especially when there are other parties involved. We can go back to the triangles mentioned above and imagine them stacked up for the three levels. If any level is not equilateral, the stack will be insecure. For example, an organization that consistently delays paying for supervision may lead to a frustrated supervisor feeling resentful towards a supervisee. A supervisee may expect the supervisor to be a subject expert who will give advice instead of the non-directive role the supervisor planned to adopt.

## Discounting

Discounting within TA is defined as minimizing or ignoring some aspects of ourselves, others or the situation (Mellor and Schiff 1975). We do this to stay sane, as when we tune out background noise to pay attention to something important, or fall asleep in front of the television. Unfortunately, we also discount to maintain our frame of reference, or the script we adopted when a young child and that we have now forgotten exists. By discounting we can maintain our limiting beliefs, continue to interact with others in familiar ways, and justify our failure to deal with problems.

Discounting is the key to why we need supervision. We need someone else who can spot what we are not allowing ourselves to notice. Mellor and Schiff (1975) identified several levels and types of discounting and matched these to six therapeutic treatment levels. These can be converted into a visual and alliterative memory aid called Steps to Success (Hay 1996; see Figure 11.1). The labels for most steps are self-explanatory in that we discount some aspect of the situation, significance (problem), solutions available, skills available, strategies available, or the possibility of success. Figure 11.1 shows the steps and the supervisor and supervisee on them. This is to illustrate that we will usually be on a higher step than the person doing the discounting. We need to go down the steps to their level and then 'coax' them back up the steps with us. It is usually worth going all the way back to the situation step to ensure that the significance of the issue has been correctly identified and the supervisee is not trying to solve someone else's problem.

To illustrate this with an example, Saroj brought a 'difficult' client to supervision. Saroj had identified that the client was discounting at the solutions level, by insisting there were no options that would resolve the problem of needing to

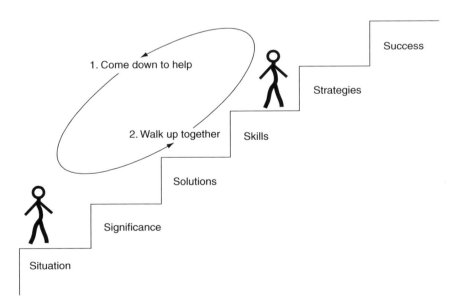

**Figure 11.1**  Walking up the Steps to Success

work with a colleague the client disliked. It was clear to me, but not to Saroj of course, that there was a parallel process (Searles 1955) in effect: Saroj disliked this client. I therefore set out to help Saroj climb the steps. We began by reviewing the situation, which in this case meant the contract with the client, the coaching plan and what had happened so far within the coaching.

When we moved up a step to significance, I was able to question Saroj about why this client was difficult whereas other clients who got stuck were not. This prompted Saroj to realize that a personal dynamic was getting in the way; the client reminded Saroj of a former colleague with whom Saroj had struggled unsuccessfully to work. This insight enabled Saroj to identify some solutions that could have been used with that colleague; this in turn prompted solutions from Saroj for working with the client. One solution involved Saroj walking the client up the client's own steps, another option was to have the client explore the psychological game being played (with Saroj and with the colleague), and yet another was to help the client identify how the ego state they typically adopted with this colleague was leading to crossed transactions.

Saroj did not need more supervision about the steps for skills, strategies and success because once the discounting at a lower level had been dealt with, Saroj was able to think clearly about how to coach the client in new skills, how to prompt the client to develop a strategy for changing their behaviour towards the colleague, and how to have the client check for potential self-sabotage of a successful resolution of the issue.

## Case illustrations

Lesley – new to TA

*Lesley did not know much TA but was interested to learn. We therefore contracted that I would use TA when supervising and would explain my thinking as necessary so Lesley would increasingly be able to undertake the analysis unaided. This involved me in some mini-teaches and also meant we frequently focused on building awareness of how personal issues affected Lesley's competence as a practitioner.*

*For example, I needed to explain contracting and especially the significance of the psychological level and psychological distances. A short input enabled Lesley to identify what was not being said with a couple of coaching clients: in one case this was the client's expectation that the coach would do the problem solving; in another it was that the organization expected the coaching to fail so they could dismiss the coachee with an apparently clear conscience. In both cases, Lesley was able to raise these issues in a non-threatening way and agree more realistic outcomes with the organizational contact: that the coach would facilitate the client's identification of options; and that the threat of dismissal would be made overt and not linked to the coaching per se.*

Robin – very experienced

*We can contrast Lesley with Robin, a very experienced coach who had attended ongoing TA training and supervision workshops for about two years and used it extensively within coaching. Robin therefore tended to arrive for supervision with excerpts of recorded sessions plus transcripts, already analysed using several TA concepts. My supervisory role was for more than listening out for accuracy of analysis – my key purpose was to be the 'discount identifier' who alerted Robin to those elements that had been outside awareness.*

*These instances of discounting tended to be linked to Robin's personal issues that were as yet unresolved. Because Robin was generally self aware and analytical, such issues could often be addressed during supervision rather than having to be ring-fenced as therapy issues. Thus, Robin's familiarity with his/her own working styles and script meant that Robin readily saw the connection when I pointed out sentence patterns that Robin had missed. Robin thus volunteered the connection between the Please People pattern with an After process script of things feeling good to start but then going wrong – and how coaching with that client had indeed seemed to be going well until the client complained that no real progress was being made and challenged Robin's professional status.*

*A less self-aware supervisee might have needed careful questioning to reach this awareness, and might have needed to take the issue to therapy in order to work on their script dynamics. Robin, on the other hand, was able to recognize this as a replay of an old pattern, and to use the rest of the supervision session to figure out how and why this client had triggered this reaction at this time – and what to do about it now.*

## Evaluation of the approach

Like the other theoretical approaches in this book, TA is a psychological framework and will therefore be useful for understanding the psychological processes of supervision and coaching. It will be used differently depending on the degree of exposure to TA concepts of the supervisee but in some ways will be even more productive for supervisees with little TA knowledge than for those who have already gleaned significant insights from prior exposure to TA.

### Supervision is not therapy

A key consideration is maintaining the boundary between supervision and therapy when applying an approach that has its roots in psychotherapy. This is particularly so for supervisees whose only previous contact with TA has been in therapy or therapy training. Students are often unaware that different fields of application exist and may complete two or three years training as potential psychotherapists before their evident lack of therapy clients, and availability of coaching clients, leads them to properly investigate the different fields of TA application and recognize they could have been on a more relevant programme.

If the distinction between therapy and supervision is not understood, unprofessional practice may be the result. A supervisor and supervisee who both come from a therapeutic background may share expectations about coaching and supervision that blur the boundaries. They may spend supervisory time engaged in personal therapy for the supervisee instead of focusing on the development of the supervisee's practice. This in turn heightens the risk that the coach works inappropriately with clients, encouraging clients to regress and offering a reparative experience by acting as the good enough parent figure that was presumably missing during the clients' childhoods. This may mean that clients become increasingly dependent on their coach, perhaps with tearfulness during sessions and much talking about childhood events. There may be little focus on the original aims of the coaching, so that an organization buying coaching to work on the client's leadership skills may find that client exhibiting even less leadership competence in the workplace because of the constant reinforcement by the coach of the client's regressed Child ego state.

Transactional analysis is not the only approach where this applies of course, but the availability of developmental TA is significant in avoiding such problems. Unlike some forms of therapeutic supervision, it is regarded as a key element of DTA supervision that we facilitate the supervisee to stay in the here-and-now. They may regress momentarily, as we all do sometimes, but need to identify they have done this and maintain a conversation about what just happened, what it means, how they need to factor it into their professional work. They may dip into script but need to be able to move back to autonomous functioning; they may recognize a driver pattern and need to let go of the belief that this is the only route to OKness; or perhaps they identify they have played a psychological game with their client (or their supervisor) and instead of berating themself or others, they need to be prompted to become engaged with analysing the dynamics and working out what to do differently in future. In other words they need to be able to stay with the process of identifying their own supervision (Hay 1992/2007) of their practice instead of expecting the supervisor to take responsibility for that; the supervisor's role is to facilitate this process.

## Knowledge of TA

Another consideration is the levels of TA knowledge of supervisor and supervisee. If the supervisee has studied TA and the supervisor knows little or none, the supervisor may see this as an opportunity to encourage the supervisee to take the lead within the supervision process. This can be a powerful permission (Crossman 1966) and great role modelling for how to maintain your potency without having to be the expert.

If the supervisor has TA experience and the supervisee knows none, the supervisor may use their TA knowledge to guide their own thinking, to form hypotheses such as what script is in effect, or to use TA concepts to analyse behaviour patterns.

These can be checked out tentatively without using TA jargon and may well provide the supervisee with valuable insights. Another option, as I described above with Lesley, is to provide mini-teaches, with a focus on a specific aspect of the supervisee's or client's activity.

If supervisor and supervisee each know only a little TA, the danger of misinterpretation is slight provided the relationship is free of co-dependency and the joint discovery process will contribute to the working alliance. If both know considerable TA, they can save time by talking in professional jargon; being able to label patterns of behaviour in consistent ways eliminates the need for lengthy descriptions of who said and did what.

### Some common criticisms

Various criticisms have been levelled at TA over the years although not specifically at TA supervision. Berne has been accused of being racist and sexist, without any recognition that this could be said of anyone writing in the 1960s – a quick look at Edward de Bono's books published around the same time show the same issues. 'Paralysis by analysis' is another common complaint and is true insofar as the psychoanalytic tradition is allowed to creep in but does not apply when clear contracts are established for client change or coach development.

Another criticism has been about the apparent lack of research into the effectiveness of TA. However, the *International Journal of Transactional Analysis Research* (www.ijtar.org) was launched in summer 2010 and the initial issue contained an extensive review of research undertaken, albeit there have been none about TA supervision yet.

## Learning more

A good place to start learning some TA is through attendance at a TA introductory course, known as a TA 101 after the way universities in the USA refer to beginners' programmes. These courses cover the major TA concepts, albeit rather rapidly because they typically last only two or three days. Put TA 101 into a search engine to find options. Although there is an internationally-agreed syllabus, examples given during a course will vary according to the experience of the trainer so the reader is advised to check qualifications before booking. Only 101 Instructors and (Provisional) Teaching and Supervising Transactional Analysts may run TA 101 courses, and it is a professional practice requirement that qualified professionals show their specialization of organizational, educational, counselling or psychotherapy as part of their professional title.

The major TA qualifications and the associated examinations are operated internationally through a collaborative process by the European, International and Western Pacific TA Associations – EATA, ITAA and WPATA. Separate qualifications exist in South America, under the auspices of the Latin American TA Association – ALAT. However, these associations do not provide training or supervision; this is done by those who have attained the relevant qualifications. Additional certifications are offered in ways that fit around the international accreditations. Some universities accredit TA training programmes at master's level and some TA training institutes award their own certificates or diplomas.

## Key texts

There are many TA books available but few relate the theories directly to coaching or supervision. An exception is *Reflective Practice and Supervision for Coaches* (Hay 1992/2007). This is written for coaches and their supervisors and the content includes more than can be provided here on: discounting and the steps to success; contracting, boundaries, multi-party contracting, ethics; suggested groundrules for supervision groups; and some material related specifically to supervision about games, strokes and working styles; change and the competence curve.

*Transactional Analysis for Coaches and Mentors* (Hay 2011) contains material on organizational contexts, leadership and coaching styles, what happens in groups, plus many of the TA concepts mentioned within this chapter.

Although not directly about coaching or supervision, *Working Together: Using Organizational Transactional Analysis to Improve Communication with Others* by Mountain and Davidson (2011) relates up-to-date TA theories to organizational cultures and leadership. As such it will provide an excellent background to coaches working with members of the book's target audience. A similar but more generally targeted book, subtitled *Understanding Attitudes and Building Relationships* is *Working it Out at Work* by Hay (1993/2009).

# References

Allen, J. and Allen, B. (1977) A new type of transactional analysis and one version of script work with a constructionist sensibility, *Transactional Analysis Journal*, 27(2): 89–98.

Barnes, G. (ed.) (1977) *Transactional Analysis after Eric Berne: Teachings and Practices of Three TA Schools*. New York: Harper's College Press.

Berne, E. (1957) *A Layman's Guide to Psychiatry and Psychoanalysis*. New York: Simon and Schuster.

Berne, E. (1961) *Transactional Analysis in Psychotherapy*. New York: Grove Press.

Crossman, P. (1966) Permission and protection, *Transactional Analysis Bulletin*, 5(19): 152–4.

English, F. (1975) The three cornered contract, *Transactional Analysis Journal*, 5(4): 383–4.

English, F. (2007) I'm now a cognitive transactional analyst, are you? *The Script*, 37: 5 July.

Erskine, R. and Zalcman, M. (1979) The racket system; a model for racket analysis, *Transactional Analysis Journal*, 9(1): 51–9.

Goulding, R.L. and Goulding, M.M. (1979) *Changing Lives through Redecision Therapy*. New York: Grove Press Inc.

Hargaden, H. and Sills, C. (2002) *Transactional Analysis: A Relational Perspective*. Hove: Brunner-Routledge.

Hay, J. (1992/2007) *Reflective Practice and Supervision for Coaches*. Maidenhead: Open University Press.

Hay, J. (1992/2009) *Transactional Analysis for Trainers*, 2nd edn. Hertford: Sherwood Publishing.

Hay, J. (1993/2009) *Working it Out at Work*, 2nd edn. Hertford: Sherwood Publishing.

Hay, J. (1996) Steps to success, *INTAND Newsletter*, 4: 3 September.

Hay, J. (2011) *Transactional Analysis for Coaches and Mentors*. Hertford: Sherwood Publishing.

Kahler, T. (1974) The miniscript, *Transactional Analysis Journal*, 4(1): 26–42.

Kahler, T. (1975) Drivers: the key to the process of scripts, *Transactional Analysis Journal*, 5(3): 280–4.

Kahler, T. (1978) *Transactional Analysis Revisited*. Little Rock, AR: Human Development Publications.

Mellor, K. and Schiff, E. (1975) Discounting, *Transactional Analysis Journal*, 5(3): 295–302.

Micholt, N. (1992) The concept of psychological distance, *Transactional Analysis Journal*, 22(4): 228–33.

Mountain, A. and Davidson, C. (2011) *Working Together: Using Organizational Transactional Analysis to Improve Communication with Others*. Maidenhead: Gower Publishing.

Proctor, B. (1986) Supervision: a co-operative exercise in accountability, in A. Marken and M. Payne (eds), *Enabling and Ensuring: Supervision in Practice*. Leicester: National Youth Bureau/Council for Education and Training in Youth and Community Work.

Schiff, J.L. (1975) *Cathexis Reader*. New York: Harper & Row.

Schmid, B. (2008) The role concept of transactional analysis and other approaches to personality, encounter, and cocreativity for all professional fields, *Transactional Analysis Journal*, 38(1): 17–30.

Searles, H.F. (1955) The informational value of the supervisor's emotional experiences, *Psychiatry*, 18: 135–46.

Stark, M. (2000) *Modes of Therapeutic Action*. Northvale, NJ: Jason Aronson Inc.

Summers, G. and Tudor, K. (2000) Cocreative transactional analysis, *Transactional Analysis Journal*, 30(1): 23–40.

# 12 Organizational psychology models in coaching supervision

*Carmelina Lawton-Smith*

## Introduction

Coaches come from diverse backgrounds and often bring a wealth of experience with a clear understanding of organizations and the wider context in which they operate. However, with that knowledge and experience can come a frame of reference that limits the scope of view. Expanding a coach's frame of reference can be a valuable skill for the supervisor because it informs and influences what individuals see or fail to see. Organizational psychology provides meta-perspective which enables this. It is a diverse field that seeks to understand how organizations and the people within them operate. It draws on a multidisciplinary approach to provide alternative perspectives and multiple levels of analysis.

The purpose of this chapter is to draw on models and ideas from the field of organizational psychology to bring new perspectives to coaches through supervision. However, to discuss all potential areas in relation to supervision would require more than one chapter. Therefore the aim is to look at the macro level at how the ideas, concepts and perspectives offered by organizational psychology can contribute to effective supervision.

## Using multiple perspectives in supervision

Supervision has primarily three functions: *developmental, qualitative and resourcing* (Hawkins and Smith 2006). The supervisor that brings new perspectives to the supervision process fulfils both developmental and qualitative roles. By focusing the supervisee on a different picture of the organization new ways of working with their client may emerge thus facilitating development and greater understanding of the situation. However, these alternative perspectives can also enhance quality as the supervisee may be subject to blind spots and personal bias that restricts their field of view when working with particular clients or situations.

Ultimately the more knowledge and understanding the supervisor can bring to the relationship the more opportunities this presents to enhance coaching development and quality. In addition, appreciating the multiple perspectives of an organization communicates to supervisees that the supervisor appreciates the complex organizational contexts in which the supervisee operates.

## Defining organizational psychology

'Organizational psychology' is not an easy term to define and does not exist as a discrete set of topics that can be listed, 'it is rather a meeting place for various sub-disciplinary interests' (Nicholson and Wall 1982: 4). Continued growth has also generated numerous sub-disciplines, including industrial psychology, work psychology, business psychology and organizational behaviour. Each sub-discipline reflects a specific interest drawn from a particular field. The concepts in this chapter are drawn from various areas but share a focus on psychology within the organizational context. The ideas have relevance to all organizations including private, public and third sector organizations. The term 'psychology' will refer to 'the study of human behaviour and experience' (Nicholson and Wall 1982) but can be interpreted in a number of ways.

All individuals working within organizations are psychological beings. Each individual creates for themselves a personal identity that may be subject to issues of confidence or self image. These are aspects of the individual's psychology that would be present whether or not the individual was in an organizational context. There is always psychology *in* an organization, but here we consider more broadly the psychology *of* the organization: those aspects of psychology that are affected in a particular way by the fact that they operate within the context of the organization.

This means that the individual may not be the only unit of analysis. When considering performance, for example, it is possible to consider individual learning plans or personal performance targets. But organizational psychology draws attention to other potential units of analysis. We might consider a task unit of analysis looking at schedules and priorities or how work is structured and assigned. The unit of analysis may be the group and how team working can be enhanced to meet wider performance goals. While the organizational unit of analysis might examine how recognition and reward systems affect performance across departments. Even the organizational environment, where competition and external concerns are affecting and driving performance requirements, may be relevant (Drenth et al. 1998). Psychology pervades many aspects within organizations in a variety of forms. Organizational psychology by virtue of its diversity and multidisciplinary nature brings with it a rich set of perspectives that can be of value to the supervisor.

## The growth of organizational psychology

Throughout its evolution organizational psychology has never had one single underlying theory (Drenth et al. 1998) but has retained multiple levels of analysis focused on the effective utlization of people in the workplace (Schein 1980). The diversity and fragmentation of the field can be partly explained by how the discipline emerged and this short historical account will summarize the scope of the topic.

As psychology became a scientific area of inquiry in the late nineteenth century interest grew in applying it to practical problems. Industrialization was increasing and profession was no longer determined by birth. Larger organizations needed a way to select workers, leading to interest in psychological testing to determine level of skill and suitability. Mechanization also created interest in 'time and motion' studies to maximize productivity. The focus was on creating industrial efficiency through 'scientific management' (Taylor 1911), drawing ideas from engineering. Scientific management sought to quantify the exact determinants of organizational success through measurement and analysis of how people function in the working context.

The First World War fuelled further interest and expansion in the area of selection and assessment as it became evident that certain specialist and newly created roles like telegraph operators required the identification of specific skills. The scientific approach became the norm until the classic Hawthorn experiments (Mayo 1933). This study aimed to define the ideal lighting conditions to maximize productivity but found that social and group factors had an unexpected and significant impact on productivity. This study saw the birth of the Human Relations movement and created a major shift in focus. Motivation, leadership and group processes came under the spotlight.

The Second World War created interest in a number of new areas such as stress, propaganda and man-machine interface, but continued to drive research into selection and individual difference for specific war roles. With the pressure to increase productivity after the war years training, learning and acquisition of skill became of interest. However, social norms were changing and the importance of quality of working life created a focus on patterns of management, group dynamics and social processes. Aspects like power, control and communication became new research areas in organizations. There was a 'humanization' of work with terms such as job enlargement and job enrichment being fuelled by the motivational theories of Maslow (1954) and Hertzberg (1968).

As the field expanded it drew in researchers from such areas as sociology, anthropology and even social administration. It also became clear that the organization itself had characteristics that needed to be considered especially in relation to the rapidly changing environment. Organizational Development (Senge 2006; Argyris and Schön 1996) and ideas about change entered the lexicon of organizational psychology together with concepts like corporate culture (Peters and Waterman 1982).

More recently psychology has started to focus on 'positive' aspects like strengths, happiness and optimism as ways to maximize human functioning. This has now been applied to organizations under the new heading of 'Positive Organizational Scholarship' (Cameron et al. 2003) or 'Positive Organizational Behaviour' (Luthans and Youssef 2007).

The necessary breadth of the field is effectively summarized by Kahn et al. (1964 cited in Nicholson and Wall 1982: 7):

> Knowledge can best be advanced by research which attempts to deal simultaneously with data at different levels of abstraction – individual, group and organization. This is a difficult task, and the outcome is not uniformly satisfactory. It is, nevertheless, a core requirement for understanding human organizations. Organizations are reducible to individual acts, yet they are lawfully and in part understandable only at the level of collective behaviour.

Organizations are therefore more than the sum of their parts and require multiple levels of analysis to understand them. Topics like personality, stress, learning and skills enhancement are most relevant at the *individual level*. Group processes, team working, recruitment and training practices, and leadership have an impact at the *management level* (Schein 1980). At the *organizational level* topics such as culture, power and change become relevant. As illustrated previously in relation to performance, each topic can reveal important features from each level of analysis. We may need all aspects to make sense of the situation.

This brief historical account is expanded elsewhere (Drenth et al. 1998). In this chapter we will review two major approaches to understanding organizations. The first is the 'open systems' model that highlights the inherent dependencies that result from interactions both inside and outside the organization. The second provides alternative perspectives that can be taken within the organization by using alternative 'frames'.

## Organizations as 'open systems'

Organizations are never self contained units. They are complex, evolving entities that respond and react to the environment and context within which they operate. Theorists have long tried to define the ideal organizational structure but this has proved elusive as many situational variables affect the organization. For example, as an organization grows it needs more bureaucracy and systems which were not required with few employees. Technological advances affect how organizations are structured and the advent of email and communication technologies allow for cross global teams and reporting lines which impact the relationships between people. These dependencies are highlighted in the open systems model which identifies the organization as being open to, and in continual interaction with external environmental factors. Mullins (2010: 90) summarizes the importance of this: 'To be effective and maintain survival and growth, the organization must respond to the opportunities and challenges, and the risks and limitations, presented by the external environment of which it is part.' Since all organizational coaching relationships take place within this organizational system, understanding the implications of that system can be valuable in supervision. Hawkins and Smith (2006) draw attention to this in the supervision context by stating:

It is often quite a shock to the system for us to look beyond the work with our clients and their organization. By doing that, we start to see what is happening beyond that session and at the influences that the larger dynamics and events have upon the internal workings of the client organization, and their impact on what initially appeared to be an individual client issue only.

(Hawkins and Smith 2006: 170)

An example of this might be a coach who reports difficulties with a senior executive suddenly unable to delegate. They may attribute this to issues of personal trust, yet a review of the wider external environment may reveal a recent legal case that culminated in a director sued for corporate manslaughter. While this may or may not be relevant in this case, the wider environmental system is worthy of consideration in the coaching space and one role of the supervisor is to encourage this wider perspective. While a supervisor and supervisee may not be able to fully appreciate the individual complexities of every specific industry or organization, it is valuable to comprehend the potential dependencies and interrelationships and adopt a systems perspective.

The open systems model also provides frameworks by which to consider potential variables within the organization, usually identified as *sub-systems*. Authors vary in the sub-systems they highlight but one example is to consider the *task*, the *technology*, the *structures*, the *people* and the *management* (Mullins 2010). A coach may come to supervision reporting a client who is having difficulty with team communication looking to review how to take the client forward. Using the open system model could broaden the conversation to discuss each 'sub-systems' in turn and to consider how areas may interact and affect each other. Possible areas for inquiry and solutions may lie as much in new systems or structures as with interpersonal skills.

Giving the coach this wider system and interrelationships to consider can help them work with clients in a more comprehensive and holistic way. The supervisor can encourage a broader context for enquiry which can clarify for the coach where they are within the organizational system. Such a model could provide a framework for discussion of an issue or it could facilitate a discussion around the supervisee's own experiences and assumptions. It may be a useful way for the supervisee to evaluate and assess how their own assumptions about 'how organizations work' influence how they are approaching a client issue.

## Alternative views of the organization

A 'paradigm' can be thought of as the philosophical and theoretical lens through which an organization is viewed and will impact what can be seen through that particular 'lens'. The concept of paradigms is often poorly understood but at a simple level 'paradigms tell us what information to consider important and how to use that information' (Weaver and Farrell 1997: 45). The analogy used is that paradigms 'illuminate some information while leaving other information in the dark'. For many what is seen is an automatic function of their meaning-making process and outside conscious awareness.

Organizational psychology advances numerous models of organizations but one that focuses specifically on paradigms may be a more useful tool for the supervisor. Bolman and Deal (2008) identify four ways that it is possible to frame an organization:

1   the structural frame – 'factories';
2   the human resources frame – 'families';
3   the political frame – 'jungles';
4   the symbolic frame – 'temples and carnivals'.

Each lens reveals an alternative perspective and helps managers and leaders devise alternative solutions to problems. Within supervision this framework can also help the supervisee see alternative ways to conceive of an organization and a situation. This can help free coaches from the shackles of past experience and the historical route through which they arrived in coaching. Both coaches and clients can be trapped within an existing frame and knowledge of alternative perspectives can help move thinking into new more fruitful areas. For example, looking at a set of financial figures can reveal how much an organization spends on employee entertainment and this can be evaluated against corporate standards. But this fails to uncover how that expenditure is received by staff; whether it is seen as worthwhile and motivating, or as a cynical abuse of expenses by the company elite. The financial perspective gives one standpoint but if we focus on the people, we may form a very different view.

## The structural frame

The structural perspective evolves from Taylor and 'scientific management' (Taylor 1911). In this frame efficiency and effectiveness are driven by the structures, policies and procedures put in place. Coordination and control are essential to achieve organizational goals. The aim is to measure, quantify and define as much as possible to reduce variability and unpredictability. This proposes that for any organization there is an ideal work flow pattern and division of labour. Therefore problems can be resolved by restructuring.

Within the structural frame we consider how authority and the chain of command may operate vertically and how lateral coordination between teams and working groups can be achieved. This results in rules, policies and procedures with strong planning and control mechanisms. In defining the ideal structure and work flow we need to consider aspects such as the size of the organization, what technologies are in place and what the external environment will require of the organization. So an organization in a volatile or uncertain environment must structure for adaptability and flexibility perhaps at the expense or economy and simplicity. The organizational goals and strategy therefore drive many of these decisions. A large scale commodity supplier of milk will operate a very different structure to that of an elite fashion product.

## The human resources frame

The human resources perspective addresses the needs of the people involved in the organization and considers the feelings and prejudices that arise. In this frame the activities of management can lead to alienation and hostility or to engagement and motivation. As a result managers need to create participative management and focus on job enrichment and autonomy to build high performance. This perspective owes much to the ideas of Hertzberg (1968) and Maslow (1954) who drew attention to how the reaction of individuals can impact organizations.

Within the human resources frame the focus is primarily on people. How to recruit the right people, how to motivate, train and reward key performers. There is debate on how to empower employees and encourage engagement and participation. There is a strong focus on interpersonal dynamics and the ideal make up of teams. Psychometrics are used to support individual development and management. Feedback is sought from employees in the form of staff surveys to assess how to improve the environment in which people work. People are seen as social animals that bring other issues to the working context. Therefore organizational success depends on managing the emotions and interactions between these social beings.

## The political frame

The political frame introduces the concept of power dynamics and conflict in the organization. The focus is on how decisions are made and the impact that the internal coalitions have on the ability of the organization to reach its goals. This is not to say that conflict is always bad, because it can drive development and growth. However, how conflict is addressed and power brokered has a significant impact on the organizational outcomes.

This frame looks at alternative sources of power and how this power is distributed and used. Power structures can be mapped to gain understanding of situations. Networking, negotiation and bargaining are vital components. Here ecosystems evolve that sometimes intersect in the form of buy-outs and take-overs. We see these power dynamics and ecosystems influencing the ground between public and private sector initiatives where quangos and lobbying is standard business practice.

## The symbolic frame

The symbolic frame addresses the meaning making and cultural norms that exist within the organization; what rituals and actions define the values and prevailing culture; how stories are transmitted and what meaning is made of the actions taken. Defining events in organizational history are often interpreted in ways that were never meant and that meaning making becomes an expression of the organization.

Myths, vision and values are important. Stories encompass the values of the organization and the core ideology permeates through rituals and history. Culture encompasses a set of shared beliefs, values and customs that communicate the 'way we do things round here'. Impressions are managed to fuel common understanding and cultural fit that creates an insider/outsider mentality.

This brief summary highlights four potential frames, but often coaches and their clients – perhaps as a result of experience or long-held values and beliefs – have a bias towards one or a number of these frames. This means they see the issue and therefore the solution primarily through the lens they currently use. 'Each of these frames has its own vision or image of reality ... we have found managers who think in ways that limit their vision and impede their ability to understand and respond to the complexities of everyday life in organizations' (Bolman and Deal 1991: 17). So a coach who values structure and organization may tend towards a structural frame. If their client wishes to address issues of micro-management and delegation and is prone to a similar frame, the focus may be on authority, coordination and control systems. Perhaps looking at how the client needs to restructure responsibilities and tasks to achieve department goals more effectively. However, a coach and client locked in a human resources frame might spend time discussing the interpersonal group dynamics that might result from increased delegation, or the impact on motivation and what training or development might be required. While neither approach is either right or wrong, both individual approaches alone present limitations. It may be possible to enable delegation purely through creating self-managed working teams and training. But if the problems are the result of expanded responsibilities a change in structure may be required so a human resources frame alone might not resolve the issue.

As a supervisor these paradigms can be used in a number of ways. First, when working with organizations, understanding each frame can support effective working relationships, ensuring supervision meets the needs of the sponsor. Second, these frames can enable the supervision process by creating a language and model for discussion with supervisees. They provide a clear framework for debate that is non-judgemental in terms of relative merits of each approach. Lastly, the model can be used to extend the perspective from each of the 'seven eyes' (Hawkins and Smith 2006):

- In mode 1 the supervisor can help the coach become aware of how the client frame may impact their descriptions and reactions expressed in coaching, helping the coach gain understanding of the client perspective. Is the client locked into one particular frame? What frame is communicated by the client's descriptions?
- In mode 2 the supervisor can draw attention to interventions that the coach can use to broaden the client perspective. Where the coach is tending towards interventions that are supporting not widening the client perspective, this would be highlighted. What interventions will broaden the frames in view? What frames are implicit in the interventions currently used?

- In mode 3 the supervisor can draw attention to potential similarities or differences of paradigm between coach and client. What frames currently inform the client and coach view? What aspects of the relationship indicate a similar or divergent view?
- In mode 4, do deeply held beliefs within the coach tend to drive them consistently into one frame? What experiences and beliefs inform their current view of organizations and the people within them?
- In modes 5 and 6 the supervisor looks at their own beliefs and frames to ensure they model and use all the frames within their own practice.
- In mode 7 we can place each of these frames in the wider open system and environment.

The supervisor is in a unique position to identify any particular habit in the way a coach sees and interprets a situation and to encourage the development of alternative frames of reference.

The following is based on a real situation which was brought to supervision. The names and context have been altered to protect the anonymity of the parties but an expression of gratitude goes to the coach who gave his consent for publication.

Robert was a business coach and came to supervision wanting ideas on how he might approach future meetings with a client. He had been working with Carl for some time but felt he was no longer enabling Carl to generate new ideas or to move forward. This is the situation as he described it to his supervisor.

## Case illustration

### The background

**Robert:** 'I am currently coaching a man called Carl who was recruited two years ago as the Business Development Director of an engineering company. The company has a long traditional history but has been struggling to develop into new and emerging markets so Carl was recruited to develop new business opportunities. Carl was expected to take at least a year to become familiar with the products and markets but after two years Carl is still struggling to meet the strategic targets set by the MD, Michael. Michael has been with the company for six years and is keen to show growth to the parent company but is worried about Carl. I was brought in by Michael because he feels Carl has potential. I have now had a number of meetings with Carl and he feels there is a major problem with the Sales Director, Simon. So we have three key players in this. Carl, my client, Michael the MD and Simon the Sales Director.

Carl says that Simon is stopping him achieving his targets. Carl reports that Simon is obstructive, fails to follow up leads he is given and undermines his suggestions in board meetings. Carl says that he has tried everything to get Simon on side and since they are the same level should not be facing this sort of behaviour.

*We talked a lot about Simon who has been with the company over 30 years and rose from the manufacturing floor to Sales Director. I have talked to Carl a great deal about his relationship with Simon and how he might win him round. We have discussed his communication style looking at his approach to Simon. But everything we have discussed Carl seems to be doing yet it is clear that despite all our work Carl is still not achieving and I am not sure how to help him.*

*I can't seem to bring anything new to this situation and do not know what to focus on now.'*

From the interventions described by Robert he appeared to have approached Carl and his situation from a human resources frame, trying to get Carl to consider the interpersonal relationship to establish how to motivate Simon into a more cooperative stance. However, despite this work no progress was being made. In fact Robert even felt that Carl had good communication skills and seemed to be doing everything they discussed in coaching meetings.

The supervisor decided to ask Robert questions from alternative frames in an effort to generate new approaches. The aim was to bring a new perspective to the situation.

**Supervisor:** *'You said that both Carl and Simon are of the same level but that your client feels he is not treated in that way. Where does Carl believe Simon gets his power from?'*

Robert stopped and thought about this question as he realized he had not discussed this aspect with Carl at all. This generated a very useful discussion about the power structures that were in place and gave Robert ideas about how he might widen the discussion with Carl. After this the supervisor raised the issue of the culture in the company and the symbols and meaning that might be attached to actions. This also gave Robert some ideas for future discussions with Carl based on the symbolic frame. It was clear that the traditional nature of the organization brought with it numerous cultural norms that needed to be discussed.

They discussed the other frames in turn and Robert came to realize that both he and Carl held a human resources frame so both were approaching the situation in a similar way. Robert and his supervisor discussed how each of the alternative frames could be used to widen the client's perspective.

### The end of the story

At the next client meeting Robert got Carl to map the current situation and the preferred situation resulting in two potential tactics emerging. The eventual solution arose from the political frame, to reduce Simon's power through increased involvement of the MD. With greater involvement in business development the MD could then have enough knowledge to back Carl when required. Carl decided to speak to the MD and gain his backing to a new development which gave him enough knowledge to support Carl when required and effectively diminish Simon's level of control. His new project was presented by the MD at the next board meeting and Carl was surprised to see Simon agree with the new proposal.

It is clear that the information that results from alternative frames may overlap. It may be that to reduce Simon's involvement in new projects may require a change to the structures and reporting lines. So a political frame analysis may generate an idea which needs to be implemented through a structural change. However, using each frame with the supervisee can help generate new ideas and insights on how to work with the client situation.

## Evaluation of the approach

Organizational psychology covers a huge range of topics that provide a diverse tapestry of concepts and approaches in relation to organizations. Individual topics may prove useful but one of the major benefits of the field is the variety of perspectives it provides. This chapter has presented a number of alternative perspectives that a supervisor can use when working with a supervisee who presents issues based in an organizational context. It highlights a number of paradigms that can facilitate new thinking about situations and thus enable supervisees to assess and develop their practice. Broadening the field of view for the supervisee can reveal new and complex dimensions worthy of investigation, enhancing both development and quality.

## Learning more

Bolman and Deal (2008) is a classic text covering the four frames in much more detail and gives relevant and current organizational examples to illustrate points.

Drenth et al. (1998) is a concise book covering historical background and the role of the organizational psychologist.

Mullins (2010) is a general textbook that comprehensively covers most of the key theoretical ideas from organizational psychology.

### Questions for reflection

1.  Are you able to identify your own preferred frames of interpretation when thinking about issues in organizations?
2.  Can you identify the preferences of key coaching or supervision clients?
3.  Which frame would it be most useful for your practice to develop further?

# References

Argyris, C. and Schön, D.A. (1996) *Organizational Learning II*. New York: Addison-Wesley.

Bolman, L. and Deal, T. (1991) *Reframing Organizations: Artistry, Choice, and Leadership*, 1st edn. San Francisco, CA: Jossey-Bass.

Bolman, L. and Deal, T. (2008) *Reframing Organizations: Artistry, Choice, and Leadership*, 4th edn. San Francisco, CA: Jossey-Bass.

Cameron, K., Dutton, J. and Quinn, R. (eds) (2003) *Positive Organizational Scholarship*. San Francisco, CA: Berrett-Koehler.

Drenth, J.D., Thierry, H. and de Wolff, D. (eds) (1998) *Introduction to Work and Organizational Psychology*, 2nd edn. East Sussex: Psychology Press.

Hawkins, P. and Smith, N. (2006) *Coaching, Mentoring and Organizational Consultancy*. Maidenhead: McGraw-Hill.

Hertzberg, F. (1968) One more time: how do you motivate employees? *Harvard Business Review*, January–February.

Kahn, R., Wolfe, D., Quinn, R., Snoek, J. and Rosenthal, R. (1964) *Organizational Stress: Studies in Role Conflict and Ambiguity*. New York: Wiley.

Luthans, F. and Youssef, C. (2007) Emerging positive organizational behaviour, *Journal of Management*, 33: 321.

Maslow, A. (1954) *Motivation and Personality*. New York: Harper.

Mayo, E. (1933) *The Human Problems of an Industrial Civilization*. New York: Viking.

Mullins, L.J. (2010) *Management and Organisational Behaviour*, 9th edn. London: Pitman Publishing.

Nicholson, N. and Wall, T. (1982) *The Theory and Practice of Organizational Psychology*. London: Academic Press.

Peters, T. and Waterman, R. (1982) *In Search of Excellence: Lessons from America's Best Run Companies*. New York: Harper and Row.

Schein, E.H. (1980) *Organizational Psychology*, 3rd edn. London: Prentice Hall.

Senge, P. (2006) *The Fifth Discipline*. London: Randon House Business Books.

Taylor, F. (1911) *The Principles of Scientific Management*. New York: Harper.

Weaver, R. and Farrell, J. (1997) *Managers as Facilitators*, San Francisco, CA: Berrett-Koehler Publishers Inc.

# 13  Systemic approaches to supervision

*Peter Hawkins*

*Why in the plenitude of God's universe, have you chosen to fall asleep in this small dark prison?*

Mevalana Jallaladin Rumi

## Introduction

In this chapter I will address how systemic supervision can help the coach to focus not only on the needs of their individual client, but also the organizational client, the organization's stakeholders, as well as the relationships between each of these parties. Thus I will look at how systemic supervision can create what Michael Porter and Mark Kramer (2011) term 'shared value' for all parties. Also I will argue that systemic supervision is an essential approach for supervising the coaching of teams and organizations.

## Systemic supervision

I have been writing about supervision for thirty years and with the wisdom of hindsight, I can see that nearly all my work has been influenced by a systemic perspective, but until this chapter, I have never stopped and defined the essential tenets of systemic supervision. I would propose the following definition.

Systemic coaching supervision is the supervision of a coach or team of coaches which:

- is informed by a systemic perspective;
- is in service of all parts of the system learning and developing;
- attends to the client in relation to their systemic context(s);
- includes and reflects upon the coach and the supervisor as part of the systemic field.

I call these the four pillars of systemic supervision, but we should be careful not to fall into the trap of seeing the approach as being contained within the pillars, rather we must keep our attention on the systemic supervisory space that the pillars create between them. With that in mind I will now explore each of these pillars in turn.

## Pillar 1: informed by a systemic perspective

Increasingly it is recognized that the most important organizational issues cannot be resolved by trying to fix problems just within one part of the organization, for the organization is an interrelated whole. Also many of the organizational challenges transcend the boundaries of the organization and involve the wider system of stakeholders, without which the organization has no life or meaning. These stakeholders include customers, suppliers, partner organizations, employees, investors, communities in which the organization operates and the ecological environment.

Gareth Morgan (1997) has written about how the dominant organizational metaphor has moved from seeing organizations as machines, to seeing them as living organisms. This shift of dominant metaphor has brought with it a shift in other perspectives and ways of working with organizational issues. This 'systemic turn' is summarized in Table 13.1.

One of the clearest writers who has defined systems and systemic thinking is Frijof Capra. He defines a system as: 'an integrated whole whose essential properties arise from the relationships between its parts' (Capra 1996: 27). He later defines systems thinking as: 'the understanding of a phenomenon within the context of a larger whole' (p. 27). Capra argues that the living systems can be viewed through three distinct, but connected lenses. These are:

- **pattern of organization:** the configuration of relationships that determines the system's essential characteristics;
- **structure:** the physical embodiment of the system's pattern of organization;
- **life process:** the activity involved in the continual embodiment of the system's pattern of organization.

Thus a living system can be a plant, a living animal or human, a family, a coaching relationship, a team or a whole organization.

**Table 13.1** The systemic turn

| From focusing on | To also focusing on |
| --- | --- |
| Parts | Whole |
| Objects | Relationships |
| Contents | Patterns |
| Quantative analysis | Qualitative inquiry |
| Stand alone events | Events in their wider context |
| Events as snapshots in time | Patterns that function over time |
| Linear thinking | Process thinking |
| Building blocks | Organizing principles |

Capra was very influenced by the great anthropologist and systems thinker Gregory Bateson who wrote:

> In accordance with the general climate of thinking in mid nineteenth century England, Darwin proposed a theory of natural selection and evolution, in which the unit of survival was either the family line or species of sub-species or something of that sort. But today it is quite obvious that this is not the unit of survival in the real biological world. The unit of survival is organism plus environment. We are learning by bitter experience that the organism that destroys its environment destroys itself.
> (Bateson 1972: 459)

Survival and success is never unitary but always relational and yet we mostly behave as if the individual, team or organization can succeed by sub-optimizing their part of the wider system.

Peter Senge (1990: 67) defined a system as: 'a perceived whole whose elements "hang together" because they continually affect each other over time and operate towards a common purpose'. He went on to say that systems thinking is: 'a discipline for seeing wholes, a framework for seeing interrelationships rather than linear cause-effect chains, for seeing underlying structures rather than events, for seeing patterns of change rather than snapshots' (Senge 1990: 68).

The implications of this pillar for supervision, is that all supervisors need to be trained, not only in coaching, individual psychology and development, understanding organizations and supervision, but also in systemic thinking. This essentially includes developing one's personal epistemology from one that focuses on individuals, problems and snap-shots in time to one that sees all issues in their wider context, over time and sees patterns and knows how to create shifts at more fundamental systemic levels.

## Pillar 2: in service of all parts of the system learning and developing

Many supervisees talk of their coaching client as being the individual they meet with. They fail to recognize that the organization where the coachee works (and who is normally paying for the coaching) and the relationship between the organization and the individual, are both important clients in their own right.

In *Leadership Team Coaching* (Hawkins 2011), I use the Parsifal myth to illuminate this issue. I call it the Parsifal trap.

The Parsifal trap is named after the legendary Knight of the Round Table Sir Percival or Parsifal, who left home very early and went on his adventures in search of the Holy Grail. His courage and innocence served him well and he, whilst still very young, arrived at the Grail Castle, where he saw the awesome sight of the Grail Procession, carrying the much sought after Holy Grail. He was intoxicated with excitement and with the splendour and privilege of having got there. But the next morning he awoke in a damp, cold, open field and the whole castle, procession and grail had evaporated into the mist. He had failed to ask the question that would have allowed him to stay. Parsifal took many more years of travails and searching to find his way back to the Grail Castle, but this time with the wisdom of experience he knew the question that must be asked: 'Whom does the Grail serve?' Supervisors can fall into the Parsifal trap when they see supervision and/or coaching as an end in itself and fail to work with their client in asking: 'What or who does our supervision and your coaching serve?'

When we fail to ask this question, we, like the young Parsifal, may well find ourselves waking up in a cold, misty, barren field, wondering why our dream has evaporated and are condemned to many more long years of searching. As a minimum my executive coaching needs to be in service of the individual client, the teams they are part of, their organization, and the wider system that the organization serves. In addition I must be in service of the relationships that connect and weave between all these parties, for none of these entities can be successful by themselves and their value is intrinsically bound together. I need to be focused on the unrealized potential in all parties and the connections between them as well as assisting in that potential being realized so the organization can fulfil its potential and make a better contribution to the wider world.

Thus the systemic supervisor needs to be clear right from the beginning of the contracting with the supervisee that the work is a joint enterprise in service of the individual and organizational clients, the relationship between them, the wider stakeholder system and the coaching profession. (The way in which contracting works is explored further in the following section and in the case illustration, later in the chapter.)

### Pillar 3: attends to the client in relation to their systemic context(s)

When I supervise a coach I follow the CLEAR process model (Hawkins 2010). This has parallels to, as well as differences from, the GROW model (Whitmore 2002; Downey 2003). It has five stages: Contract, Listen, Explore, Action and Review. When supervising systemically each of these stages has a different and more extensive focus than when supervising with a more individual client and performance focus.

I usually begin the session by asking the supervisee what will make this session of value to them, their individual clients, the organizations those clients work for and the wider systems they serve (**Contract**). Then, as they engage in bringing material from their work, I will **Listen** with systemic ears, listening to the reality of the coach, their individual client, the organization they work for and the relationship between the organization and the individual. Clients' stories are often 'sticky' so that the coach can arrive caught within the story and frame of their client. It is important that the supervisor can listen from multiple perspectives, not only to what is shared but what is not said and possibly ignored.

In the **Explore** stage I might ask the supervisee to embody the perspective of the client, their team, their organization or the wider stakeholders. I might, for instance, encourage them to sit on different chairs to represent different aspects or make a picture sculpt (see the example below).

If I am helping the coach to explore their own development, I will often adopt my favourite strategy question (Hawkins 2005), which is: 'What is it that you can uniquely do, that the world of tomorrow needs?' This question can be valuable not only for the coach, but can be asked at all different levels of the system to benefit the individual, team, division, business unit, organization, stakeholder community, business sector, nation, etc.

In the **Action** stage the focus of the supervision is on helping the coach to embody the transformational shift (Hawkins and Smith 2010) that is needed to enable the shift in the client. If this is done sufficiently the coach can have the desired impact on the wider system with which they engage. This stage often involves a 'fast forward rehearsal' (Hawkins and Smith 2006: 224, 2010: 232).

In the final **Review** stage it is important to reflect back on the agreed contract and the value we have jointly created for all parts of the system, as well as the experiments that the coach has committed to trying out. We will review these at the beginning of the next supervision session.

### Pillar 4: includes the coach and the supervisor as part of the field that is being reflected upon

The seven-eyed supervision model (Hawkins 1985; Hawkins and Shohet 2006; Hawkins and Smith 2006; and Hawkins and Schwenk in Chapter 2) is fundamentally a systemic model, based on how the supervisory system can attend to its own system, the coaching system and the wider systemic contexts in which both are embedded. The model does not just focus on the individual client (mode 1) and their relation with their systemic context (mode 7), but also focuses on the system of the coaching relationship (modes 2, 3 and 4) and the system of the supervisory relationship (modes 4, 5, 6 and 7).

In training supervisors we nearly always find that supervisors start the training already proficient in one or two of the seven modes, but rarely do they utilize the full palate of possibilities. Often they work with the supervisee/coach to better understand their individual clients (mode 1) and under-focus on the wider systemic context (mode 7). As they progress in their training they often report how they tune in more to the wider system needs (mode 7) as well as finding that the most impactful interventions often come from modes which reflect on their own felt responses (modes 5 and 6). In these they reflect out loud on what is happening inside themselves and focus on what needs to shift in the here and now relationship (mode 5) to enable a shift for the coach (mode 4). It is easy to forget that the only place and time that change can happen in, is *here and now*, and the only part of the wider system within which the supervision can create an embodied shift, is within the coach.

The seven-eyed model emphasizes that systemic supervision is not only attending to the system externally but also the supervision system itself that both the supervisor and supervisee are part of. This supervisory relational system is also embedded in a wider systemic context. This includes the organizations that both the supervisee and supervisor work for and the ambitions and expectations of these bodies, as well as the professional context and organizations that both parties belong to. It is possible also that the supervisee may still be in professional training or seeking accreditation and these become important features of the field that the needs to be attend to by the supervision process.

## Roles and responsibilities of the supervisor

To work systemically as a supervisor requires vigilance. First and foremost the supervisor must be vigilant in attending to their own assumptions and limiting ways of thinking. If we are human beings brought up and educated in twentieth-century western ways of thinking, our basic epistemology, or way of knowing about the world, will be inherently non-systemic. We are taught from a young age to:

- see things not relationships, and events not patterns;
- think dualistically – within polarities – night-day, good-bad, right-wrong;
- focus on the world out there as though it exists independently of our engagement with it;
- be problem focused;
- see leadership and learning and development as residing in, and belonging to, individuals rather than being relational phenomena.

(Hawkins 1994: 257)

If we do not constantly attend to unlearning the fixity of these frames through which we see and understand the world, we cannot supervise systemically.

Second, we must be vigilant to the limiting assumptions and patterns of behaving in our supervisees. As supervisors we add more value by helping the supervisee become aware of, and then transcend their limiting frame of reference, than by attending to the presenting issue or 'problem' within the frame in which the supervisee presents it.

Third, we must be vigilant not to become individualistically centred on the presented clients, but always to be curious and inquire about the wider system in which their behaviour and personality and presenting issues are forged.

The supervisor must also adopt an appropriate systemic humility including recognizing that it is not possible to hold all of the whole system's perspective in awareness at any one time, as we will be limited by the particular position we occupy in the system and by our particular point in time. The supervisor needs to remember that supervision is not done by the supervisor, but is a joint endeavour between the supervisor and the supervisees, in service of the coachees/mentees, their organizations and their relationship within them and the wider stakeholders. The supervisor should avoid knowing better and knowing first, and rather use the privilege of their relative distance from the presenting issues to open up new systemic perspectives that can be inquired into within the supervisory dialogue.

The most important insights and transformations do not come from the knowing of the supervisor or the knowing of the supervisee, but emerge out of the dialogical inquiry that happens between them (Bohm 2004). Thus for systemic supervision what is most important is not what the supervisor does, but the attitude and perspective they bring and hold in the supervisory relationship. This attitude needs to be built on a systemic perspective that embraces all the four pillars mentioned above and explores in the space created between them.

To help with these dynamics and complexities, I have developed a specific team coaching supervision model (Hawkins 2011), which, although designed for supervising team coaching in a group setting, can be adapted for other supervision contexts. This model provides a discipline and framework that ensures the balance of attending to the minimum requisite amount of data that one needs in order to be able to explore the many levels of dynamic (individual, interpersonal, team, organization, wider system, coach relationship with team and team coaching sponsors), before moving on to discover live, what needs to shift in the team, the coaching relationship and in the coach.

The following is an anonymized example of supervising a team coach written jointly with her, showing each stage and then, in italics, the supervisee's responses and how the supervision progresses.

## Case illustration

### Step One: contracting

Asking the team coach/supervisee what they want and need from the supervision on this team. This can most usefully be done by starting with the end in mind and asking them:

'For this to be a successful supervision for both you and the team and the client organization, what do you need to leave this session having achieved?'
*From this supervision, I need clarity on how to resolve the blurred boundaries and conflicting agendas I now experience in relation to the team coaching I am doing with a senior team, and the one-to-one coaching I'm doing with individuals within it.*

'And what do you most need from myself as supervisor to achieve that success?'
*As supervisor, I need you to help me to unpick what's going on and challenge me to see the way forward, so that I can best serve the needs of all involved. Whatever emerges from these two inquiries needs to inform the balance of my attention in the rest of the process.*

### Step Two: setting the scene

The team coach is asked to take less than one minute to say what type of team they are working with and some brief data on the team.

*I am working with the executive team of a UK subsidiary of an international orga-
nization. The work has evolved piecemeal from one-to-one coaching with certain
members of this team (who are perceived by the MD as not meeting the level he
expects of his Board), through a 360 feedback process with all nine members, to
acting as team coach with five of the team who are establishing themselves as the
senior tier of a two tier 'Board'. I find myself in a messy situation where I have begun
coaching part of the team without the knowledge of the excluded individuals, who
I am still coaching one-to-one.*

### Step Three: exploring the dynamics

The team coach is invited to draw on a large sheet of paper, symbols, images and
colours representing the individual team members, the connections between
them and then the stakeholders who surround the team. At each stage the
supervisee is asked to draw and then speak about what she has drawn. This is a
form of picture sculpting (Hawkins 2011).

**a) Individuals:** 'what is happening for the individuals in this team?'
*The MD hired the FD, Commercial Director and IT Director about 18 months ago, at
a more senior level than the existing functional directors. There is in effect a two-tier
board, although this is not openly discussed in the team. This disparity is a source
of resentment for the older members of the team, whilst the newer team do not rate
the old team members' skills.*

**b) Interpersonal:** 'what is happening in the spaces between the
individuals?'
*There is a 'love in' between the MD, FD and Commercial Director. I see myself
as holding the MD's hand, and seem to have been put on a pedestal by the
'inner circle'.*

**c) Team dynamic:** 'If this team was a piece of music, a meal, a geographical
place, etc. what would it be?'
*If this team was a piece of music, it would be by Schoenberg – discordant with some
virtuoso performances but each member of the orchestra doing their own thing.*

**d) Team mission and intent:** 'What are the team wanting/needing/
aspiring to achieve that is currently beyond their reach?'
*The team have been very 'heads down' in their own areas for 18 months, sorting
out the financial and organizational mess they inherited and completing a rebrand
of the business. They now wish to take a more collective strategic focus to drive the
business through the next phase of its development, and are keen to improve the
level of operation and level of challenge of the team.*

**e) Stakeholder engagement:** 'Who are the key stakeholders the team
needs to engage with and what needs to shift in each of these relationships?'

*Their key stakeholders are the parent organization, customers, suppliers and the staff team. There are some good relationships between individual members of the team and their stakeholders, but there needs to be a shift to a more coordinated collective way of connecting.*

**f) Wider systemic context:** 'What is the shift the team needs/wants/ aspires to create in its wider systemic context and what needs to shift in the team in order for them "to be the change they want to see"?'

*The team have made significant improvements to the brands to increase their profitability and market share. Now they believe the market is saturated, the focus is on margin improvement and profitability through improving processes and delivery. This will require the team to be much smarter in the way they work together to increase operational efficiencies business-wide, and become much more strategic in identifying possible growth opportunities.*

### Step Four: clarifying the three way contract and intent and deciding where on the coaching continuum the work needs to focus

**a)** The team coach is invited to step into the role of the collective team and, speaking as the team, states what the team wants and needs from the team coaching and the team coach.

*As the team, what we need from the team coach is someone to enable us to bring greater levels of challenge and honesty to our board meetings . . . to challenge us to name the elephant in the room and have the conversations we shy away from addressing.*

**b)** The team coach is then asked to change back to being themselves as the team coach and voicing their intent/interest/investment in working with this team.

*As the team coach, my intent for this team is that they be able to have difficult conversations in an upfront way, and that they become a strategically focused board able to hold each other to account individually and collectively, whilst really focusing on delivering for their stakeholders.*

**c)** Then they are asked to move to the side and step into the role of the wider organization or system, in which the team exists. In this role they are invited to voice what the wider organization wants and needs from the team coaching relationship. They can be asked their view of the return on invest-ment the organization is implicitly or explicitly looking for.

*As the wider organization, we need the team coaching to enable this team to work together effectively to lead us to sustainable growth in a challenging market, to coordinate the processes between the different teams and make our working lives easier through overcoming some of the disjointedness between us.*

### Step Five: developing the shift required in team and team coach

The team coach is encouraged to answer the following questions, based on what she has discovered in the first four steps.

(a)   What is the shift needed in the team to meet the aspirations of all parties?

(b)   What is the shift required in her relationship with the team?

(c)   What is the shift required in her as the coach, to be the change she wants to see in the client?

(d)   What is her specific commitment?

In this process it is important to facilitate the team coach moving beyond insight, awareness and good intention to embodied learning and commitment (see Hawkins and Smith 2010). This may entail the coach rehearsing the most important lines she needs to use when she next meets the team, or finding and enacting the right emotional state to shift the dynamic within herself.

- *The shift needed in the team to meet the aspirations of all parties is a willingness to be more open with each other and to other points of view, offer and receive more challenge, take a cohesive view of the business, not just their own areas, and to look outside the team at the needs of the stakeholders to guide their focus.*

- *The shift required in my relationship with the team is to step outside the 'inner circle', giving up my 'favoured one' status, by offering more of a challenging mirror to what I see happening, or not happening. This will mean me not taking on their difficult conversations for them!*

- *The shift required in me as the coach, to be the change I want to see in the client, is to have more upfront conversations, and to define my role in relation to the team more explicitly, including what I will and won't do with them.*

- *My specific commitment is to call the MD to discuss how I can be most helpful to the team in their journey going forward . . . specifically in helping them to have the difficult conversations they shy away from. In this conversation I will address my discomfort with coaching individuals in the team when also coaching the upper tier of the team on issues that affect them, but are not addressed with them.*

### Step Six: review

It is important to end the supervision by returning to the contract and checking back with the supervisee what has been most helpful from the session and anything that could have been even more helpful for her work and learning.

*This supervision has really helped me to see clearly the whole picture of the situation I am in. Particularly useful is thinking about what the system needs from this team. I can also see that the system has found a way of having me experience the dynamics of the system ... I have been sucked into the 'secrets' and meeting furtively without addressing issues upfront.*

## Evaluation of the approach

Systemic supervision is more relevant to the supervision of executive coaching and mentoring where there is an expectation of organizational benefit and learning, than where there is merely a focus on individual learning and awareness. It is 'clients centred' rather than 'client centred' insofar as it always assumes that the work is in service of multiple clients and not just the coachee or mentee. Some coaches struggle with a systemic perspective, because of the levels of complexity it brings even to individual coaching. Some activist learners also find some of the theories that underpin this approach both demanding and challenging. Here supervision can help by the systemic learning emerging out of practical issues in their coaching experience.

To date there has been no substantial research on the impact of supervision on coaching outcomes. Indeed there is little research on the benefits of coaching for the wider system beyond the coachee. What I believe is needed in the field is a comparative research between the individual and organizational benefits derived from:

1  executive coaching with no supervision;
2  executive coaching with individually focused supervision;
3  executive coaching with systemic supervision.

If coaching is to truly serve the multiple stakeholders of the coachee, their team, division, organization and the organization's wider stakeholders, coaches need to develop a greater systemic approach to their coaching. Many coaches try to do this by reading the growing literature on systemic, complexity and chaos theories, but struggle to apply what can be complex and abstract concepts to their work with individuals and teams. Systemic supervision is a key methodology in the journey to systemic coaching, where the supervisor can help the coach not only reflect on the coaching client within a wider systemic context, but also on their own role in the web of systemic relationships.

In my own long journey as an ever-developing and learning coach I have always required and often received supervision that has helped me see a wider perspective and step into a bigger field than I had previously dreamt possible. Without such systemic supervision, I believe I would have failed to serve the needed development in the clients and their wider systems. Further I believe that a systemic way of thinking is fundamental to a wider shift in human consciousness and action that the world urgently requires.

## Learning more

To learn more about practising systemic supervision a good first base is to read the chapter in this book on the 'seven-eyed model' that I have co-authored with my colleague Gil Schwenk. If you want to go deeper you can read *Coaching, Mentoring and organizational Consultancy: Supervision and Development* (Hawkins and Smith 2006) which outlines the whole field of coaching supervision from a systemic perspective. The particular approach to systemic supervision of team coaching of all kinds can be found in *Leadership Team Coaching* (Hawkins 2011).

The best introductions to systemic thinking are Fritjof Capra's 1996 book *The Web of Life* and Bateson's (1972) seminal work *Steps to the Ecology of Mind*. The latter is very dense and demanding to read and the reader might find my paper 'Gregory Bateson: his contribution to action research and organization development' (Hawkins 2004) a helpful introduction.

Trainings in systemic supervision are also available from a number of training bodies.

## References

Bateson, G. (1972) *Steps to the Ecology of Mind.* Chicago: University of Chicago Press.
Bohm, D. (2004) *On Dialogue.* Abingdon: Routledge Classics.
Capra, F. (1996) *The Web of Life.* New York: HarperCollins.
Downey, M. (2003) *Effective Coaching: Lessons from the Coach's Coach.* New York: Thomson, Texere.
Hawkins, P. (1985) Humanistic psychotherapy supervision: a conceptual framework, *Self and Society*, European Journal of Humanistic Psychology, 13(2): 69–77.
Hawkins, P. (1994) The changing view of learning, in J. Burgoyne (ed), *Towards the Learning Company.* Maidenhead: McGraw-Hill, 19–27.
Hawkins, P. (2004) Gregory Bateson: his contribution to action research and organization development, *The Journal of Action Research*, 2(4): 409–23.
Hawkins, P. (2005) *The Wise Fools Guide to Leadership.* Chichester: O Books.
Hawkins, P. (2010) Coaching supervision, in E. Cox, T. Bachirova and D. Clutterbuck (eds) *The Complete Handbook of Coaching.* London: Sage, pp. 381–93.
Hawkins, P. (2011) *Leadership Team Coaching.* London: Kogan Page.
Hawkins, P. and Shohet, R. (2006) *Supervision in the Helping Professions*, 3rd edn. Maidenhead: Open University Press.
Hawkins, P. and Smith, N. (2006) *Coaching, Mentoring and Organizational Consultancy: Supervision and Development.* Maidenhead: McGraw-Hill/Open University Press.

Hawkins, P. and Smith, N. (2010) Transformational coaching, in E. Cox, T. Bachkirova and D. Clutterbuck (eds), *The Complete Handbook of Coaching*. London: Sage, pp. 231–44.

Morgan, G. (1997) *Images of the Organization*. London: Sage.

Porter, M.E. and Kramer, M.R. (2011) Shared value: how to re-invent capitalism and unleash a wave of innovation and growth, *Harvard Business Review*, 89(1/2): 62–77.

Senge, P. (1990) *The Fifth Discipline: The Art and Practice of the Learning Organization*. New York: Doubleday Currency.

Whitmore, J. (2002) *Coaching for Performance: Growing People, Performance and Purpose*. London: Nicholas Brealey.

# Part III

# Contexts and modes of supervision

# 14 Supervising the internal coach

*Alison Maxwell*

## Introduction

Internal organizational coaching is a growth area – coaching surveys (e.g. CIPD 2009) chart increasing reliance on internal coaches, particularly for coaching below senior levels. External coaches are therefore being employed more selectively, but may be asked to support the internal resource pool in other capacities, including provision of coaching supervision. While there is a growing body of literature (Hawkins and Smith 2006; Hay 2007) discussing supervision of the coach, this is largely targeted at independent professional coaches and there is little in the coaching literature that discusses specific issues relating to supervision of the internal coach.

This chapter briefly reviews the rise of internal coaching within organizations. However, before addressing the specific challenges facing the internal coach, it is important to explore the variety of developmental activities in organizations that are bannered under the term. 'Coaching' is a broad term and internal organizational 'coaches' work in extremely varied ways with different associated risks and issues. Their need for oversight, development and support consequently ranges from minimal supervision which can be provided adequately through normal management channels, to more specialist support.

The second half of the chapter looks more specifically at the work of the 'internal developmental coach' and discusses their unique supervision needs and the current ways that organizations are choosing to support them. Selection of internal coach supervisors is briefly discussed, along with some of the more challenging aspects of this role.

## The rise of the 'internal coach'

While many organizations still reserve the use of external coaches for more senior executives, or for particularly problematic performers, investment in internal coaching is now common place (e.g. Eaton and Brown 2002; Silva and Doss 2007; McKee et al. 2009). It is perhaps not surprising that cost drivers are most frequently cited (Corporate Research Forum 2006, 2008) as a prime motivation for use of internal coaches over external. However, cost is not the only driver – many argue (e.g. Strumpf 2002; Rock and Donde 2008) that the internal coach is far from a second best option and believe that internal coaches, assuming they are appropriately skilled and supported, are ideally placed because of their detailed knowledge of organizational mechanics, politics and culture. They are also well positioned to observe their clients in action close-up rather than from afar. Whatever the motive, many large organizations are actively developing their own in-house coaching capability, as well as extensively promoting the value of coaching skills as general performance enhancement tools for all managers.

As organizations become increasingly shrewd purchasers of coaching services (CIPD 2009), many more are demanding that competence to practise is more clearly demonstrated by all providers – internal or external. This has driven increasing professionalization in the external coach market place (Grant and Cavanagh 2004), and a growing dialogue around competencies, standards of practice, ethics, continuous professional development and use of qualified supervision to oversee and regulate practice (BPS 2007). However, as Frisch (2001, 2005) says 'internal coaching has been flying under the radar of mainstream coaching' and the equivalent dialogue for internal coaches has up to now been limited. However, in parallel with the growth of internal coaches, many large organizations are also investing in provision of a number of support roles (including coach supervisors) tasked with ensuring the efficacy of the organizational resource.

## Defining 'internal coaching'

An initial challenge in this area is to define what is meant by 'internal coach' as in many organizations this is a broad catch-all term for any individual tasked with performance improvement, organizational change or even general management. While little hard data exists, a recent CIPD report (2009) reported that while more than 90 per cent of organizations report using coaching, in practice the majority (63 per cent) was delivered by line management supported by dedicated internal resource or use of externals (15 per cent).

For the purposes of this chapter, a distinction is drawn between four types of activity that fall broadly under the banner of 'internal coach' (Figure 14.1). Each of these is qualitatively different and potentially requires different forms of oversight depending on the 'depth' and duration of the work concerned. Internal coach supervision could therefore be conceived as an activity which fits within the normal functions of line management supervision to a specialist activity provided by dedicated qualified resource.

### Manager as coach

'Manager as coach' is defined as a line manager who draws on a coaching mindset and coaching skill set (Starr 2008: 25) in order to improve the task performance and delivery of their immediate subordinates and teams. This form of coaching

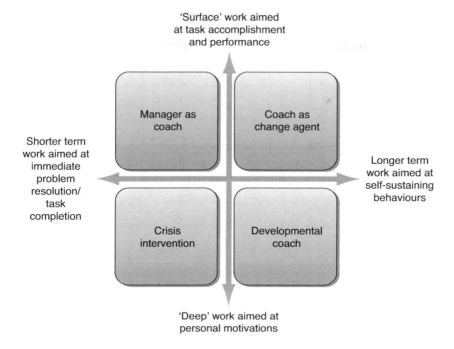

**Figure 14.1** Forms of internal coaching

could be regarded as largely tactical or short term – focusing on immediate task performance and problem resolution. Many managers and team leaders in organizations attend short trainings to teach and practise basic skills. 'Supervision' of their coaching in this context is likely to be provided through the normal channels of line management (i.e. manager to manager), and emphasize task delivery over support and development of the individual coach (Peach and Horner 2007).

This form of 'coaching supervision' could therefore be seen as wholly appropriate as long as the 'manager as coach' stays within the boundaries of task accomplishment, and does not attempt to address more in-depth and/or complex issues and transgress beyond the boundaries of the manager–subordinate relationship.

## Crisis intervention

In contrast to 'manager as coach' is 'crisis intervention'. Here an employee may present to their line manager (or HR) with an issue which may have erupted as some form of personal crisis, e.g. bereavement, alcoholism, drug abuse, depression or relationship issues. The function of supervision in this context is therefore to help managers funnel distressed individuals to the appropriate referral points rather than provide support for any attempt to work with presenting issues.

## Coach as change agent

In many organizations the term 'coach' is used as a short hand for individuals working in a change capacity, perhaps on a strategic initiative lasting a number of months or years (e.g. Lean coach, Agile coach, Vision coach, etc.). Here, like 'manager as coach', the salient part of the role is to ensure task accomplishment and the focus therefore for supervision is on the work not the worker. Coaching supervision to the change agent may therefore be divided among a number of parties, with formative support provided by subject matter experts, and normative support provided by line management to ensure timely, quality delivery. In addition organizations may also use communities of practice and action learning sets to provide opportunities for sharing best practice. Risks to this group of 'internal coach' are primarily around their ability to deliver sustainable change into the organization, rather than boundary, confidentiality or other ethical considerations.

## Developmental coaching

The 'developmental coach' is defined as an individual who offers developmental or remedial coaching to employees of the same organization, as a recognized part of their job description. Thus defined, the internal developmental coach offers an equivalent service to many external coaches, differing only perhaps in the level in the organization at which they operate. The attendant risks are therefore largely similar to that of the external coach – competency to practise, ethical awareness, boundary management, etc. – as well as ensuring a return on investment. This therefore potentially requires the internal developmental coach to operate at least at the same standards expected of an external coach, and be subject to the same rigour in selection, development and measurement of effectiveness.

Similarly, the argument for supervision of internal developmental coaches is equivalent to that for external coaches. Hawkins and Smith (2006: 142) argue that supervision provides coaches with development and support and a level of quality assurance to ensure that the end client benefits (and does not suffer) from the work, and it would be hard to argue that the internal developmental coach needs any less oversight or support. Indeed it would be paradoxical for organizations to insist on stringent standards of practice for externals and not enforce similar standards for their internal equivalents. The rest of this chapter therefore focuses on this type of internal coach and their particular supervision needs.

# Internal developmental coaching in organizations

Internal developmental coaches may encompass individuals who offer coaching as a part-time add-on activity (e.g. as an extension of HR responsibilities as at Alliance Boots), part of their formal role (e.g. Vodafone, NHS) or indeed as a full-time in-house resource (e.g. Sainsbury's, PricewaterhouseCoopers). Many HR functions have seized this territory with alacrity as a natural concomitant of

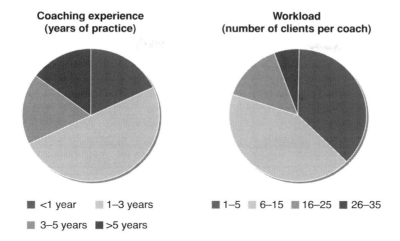

**Figure 14.2**  Coaching experience and workload for 123 internal coaches in 40 UK-based organizations
*Source:* St John-Brook (2010), reproduced with permission.

'business partnering' (Ulrich 1997), and indeed may be seen only as a formalization of an existing informal role. However, the internal coach cadre may also include talented individuals from line functions who demonstrate an aptitude for the work, and indeed some sources suggest that half of all internal coaches come from operational or corporate (non-HR) roles and were coaching on top of the 'day job' (Fletcher and Macann 2011).

It cannot be assumed that internal developmental coaches are necessarily less experienced or skilled than external coaches, and indeed many internal coaches appear to carry an at least equivalent coaching workload to those of externals. For example the St John-Brooks (2010) quantitative study of 123 developmental coaches from 40 UK-based organizations indicated a substantial workload (see Figure 14.2). It is also probably fair to assume that internal coaches meet the same diversity of clients as externals, and therefore meet their share of problematic clients.

While most organizations are still at an early stage, there is evidence (e.g. NASA 2007) that some organizations are now putting more formality, governance and structure around their internal coach resource, and rigorous selection, deployment and development programmes are coming into existence. These governance structures are in turn, being managed by an emerging role – the coaching practice manager or master coach – often an HR professional tasked with coordinating and deploying the internal coach resource. Whilst this may initially have been in response to experiences of poor practice, many organizations are now understanding that developmental coaching can be integral to impel other organizational initiatives, particularly cultural, behavioural and leadership development interventions,

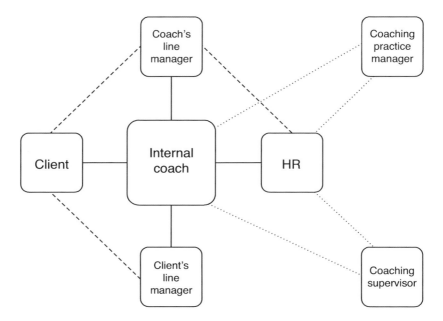

**Figure 14.3**  System of relationships for the internal coach

including deployment of 360 feedback (Frisch 2005). As such, investment in a coaching infrastructure is a necessity for many large organizations.

However, this also means that the internal coach is potentially subject to a much more complex web of relationships and political pressures than the external coach (see Figure 14.3).

This is particularly acute for the 'HR professional turned developmental coach' who might be put in the awkward position of coaching an individual on their performance one day, and perhaps disciplining them the next. Thus the Corporate Research Forum (2006: 6) note: 'Trust and confidentiality become more important because of the executive's awareness of what the HR director knows – and who else he or she talks to privately about pay, performance and promotion'. There is therefore more obvious complexity to forming the necessary confidential and trusting relationship between coach and client (Bluckert 2005) than may be the case where the coach is externally sourced. Further, the internal coach, perhaps mindful of their career prospects, may feel inhibited in giving frank feedback, and may find it difficult to coach 'upwards' (Strumpf 2002).

Some organizations have side-stepped this dilemma by ensuring coaching re-lationships are not set up within the same business unit and some even go to the lengths of swapping their internal coaches with their equivalents in non-competitive organizations in order to avoid these potential conflicts. However, it is not always possible to achieve this, and there is a high probability that a coach and client may have some form of pre-existing relationship. While this

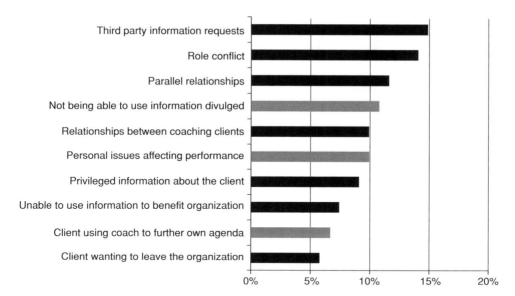

**Figure 14.4** 'Top 10' commonly occurring ethical dilemmas for internal coaches
*Source:* St John-Brooks (2010), reproduced with permission.

does not necessarily automatically imply an ethical dilemma for internal coaches, the St John-Brooks study (2010: 61–2) found a predominance of concerns related to managing internal boundaries, confidentiality of relationships and the potential for divided or conflicted loyalties (Figure 14.4). These issues would therefore appear to be more acute for the internal coach.

## Supporting the internal developmental coach

Some organizations appear to take their responsibilities towards the internal developmental coach very seriously and there are many examples of rigorous approaches to internal coach selection, development and ongoing support (e.g. NASA 2007). However, this is far from universal, and again drawing on the St John-Brooks study it would appear that there is a wide diversity of support perceived by internal developmental coaches (Figure 14.5), with a tendency to wane after initial training has been completed.

The same study also showed that organizations draw upon a wide range of means to provide ongoing support, ranging from the voluntary and self-directed to more mandatory and/or prescribed (Figure 14.6). In terms of the focus of this chapter, it is interesting to note that some 45 per cent of this particular sample noted access to one-to-one supervision and 37 per cent to group supervision. However, while all respondents were supervised 'out of the line', supervision was

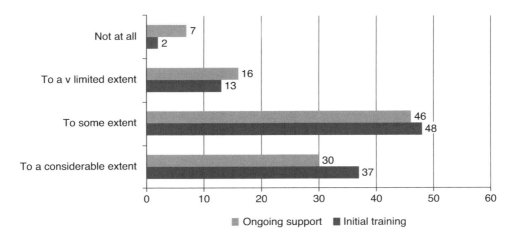

**Figure 14.5** Support for internal coaches, initial training vs. ongoing support
*Source:* St John-Brooks (2010), reproduced with permission.

provided by more experienced coaches or by training providers, rather than necessarily by qualified and experienced coach supervisors.

## Supervising the internal coach

Hawkins and Shohet (2006) discuss the concept of 'good enough supervision', and there is a persuasive argument that organizations should tailor the nature and

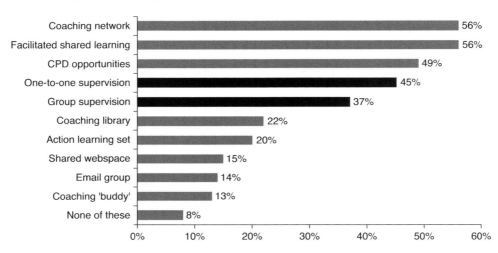

**Figure 14.6** Range of developmental support offered to 123 internal coaches in 40 UK-based organizations

format of supervision according to the type of coaching underway. It has been argued above that where coaching is largely task-oriented (e.g. 'manager or coach' or 'coach as change agent') it may be 'over-kill' to provide in-depth out-of-line specialist supervision. However, albeit with a vested interest, the BPS's Special Group in Coaching Psychology (SGCP) (2007) in their 'Guidelines for supervision for coaching psychology' argue that whether framed as task or developmental coaching, coaches are always potentially implicated at a deeper level.

> Some forms of coaching applied in work settings are described as being largely performance-based and aimed at achieving specific work based goals that are pre-determined by management performance appraisal. These activities may provide little scope for working directly with clients on deeper issues of personal motivation. However, even when services do not involve working with underlying issues, they can impact on clients at a very deep level or require the practitioner has a sophisticated understanding of the deep motivational drivers to succeed in implementing the 'surface' level of implementation.
>
> (BPS 2007)

If this argument is accepted, organizations are faced with a duty of care to both their coaches and their employees, particularly where developmental/personal work is undertaken. If the same standards of practice are applied to internal (developmental) coaches as external then similar codes of practice and ethics must also apply. For example the Association for Coaching (2010) states that 'coaches are expected to have regular consultative support for their work' and some authorities recommend one hour of supervision for every 8–15 hours of practice, depending on experience (e.g. Bluckert 2010).

A best practice survey of coaching supervision for the EMCC (Arney and Schwenk 2006) suggested that while organizations talk about the importance of coach supervision, the actual practice lags behind. Indeed there is a suggestion that (internal) coaches see supervision as only necessary in a crisis (Coaching at Work 2010) or as a time-expensive luxury (Butwell 2006), rather than a necessary form of ongoing learning, reflection and quality control. It could be argued that 'supervision' in the coaching context is not clearly understood in the corporate world, with confusion at one end of a spectrum with the surveillance functions of line management (Peach and Horner 2007) or at the other extreme, with the group counselling and therapy practices. Coaching has indeed largely inherited a psychological model of supervision from the therapeutic world (e.g. Hawkins and Shohet 2006), and some argue that this is insufficiently pragmatic or unpalatable for the internal organizational coach community (Pinder 2010). More familiar forms of organizational learning such as action learning sets (Revans 1993), and facilitated reflective practice (Mezirow et al. 1990) may be better understood and therefore accepted.

The best format for coaching supervision is also a matter of debate. From a practical stance, case supervision can be offered to internal coaches in one of three major forms – one-to-one, peer and group, with cost-drivers weighing against provision of the former. While peer supervision has much to commend it, Pinder (2010) strongly argues for the necessity of role models, especially for embryonic coaches, and the use of expert facilitation to hold the process. However, group supervision is not without its problems and confidentiality issues are a particular concern as there is a high likelihood of coaches knowing each other's clients. Indeed Butwell (2006: 49) notes that pre-existing co-worker relationships may also form an inhibition to effective use of supervision in organizations.

While an internal master coach is an obvious choice as group facilitator, Strumpf (2002) argues that they may be subject to and unaware of the same organizational/ systemic dynamics as other internals, rendering them less effective. Many organizations therefore choose to use an experienced external coach to manage and run their coach supervision programme. However, expertise and experience in coaching per se may be insufficient for the role. As well as an understanding of the processes and purposes of supervision, the group coach supervisor must have a complex understanding of the organization, the developmental path of a coach, as well as providing an adequate 'psychological back-stop' for coaches. The internal coach supervisor therefore treads a delicate balance between the needs of the individual coach and their clients, the needs of the supervision group and those of the commissioning organization.

## Evaluation of the approach

It is likely that organizations will continue to expand their internal coach capability, partly in response to cost-drivers, and as coaching continues to be an increasingly valued form of development. The 'internal coach' comes in many flavours and their ongoing support and supervision needs vary widely. Particularly at risk is the internal developmental coach, who may be faced with emotional/ psychological issues rather than task-related issues and it is difficult to argue that this type of internal coaches should operate at lower standards of practice and ethics than their external equivalent. It is also important that other forms of internal coach do not stray into the territory of the internal developmental coach without the appropriate level of training and ongoing support.

While professional qualified supervision is a relative rarity, organizations are increasingly providing a range of support mechanisms for their internal coaches, including one-to-one and group supervision. However, there appears to be a lack of understanding of the potential benefits of supervision in some quarters and it is regarded as a luxury rather than a necessity for professional and ethical practice. Group supervision provides a cost-effective environment for coach development, support and quality assurance and it is probable that this form of support will grow as the trend towards the internal coach continues. However, there is still a dearth of professionally qualified and experienced coach supervisors and this may drive further demand in this area.

## Key questions for further reflection

- Should internal coaches subscribe to a code of ethics? Should organizations develop their own codes, and if so, how might these differ from the codes that apply to external professionals?
- Who is best placed to supervise the internal coach resource – an external professional or an internal 'master coach'?
- What should be the partnership relationship between internal and external coaches and how could this best be achieved?
- Is a supervision model based on action learning the most appropriate model for internal coaches? What might a supervision process based on this approach miss?
- What governance structures does an organization need in place to protect its coaches, clients and return on investment?

### Development activities

- How would you explain the purposes and processes of supervision to a new group of internal coaches? How is this different/similar to other forms of organizational learning, e.g. action learning set?
- What might a new supervision group in an organization need to contract for? With each other, with clients, with the organization/HR?
- What would you agree to share with the contracting organization about the discussions within a supervision group? How can the organization garner potential organizational intelligence from its coach community whilst maintaining the confidentiality of the supervisor/coach and coach/client relationship?

## Learning more

Hunt, J.M. and Weintraub, J.R. (2006) *The Coaching Organization: A Strategy for Development*. London: Sage.
This text is unusual in that it focuses on the coaching organization rather than on coach development. It contains useful chapters on the issues relating to internal coaching and case study material.

Frisch, M.H. (2001) The emerging role of the internal coach, *Consulting Psychology Journal*, 53(4): 240–50.
One of the first articles to discuss the rise of the internal coach and the associated opportunities and issues.

Peach, J. and Horner, N. (2007) Using supervision, support or surveillance?, in M.E.F. Lymbery and K. Postle (eds) *Social Work: A Companion to Learning*. London: Sage, pp. 228–39.
A short article from the world of social work supervision debating some of the tensions between developmental supervision and managerial surveillance.

# References

Arney, E. and Schwenk, G. (2006) *A Best Practice Survey of Coaching Supervision.* http://www.bathconsultancygroup.com/documents/EMCC%20Supervision%20Presentation.pdf (accessed 2 February 2011).

Association for Coaching (2010) *Code of Ethics and Good Practice.* http://www.associationforcoaching.com/about/about02.htm (accessed 12 October 2010).

Bluckert, P. (2005) Critical factors in executive coaching – the coaching relationship, *Industrial and Commercial Training*, 37(7): 336–40.

Bluckert, P. (2010) *Coaching Supervision: An Article by Peter Bluckert.* http://www.pbcoaching.com/article-coaching-supervision.php. (accessed 12 October 2010).

British Psychological Society (BPS) (2007) *Guidelines on Supervision for Coaching Psychology.* http://www.bps.org.uk/sgcp/in-practice/supervision.cfm (accessed 8 October 2010).

Butwell, J. (2006) Group supervision for coaches: is it worthwhile? A study of the process in a major professional organization, *International Journal of Evidence Based Coaching and Mentoring*, 4(2): 43–53.

CIPD (Chartered Institute of Personnel and Development) (2009) *Taking the Temperature of Coaching.* http://www.cipd.co.uk/NR/rdonlyres/BC060DD1-EEA7-4929-9142-1AD7333F95E7/0/5215_Learning_talent_development_survey_report.pdf (accessed 8 October 2010).

Coaching at Work (2010) Internal NHS coaches reject free supervision, *Coaching at Work*, 4(4): 8.

Corporate Research Forum (2006) *Workshop: Managing Coaching in Organisations.* http://tools.ashridge.org.uk/Ashridge/VLRC.NSF/site/APcrfcoaching.htm/$file/ManagingCoachinginOrganisationsJULY06.pdf (accessed 9 October 2010).

Corporate Research Forum (2008) *What's new in Coaching and Mentoring.* http://www.ashridge.org.uk/Ashridge/VLRC.NSF/site/APcrfcoaching.htm/$file/what_s_New_In_Coaching.pdf (accessed 9 October 2010).

Eaton, J. and Brown, D. (2002), Coaching for change with Vodafone, *Career Development International*, 7(5): 284–7.

Fletcher, A. and Macann, L. (2011) *Balancing Act.* http://www.coaching-at-work.com/2011/01/09/balancing-act/ (accessed 2 February 2011).

Frisch, M.H. (2001) The emerging role of the internal coach, *Consulting Psychology Journal*, 53(4): 240–50.

Frisch, M.H. (2005) Extending the reach of executive coaching: the internal coach, *Human Resource Planning*, 28: 23.

Grant, A.M. and Cavanagh, M.J. (2004) Towards a profession of coaching: sixty five years of progress and challenges for the future, *International Journal of Evidence Based Coaching and Mentoring*, 2(1): 1–16.

Hay, J. (2007) *Reflective Practice and Supervision for Coaches.* Maidenhead: Open University Press.

Hawkins, P. and Shohet, R. (2006) *Supervision in the Helping Professions*, 3rd edn. Maidenhead: Open University Press.

Hawkins, P. and Smith, N. (2006) *Coaching, Mentoring and Organizational Consultancy: Supervision and Development.* Maidenhead: Open University Press.

Mezirow, J. and associates (1990) *Fostering Critical Reflection in Adulthood: A Guide to Transformative and Emancipatory Learning*. San Francisco, CA: Jossey-Bass Inc.

McKee, A., Tilin, F. and Mason, D. (2009) Coaching from the inside: building an internal group of emotionally intelligent coaches, *International Coaching Psychology Review*, 4(1): 59–70.

NASA (National Aeronautics and Space Administration) (2007) *NASA Handbook on Building Internal Coaching Capability: A Guide for NASA Internal Coaches and HR Executives*. http://www.coachutbildning.se/files.aspx?f_id=41242 (accessed 8 October 2010).

Peach, J. and Horner, N. (2007) Using supervision, support or surveillance?, in M.E.F. Lymbery and K. Postle (eds), *Social Work: A Companion to Learning*. London: Sage, pp. 228–39.

Pinder, K. (2010) Experiences of supervision, *The International Journal of Mentoring and Coaching*, VIII(1): 124–9.

Revans, R.W. (1993) What is action learning?, *Journal of Management Development*, 1(3): 64–75.

Rock, D. and Donde, R. (2008) *Driving Change with Internal Coaching Programs*. http://www.davidrock.net/files/Driving_Organisational_Change_with_Internal_Coaching_Programs.pdf (accessed 1 October 2010).

Silva, K. and Doss, C. (2007) The growth of the agile coach community at a Fortune 200 Company, *Proceedings of the AGILE 2007*: 225–8.

Starr, J. (2008), *Brilliant Coaching: How to be a Brilliant Coach in your Workplace*. Harlow: Pearson Education Ltd.

St John-Brooks, K. (2010) What are the ethical challenges involved in being an internal coach?, *The International Journal of Mentoring and Coaching*, VIII(1): 50–66.

Strumpf, C. (2002) Coaching from the inside: when, why and how?, in C. Fitzgerald and J. Garvey Berger (eds), *Executive Coaching: Practices and Perspectives*. Mountain View, CA: Davies Black Publishing, pp. 225–42.

Ulrich, D. (1997) *Human Resource Champions: The Next Agenda for Adding Value and Delivering Results*. Boston, MA: Harvard Business School Press.

# 15  Group supervision

*Kate Pinder*

## Introduction

This chapter discusses coaching supervision in groups, using my experience gained through counselling group supervision and action learning sets. Group supervision has a number of attractions for coaches, especially in the current economic climate, where it may be cheaper than one-to-one supervision, covering more hours and different experiences of coaching colleagues. Many coaches work on their own and have reduced professional contact, hence the need for professional networks and network meetings, conferences and other methods of connecting with colleagues. Group supervision meets the need for supervision with an experienced supervisor, an extension of practice by understanding some group processes, and the chance to learn and experience different coaching scenarios through colleagues. Supervisees get mutual support, share experiences, potentially solve complex tasks if in training, and may further develop interpersonal competencies and increase insight (MacKenzie 1990). It is possible to have both group and individual supervision.

## Description of the context/mode of supervision practice

Hawkins and Smith (2006) define supervision as the process by which a coach or mentor, with the help of a supervisor who is not directly working with the client but with the coach or mentor, can attend to understanding better both the client system and themselves as part of the client–coach/mentor system, and transform their work, a definition widely used in this book. For some, this comes from the psychotherapeutic school and they look for something more pragmatic. According to Hay (2007), supervision is the process of helping you to stand back from your work to take a broader view of your practice. This second definition allows for group or peer supervision whether facilitated by a qualified supervisor or not.

It is worth looking at different modes of group supervision and asking questions such as: Who might be the stakeholders in group supervision? What constitutes a group? Is there a leader/facilitator/supervisor? Is it peer supervision where there is no designated leader?

Like much of the current coaching supervision practice, group supervision has its roots in psychotherapeutic practice and counselling, and the literature which supports its use depends heavily on that from those disciplines. A supervisor may draw from their own models of practice to inform their management of the group; for example, someone with a personal construct methodology and training will use that in supervision (Viney and Truneckova 2008).

The translation from group therapy for the clients to group or case work supervision for the therapists is one that is well documented and found its way into a number of disciplines including that of the Marriage Guidance Council (now RELATE). Group supervision is usually within the context of a wider professional relationship, for example, on a training course, within an employer as part of team of coaches, or an agency for freelance or employed coaches, or across a professional body, on a regular or ad hoc basis. That may mean that the contract for supervision is prescribed in some way by someone other than the participants, and that ground rules such as confidentiality differ since they take place within this context.

## Group supervision in peer groups

Peer supervision has the advantages of there being parity between the participants, potentially mirroring the equality the coach has with their client. It can be 'free' of cost, inasmuch as each gives their time and receives supervision; and developmental, inasmuch as each appreciates the different style and focus of a fellow professional. It can be challenging as all participants have to hold the security and safety of the set, and come to agreement about issues such as time for each person; what happens if someone doesn't present for some time; what the ground rules are and what happens if they are disregarded; and who takes the convenor role to arrange dates, venue, etc. Attendance and commitment need to be consistent, or the dynamics are different on each occasion, an issue for group supervision generally but more prevalent, in my experience, in peer supervision. The different dynamics caused by sporadic attendance are not necessarily a negative thing, although it means there is a differential level of familiarity of each participant by other participants. My experience of peer supervision would suggest that the role of supervisor can be passed around the group, once members are sufficiently mature, either through volunteering or some rotation agreement, and that the maintenance tasks of date, venue and time are best left to one volunteer.

Peer-group supervision is often with a very small group, i.e. three people, so that mitigates some of the disadvantages indicated above and may heighten the commitment to attend. Groups exist which operate without a trained supervisor, but operate best where all the coaches are very experienced. A coach at the latter stages of development as a coach/supervisor will require less leadership from their supervisor or colleagues; often a more equitable relationship or working alliance has developed, with the lightest of touches sufficient to invoke the learning and train of thought. To introduce this too early in the coach's development may be close to an existential approach to supervision where there is faith in the coach's abilities to see their own answers (Walsh and McElwain 2002) but may not support their learning and development as rapidly without the understanding that comes from experience, study and appropriate development.

Where all the coaches are part of an organization, there can be positive benefits in terms of sharing organizational knowledge between participants as well as having the shared overall knowledge of the organizational context, needing less explanation. The maintenance of confidentiality is key, more difficult where all belong to the same organization. Coaches need to have similar positions in the organization, otherwise the hierarchical arrangements outside the group may intrude.

## Group supervision with a qualified or experienced supervisor

Inskipp and Proctor (2001) identify four types: authoritative – where the supervisor works with each person in turn whilst others observe; participative – where the supervisor takes the responsibility but develops the rest of the group as co-supervisors; cooperative – where the supervisor monitors and supports the group in developing their own system and skills of supervision; and a peer group – where there is shared responsibility. Berne's (1961) three types are simply expressed – supervision in a group; with the group and by the group. These two typologies are not mutually exclusive and any one group may use different modes within a meeting, as long as all are familiar with the types and mores for each type; or a group may develop from one type into another over time.

For many, the initial experience of group supervision will be as part of a coaching course where novice coaches explore and discuss their practice. For some, this may be a difficult experience where they feel vulnerable, and some coaches have associated their difficulty coping with this with the practice of group supervision and rejected the idea of participating in supervision in this way. Individuals may have had bad experiences in a group setting, whether early at school or later in a professional setting, and they bring these experiences to the fresh setting. The power relationship is different in a situation where the coach is on a formal learning programme and if the supervisor has some responsibility for a pass/fail judgement. Participants may find it difficult to share their apparent lack of expertise with a tutor acting as supervisor, whether closely connected with marking the student, or just a colleague from the faculty. There may be a sense of competition among students, as well as an internal anxiety about performing well. There is something more of the educative role here, as the coaches/mentors are studying; they can practise asking open questions and demonstrating different styles; coaches learn from each other's styles as much as from the 'theory'. An exploration of someone's issue may be followed by some references and further theory for them to follow up for their further learning. Where it is possible, it may liberate the coaches if the supervisor comes from elsewhere and has no or little reward or coercive power in terms of the participants passing the programme.

Applying the Inskipp and Proctor (2001) model of the four types of group supervisor, the first two were available through a transactional analyst in group supervision of people trained at different levels, where people could choose supervision by the group or supervision in front of the group. It followed two days of training with each other on a particular topic by Mountain Associates, with a third day of supervision (although people could come just for the third day). Some participants knew each other somewhat from previous occasions, others had spent the previous two days together, and some had had no previous contact, so a different level of trust was established among participants. The trust had to be generated by and in the supervisor, and coaches could opt for individual supervision by her in front of the whole group (Inskipp and Proctor's authoritative), or by the group (Inskipp and Proctor's participative), which she facilitated. If individual supervision was chosen, the instruction to the whole group watching was to be aware of: (a) what was happening within themselves (self-awareness and learning to listen to one's inner self); and (b) the supervisor's choice of questions/exploration. Exploration then followed of the supervisor's choice of intervention as a process review, rather than revisiting the issue or questioning the presenter. This offered the opportunity to explore any transference and counter-transference, parallel processes, key issues and the meta-perspective, enabling the group to reflect on the process and so develop their own learning, whether that be by discussing their own experience or asking about the supervisor's interventions and why she did what she did. The group was an experienced group of coaches, operating internationally, and most coaches were fluent in English, but not operating in their mother tongue. This may have influenced their choice of mode, authoritative or participative, as might the position the supervisor held in terms of support and assessment of several members of the group, either through one-to-one supervision or through their own training.

A similar group, on a different occasion, also undertook cascade supervision, which added an additional dimension. A trainee supervisor supervises in front of the actual supervisor and the group, and the group may ask questions after watching the supervision, whilst the actual supervisor offers comment and theory. During this sort of trainee supervision, the trainee can stop the process and ask for support or comment from the group or the supervisor, in order to help him/her on their way; or the actual supervisor could call 'time out' to discuss what is happening during the process. A major challenge for the supervisor (and therefore for the whole group) is the issue of clarity of contracting between the facilitator/supervisor, the supervisor for the piece of work and the supervisee. Such a challenge enables stretch for all those concerned and addresses the different levels of knowledge and expertise. Again a process review is ideally undertaken following this process.

Some further ideas for group supervision follow:

## Gordon Law's model

This is a fun quick group-supervision model. The story/problem is briefly related to the group by the supervisee. Each member of the group asks the supervisee a question, which remains unanswered. Each person in the group then formulates a hypothesis regarding the questioner's reason for asking the question. This hypothesis is then related to the supervisee, without comment by them. The supervisee then goes through the questions and hypotheses one by one, saying which is most useful/least useful and why.

### Fan supervision

In this exercise all the group members are assigned specific tasks to supervise such as particular modes of the seven-eyed model, particular aspects of the issue, etc.

### Devils and angels

In the devil's advocate part someone presents an issue and their next step, including thoughts and feelings about what they are going to do (5 minutes). The group asks questions of clarification (5 minutes). Then group members act as devil's advocates and state any concerns, doubts or niggles about the next step, for example, I'm uneasy about.../I noticed that... The presenter listens in silence, sifts and sorts and takes what s/he wants and leaves the rest.

In the angel's advocate part the group gives positive feedback – I like your idea of the next step because.../That was expressed positively when you said... Presenter responds and says what s/he now thinks with reflections and additional ideas for future action.

## Roles and responsibilities of the supervisor

The group supervisor will need those contracting skills of administration, professionalism and psychological aptitude that a coach uses, all the skills of a supervisor who works with individuals, as well as an understanding of group processes and how they may be used to enable the group to function. I had to have some ideas about the way the group might work and set out at least a draft contract and way of working for the group. The format and subsequent success of the group may depend on the supervisor's style; different styles will suit different groups.

To generate and maintain trust, the supervisor holds the safety of the group and each individual so they can relax into the group meeting and gain the maximum benefit from it. S/he is the 'prime keeper' of the ground rules and challenges anyone who behaves inappropriately. Haboush (2003) highlights this need for the supervisor to support self-esteem and reduce anxiety when necessary.

To do this, s/he role models, supports and re-frames, keeping the attention of the group on the issue whilst enabling freedom of exploration, having alternative models and processes in mind should the group need them, using creativity and experience.

Proctor (2008) reflects on the role of the supervisor as group manager and adds the skill of a group supervisor learning to trust his [sic] senses – to think in physical imagery, i.e. Who has the reins here? Who is out in the cold? I contend that any supervisor, group or individual, has to do that but the skill is using the information and questions in a group context.

Competitiveness, not only in terms of air time, has to be managed, whether an internal, or external, peer group. Coaches may also fear demonstrating vulnerability whilst exploring issues. Where coaches are operating in a competitive market, the anxiety and destructive possibilities of this can be exacerbated. The group needs to be aware of other group issues such as gender, parallel process, pairing and flight or fight (Bion 1961), but these can all be used positively to enhance learning, particularly where the coaches themselves are involved in team coaching. Working within a group means there can be discussion of the behaviour in groups in general, this group in particular, and the client group as well. There is also a wider opportunity for feedback from group members, as well as the chance to practise listening and observation. By hearing others' experiences, the coach can establish a store to draw upon and strengthen their own understanding and practice.

## Case illustration

The model I currently use is based on the above, and the description that follows is of a group with which I work. The group was formed from a larger cohort of mature students who attended a training programme. All six supervisees are currently associates of a particular agency, as is the supervisor. I potentially have some power with this group as I often choose a shortlist of coaches to present to clients. However, it would be unethical for me to favour any of my own supervisees, so the criteria on which selection for a shortlist are made is clear and transparent. Geography is a key criterion, as is experience of the client's professional own expertise. Group members come from the north, but are sufficiently widespread to be on the same shortlist relatively rarely, and the two with the same expertise, law, are over a hundred miles apart. Inevitably, nevertheless, I know my own supervisees better than the other pool members and can select them with more understanding of their particular attributes. This could be both positive and negative for the supervisees, so I have the task of gaining and keeping the supervisees' trust and creating safety, so they can use the opportunity to learn. The set meets for a six hour day three times a year, and has completed its third year.

The format follows a similar one to Reg Revans's action learning sets (Pedler 1997) with an 'arrival' round with each person commenting on what has happened since the last meeting and any update on whatever was presented by that individual at the last session. The set then moves into agenda setting and some negotiation on the use of time. There are a number of alternative modes, for example, a half hour session which is five minutes for the presentation, five minutes for questions of clarification, 15 minutes where the presenter is silent and can take notes whilst the group discusses the issue, and five minutes where the presenter talks about what s/he has found useful and why. The seven-eyed model is used (see Hawkins and Shohet 2002) to think about which area of the model the questions are coming from and reflect on whether a different area might provoke new thoughts.

The contract is checked with each presenter – 'if this session is to be successful, what will have happened?'; and a time indicated to the whole group. The facilitator may offer a mirror to the set – either on behaviour (verbal and non-verbal), content, process (e.g. parallel process), projection or avoidance – often by asking the set 'what do you see happening here?'; the varied insights offered by the group add to everyone's learning. As the set grows more sophisticated, they themselves may spot a parallel process; for example, one coach brought the case of a client who kept saying 'I don't know what to do . . .'. It was mirrored by the coach who was saying 'but a good coach wouldn't tell them what to do', so (implying) 'tell me what to do'. Recognizing the parallel process helped them to say, 'OK, what would you like us to do when you are stuck?' – 'I'd like you to give me some options' . . . 'OK, how could you use that approach with your client?' 'What other ideas do you have?', and so on. The coach was able to take 'permission' to explore with her client, listing options together. The whole group participated in the coach's learning, members often building on a previous comment as the parallel process dawned for each in turn. Not only did the coachee learn, but every group member took that memory away to apply in their own practice.

Once round the group for a final question leads into the facilitator/supervisor asking the presenter what s/he takes away from the session, giving feedback to members of the group as to what was helpful/less helpful. Each individual is then asked to give the presenter feedback, for example, 'I noticed your face changed when you talked about this client feeling sad; and how joyful you were when she found her way through the issue'; 'I was impressed by the real conviction you showed and the passion to help this client'.

Issues vary from boundary management – for example, working in an organization not as a coach, but being used 'unofficially' as a coach; being 'stuck' with a client; being so close to a client that the issues are obscured; acting as 'parent' (in transactional analysis terms) rather than coach; being sucked into the client's helplessness; looking for work in recession – all the issues taken to an individual supervisor, but with the group understanding of parallel process (usually with the supervisor's help and several brains to help and support and to learn from the issue for themselves).

Using Reg Revans' action learning means that the group is likely to be operating more in the cooperative mode, as in the case illustration above, particularly if the group has been together for some time and the supervisor has established this way of working from the outset. As the group grows in confidence in themselves and with each other, supervision flows between group members. The supervisor's task is then to keep the group's interest by using creative and different methods, and to prevent them falling into the trap of over-familiarity – not listening afresh – as they might assume they already know what the coach is saying or doing.

Obviously, the theoretical basis of the group, for example, the personal construct therapy groups discussed by Viney and Truneckova (2008), will affect the group process, whether led or peer, just as the transactional analysis group used that theory.

# Evaluation of the model

Group supervision is more unusual than one-to-one supervision in coaching, although more common in counselling and psychotherapy. The number of supervisors trained and experienced in coaching is limited, and even more so with the addition of understanding and experience of group processes. Given the cost and expectation of supervision, it seems both economically and educationally sound to be offering and to participate in such forms of development. As more people are setting themselves up as coaches and mentors and being trained as such, their experience of group supervision during training is key to determining how and when they access it once they have moved through the categories of novice, to apprentice, journey person and master craftsperson as outlined by Hawkins and Shohet (2002). The logical place for the coachee to have experience of both one-to-one and group supervision is in training, as the group is already formed by the shared experience of the training. However, a number of people at an EMCC meeting indicated their less than positive experience of group supervision, citing the style of being supervised in front of a group as uncomfortable.

Group supervision need not replace individual supervision but can be part of a package which the coach decides will meet their needs at a given moment in time. As with a single supervisor, when participants are no longer challenged by the process, it is time to move on, and select a different supervisor or a different group.

# Learning more

Questions for further reflection might include:

- What ethical considerations might need to be considered which are different for a group and individual supervision?
- How are the needs of every member of the group balanced? How much responsibility does the designated supervisor take and how much the individual in that process?
- How far might the group process mirror the individual, whether as a coach with the client, or a supervisor with a coach? It is important to be able to translate what was true in the group into the coaching – projection, parallel process – and how it was dealt with among fellow professionals.

### Recommended reading

Hawkins, P. and Shohet, R. (2002) *Supervision in the Helping Professions*. Maidenhead: Open University Press, McGraw-Hill.
This book has useful models of supervision; in particular the seven-eyed model is explained and illustrated. There are two chapters on group supervision, looking at the advantages and disadvantages, contracting and issues in group process. Their own approach is called practicum groups where the shadow supervisors (i.e. the rest of the group, apart from the supervisee and supervisor) are responsible for monitoring some part of the process. The supervisor retains control and

responsibility in a different way to the action learning facilitated way described in this chapter.

Hay, J. (2007) *Reflective Practice and Supervision for Coaches*. Maidenhead: Open University Press.
A clear and very helpful exposition of supervision, in accessible language and style. The book supports improving as a coach by encouraging reflective practice. It explains how readers can develop their practice alone, with peers or with a supervisor with a number of suggested techniques and exercises.

Proctor, B. (2008) *Group Supervision*. London: Sage.
This book has a clear and comprehensive discussion of group supervision issues in the counselling world, and is easily applicable to coaching. Proctor examines the roles and responsibilities of supervisor and supervisee, with case studies and examples. It includes research findings on group supervision in organizations and explores the ethical issues in group supervision. It is well laid out and very readable.

# References

Berne, E. (1961/1993) *Transactional Analysis in Psychotherapy*. London: Souvenir Press.
Bion, W.R. (1961) *Experiences in Groups*. London: Tavistock.
Haboush, K.L. (2003) Group supervision of school psychologists in training, *School Psychology International*, 24: 232–55.
Hawkins, P. and Shohet, R. (2002) *Supervision in the Helping Professions*. Maidenhead: Open University Press/McGraw-Hill.
Hawkins, P. and Smith, N. (2006) *Coaching, Mentoring and Organisational Consultancy*. Maidenhead: Open University Press.
Hay, J. (2007) *Reflective Practice and Supervision for Coaches*. Maidenhead: Open University Press.
Inskipp, F. and Proctor, B. (2001) *Becoming a Supervisor*. London: Cascade.
MacKenzie, K.R. (1990) *Introduction to Time-limited Group Therapy*. Washington, DC: American Psychiatric Press.
Pedler, M. (1997) *Action Learning in Practice*. Aldershot: Gower Publishing Ltd.
Proctor, B. (2008) *Group Supervision*. London: Sage.
Viney, L.L. and Truneckova, D. (2008) Personal construct models of group supervision: led and peer, *Personal Construct Theory and Practice*, 5: 131–8.
Walsh, R.A. and McElwain, B. (2002) Existential psychotherapies, in D.J. Cain and J. Seeman (eds) *Humanistic Psychotherapies: Handbook of Research and Practice*. Washington, DC: American Psychological Association, 253–78.

# 16 Supervision in mentoring programmes

*Lis Merrick and Paul Stokes*

## Introduction

Supervision in formal mentoring programmes is a form of supervision that has been minimally researched and there is little evidence of good practice in programmes in the UK. Both authors spend considerable time developing and designing mentoring programmes and from their practice and research have examined the relationship between the developing experience of the mentor against the formality and functions of supervision required in mentoring. In this chapter we discuss the rationale for using supervision in mentoring, offer an updated conceptual schema linking mentor development and supervision and use it to examine supervision in a mentoring scheme case study. Broader implications for mentoring supervision are considered.

## The context and mode of supervision practice in mentoring programmes

Research by Willis (2005) into mentoring and coaching standards undertaken by the European Mentoring and Coaching Council (EMCC) suggests that in practice there is much common ground between mentoring and coaching. Garvey et al. (2009), when comparing mentoring with coaching, found that mentoring activity is found in all sectors of society and includes both paid and voluntary activities. It is also associated with 'off line' partnerships. For the purposes of this chapter we are defining mentoring as an off line developmental dialogue with mutual benefits, but acknowledge many of the similarities with coaching.

In the course of our practice when developing mentoring programmes, we have been faced with the challenges of how to support and educate mentors at varying stages of development in order to facilitate their ethical practice and ongoing progression as a mentor. This may be frequently complicated by the mentors being part of a wider organizational programme, where access to the mentors, resources (people and funding) and motivation to spend more time on the programme can all be very limited. Mentors tend to be volunteers who are mentoring for a very small part of their working time and tend to have busy and stressful day jobs. In contrast to professional full-time coaches, selling the benefits of mentor supervision to part-time voluntary mentors can be harder.

First of all, we need to address some key questions: what is mentor supervision? How does it differ to coaching supervision? What implications might these differences have for mentor development? Our initial research, conducted in 2003, revealed the following common functions of mentor supervision in schemes as understood by participants:

- being a mentor to the mentors;
- being able to explore techniques and help with problems;
- an opportunity to reflect on own practice;
- to support a mentor who feels out of their depth;
- as a mark of good practice for the profession;
- to support with ethical issues;
- to be available for the mentor as an emotional safety valve.

This echoes Barrett's (2002) work in mentoring, which puts forward the following benefits of being supervised:

- preventing personal burn-out;
- a celebration of what I do;
- demonstrating skill/knowledge;
- helping me to focus on my blind spot(s);
- discovering my own pattern of behaviours;
- developing skills as a mentor;
- a quality control process; and
- providing a different angle on an issue.

Barrett's (2002) work aside, there has been relatively little attention focused on mentoring supervision in the literature. However, the importance of the supervision role is apparent in other helping professions, with critical discussions emerging in psychoanalysis (Kutter 2002); medicine (Marrow et al. 1997); education (Blasé and Blasé 2002) and social work (Maidment and Cooper 2002). These critical discussions may be due to changes in the way other helpers understand the supervision process. However, it is interesting to reflect on the mentoring theme that runs through this literature. For example, Lawton (in Lawton and Feltham 2000), when exploring counselling, argues that 'the original concept of supervision as primarily an element of training has altered and its role as a means of providing monitoring, support and education for counsellors throughout their careers has taken on greater significance' (p. 27). This suggests a more holistic view of helping through supervision than simply training or advising hence drawing it closer to mentoring in terms of its breadth of scope.

This widening of the notion of supervision in other professions has coincided with increasing concerns with how mentors might be developed within the mentoring community (see Garvey and Alred 2000 for a useful discussion of educating mentors). These concerns prompted us, in 2003, to develop a heuristic, which linked together the needs of the mentoring supervisee with their development as a mentor.

It made sense to start with the literature on counselling development as Kram (1985) identifies counselling skills as an integral part of mentoring as part of its psycho-social function (see Stokes 2003 for a more critical discussion of the relationship between counselling and mentoring).

Hawkins and Shohet (2002) offer four categories of counsellor development:

- the novice
- the apprentice
- the journey person
- the master craftsperson

We generated some similar stages for mentor development to be used as a device for mentoring practitioners to aid reflection on their own practice and have used them in our own practice since then:

- novice mentor
- developing mentor
- reflective mentor
- reflexive mentor

For each of these stages we offer a brief description, summarizing the benefits and challenges and the role and responsibilities of the supervisor (see Figure 16.1).

## The novice mentor

A novice mentor is someone who may be new to mentoring, with little or no experience of mentoring in practice. This does not mean that they are untrained or unskilled, but that they have relatively little experience as a mentor and of participating in a live, dynamic human mentoring process. As a result, such a mentor may well have development needs that are different and distinct from more experienced mentors. For instance, they will need to become familiar with the protocols of mentoring within their particular programme and what its aims and objectives are. They will therefore need help and support in defining/refining their approach, so that it is consistent with their programme. Clearly, they will also need help in gaining access to the various theories and models of mentoring that exist.

## *Implications for supervision – description of practice*

Whilst there will be a number of development agendas for the novice mentor, one of the important functions of the supervisor at this stage is to ensure that mentoring is operating in a way that is congruent with the aims of the programme.

**Stages of mentor development**

**Increasing mentor development** →

| Reflexive Mentor | Reflective Mentor | Developing Mentor | Novice Mentor |
|---|---|---|---|
| • Extend range of skills<br>• Reflexive practice<br>• Self development and improvement<br>• Avoid complacency | • Look at own experience<br>• Critically reflect on own practice in relation to others<br>• Build on skills required | • Process knowledge<br>• Awareness of boundaries<br>• Three Stage Model<br>• Awareness of skills required | • Need to know the rules<br>• Require scheme knowledge and context knowledge of process |

**Functions of Mentor Supervision**

| Challenge Function | Development Function | Training Function | Quality Assurance/Audit Function |
|---|---|---|---|
| • Critical friend to the mentor<br>• Devil's advocacy<br>• Constructive and/or challenging feedback<br>• Spot mentoring | • Opportunity to reflect on practice<br>• Learning from other mentors<br>• Reflecting on skills | • Identifying a mentoring process<br>• Understanding different phases/stages in process | • Audit function, i.e. checking mentor's ability<br>  – Acceptance<br>  – Empathy<br>  – Congruence<br>• Quality Assurance to bestow 'aura of professionalism' |

**Increasing formality of supervision** →

**Figure 16.1** A Schema for mentor development and supervision
*Source:* Merrick and Stokes (2011)

This closely resembles what Hawkins and Shohet (2002) call the management/ normative function of supervision.

This 'quality assurance'/audit function has two main purposes:

- to check the mentor's ability as a mentor, i.e. are they using the key skills of acceptance, empathy and congruence with their mentee?
- to bestow what Feltham (in Lawton and Feltham 2000) calls the 'aura of professionalism' to ensure scheme credibility in the eyes of its sponsors.

With this level of mentor development, most supervision occurs through running small focus group activity for the mentors at regular intervals during the mentoring programme duration, so for instance a programme that has been set up over a year may bring mentors together every four months for a short period of time to review how the mentoring is going and to provide further education about the programme. The type of facilitated discussion in these groups will be to check progress around the programme aims and objectives, ensure the mentors are adhering to the type of mentoring that the programme is advocating, e.g. developmental not sponsorship, and have a largely educative input to equip the mentors to move up to the next stage of their development.

Questions for a focus group may include:

- What has really gone well/less well in your mentoring relationship?
- To what extent do you feel you have contributed to this?
- Which stage of the relationship do you think you have achieved?
- What aspects of mentoring do you feel least confident about?
- Would any further support be helpful?

## The developing mentor

In one sense, all mentors might be considered to be developing and continuing to learn but in this context, the developing mentor is someone who can no longer be considered to be a novice, as they have some experience of mentoring 'under their belt' and understand the 'rules' within their particular scheme/context. They can use a well-known mentoring model/process (e.g. Kram 1983) that they can follow within a mentoring conversation and they will have an awareness of some of the skills and behaviours required by an effective mentor (see Clutterbuck and Megginson 1999 for examples of skills/roles involved). However, this knowledge and repertoire of behaviours is basic and their comfort zone as a mentor is still fairly limited and confined to a small repertoire of behaviours.

## *Implications for supervision – description of practice*

At this stage, the developing mentor needs to start to identify other ways of mentoring so as to expand their effectiveness as a mentor. The supervisor may therefore need to pay more attention to supporting the mentor in their process development and in recognizing the dynamics within a mentoring relationship.

This closely resembles what Hawkins and Shohet (2002) originally refer to as the educative/formative supervision role. The supervisor will need to model some of the behaviours involved in order to help the mentor acquire these skills and may indeed coach them specifically in these areas where appropriate.

The supervisor needs to support the mentor in identifying a mentoring process that is effective for them to utilize and in working with them to aid their understanding of the different phases and stages of the process, skills required, etc.

Some schemes, where it is feasible, provide one-to-one supervision utilizing the scheme organizer as the supervisor or bringing in an external supervisor. Some of the challenges with this level of supervision are around the capability of the organizer, particularly if working with the mentor on a one-to-one basis, and the availability of the mentor to participate in the supervision. Due to logistical and budgetary constraints most formal programmes will still use small focus group activity to supervise mentors at this stage, or begin to bring in peer discussion and reflection around areas such as:

- outcomes
- objectives for programme
- your own goals for relationship
- processes:
  - Have we met often enough?
  - Have we spent enough time in the meeting?
  - Have we challenged each other sufficiently?
  - Have we agreed actions?
  - What processes have worked best?
- relationship:
  - Have we established trust?
  - Have we created a 'safe protected space'?
  - Are we able to be honest with each other?
  - Do we give each other feedback?
  - What have we done to achieve this in our relationship?

## The reflective mentor

The reflective mentor is someone who has a fair amount of experience as a mentor and has successfully extended their repertoire of skills beyond that of the developing mentor.

They are probably aware of most of the different approaches to mentoring theory and practice and have developed an awareness of context and their own identity as a mentor within the mentoring community. They are now in the position, on the basis of both their experience of mentoring and of being supervised, to begin to critically reflect upon their own practice and to further develop their skills and understanding of different mentoring approaches, drawing from other mentors, their supervisor and from other helping professions.

## Implications for supervision – description of practice

One of the important aspects of effective supervision for the reflective mentor is that the supervisor is able to demonstrate emphatic attention and insightful reflection to the mentor.

This development function is a combination of Hawkins and Shohet's (2002) role of educative/formative support and of a supportive function, where through reflecting on and exploring the supervisee's work, the supervisor focuses on developing the skills, understanding and ability of the mentor they are supporting. Therefore, there are two changes in focus here. First, the supervisor is focusing more on the mentee and the 'work' of the mentor whilst at the same time encouraging the mentor to begin to recognize how the mentor's own experiences (including those as a mentor/supervisee) are beginning to impact upon their mentoring work. Second, the supervisor is supporting the mentor to develop his or her own internal critically reflexive capacity.

### The reflexive mentor

The reflexive mentor is someone with considerable experience as a mentor and may even be a mentor supervisor themselves. They have developed sufficient self-awareness, with the help of their supervisor, to critically reflect upon their own practice and to identify areas for their own development, as well as being more competent in detecting and using their own feelings within mentoring conversations to inform their practice. They are, however, astute enough to recognize that there is nevertheless a need to continue with their development and to understand the dangers that lie in complacency in terms of rigidity of approach. In this sense, the reflexive mentor who needs supervision to assure the quality of their helping skills and to prevent blind-spots or damage being done through arrogant or careless interventions.

## Implications for supervision – description of practice

For the effective supervision of a reflexive mentor, the supervisor would need to be a highly competent, flexible and experienced mentor themselves as the range of supervision required might range from very gentle support when a problem occurs, as a 'spot mentoring' transaction, or conversely adopting a strong critical position in order to challenge the potentially complacent mentor supervisee. As a result, the frequency of supervision may differ, depending on the needs of the supervisee. For instance, Feltham (in Lawton and Feltham 2000) refers to a highly experienced psychotherapist Arnold Lazarus who does not use regular supervision: 'I probably ask for help or input from others mainly when I run into barriers or obstacles or when I feel out of my depth. If things are running along smoothly, why bother, but if there are some problems that make you feel lost or bewildered, or when you feel that you are doing OK, but could do better, why not bring it to the attention of somebody else, and discuss the issues?' (Dryden 1991: 81).

With these four stages in mind, we will now examine a mentoring supervision programme.

## Case illustration

The NWDA business mentoring programme commenced in September 2009 and is seeking to support 3000 SME leaders and managers in the North West of England over a three-year period. The aim of the programme is to establish an exemplary one-to-one mentoring programme demonstrating accredited quality standards. The focus of the mentoring is on small businesses with the potential to grow, which is a core objective of increasing the availability and standard of mentoring provision in the region and robust evaluation. The delivery model has four key elements to it to ensure these deliverables: a quality framework based on the ISMPE standards (International Standards for Mentoring Programmes in Employment); a central coordination team; delivery through a trained and quality controlled provider network; and ongoing monitoring and evaluation. Given the number of people involved in the scheme, a train-the-trainers approach to mentor development was adopted, with a number of professional mentoring organizations (the providers) being contracted to actually deliver the mentor development to the mentors.

The ongoing support and supervision for the programme has been provided at two levels: for the provider organizations and the mentors themselves:

### Supervision for providers

Provider networking events are run by the central team three times a year to disseminate knowledge and share best practice. These sessions are an opportunity for the organizations to be versed in further mentoring themes and theory, which they can then deliver at their own mentor focus groups. New research and cutting edge best practice is shared at these sessions. It is also an opportunity to share evaluation results from the programme and discuss aspects of interest to the providers to enable them to use this formative evaluation wisely. In our heuristic, this provider supervision is providing a development function to the professional mentors. In the programme set up, the providers attended a workshop where they were given details about the expectations of them on the programme as well as some approaches and models to practise within the session. Hence, these workshops provided both the quality assurance and training functions of supervision for these providers.

### Supervision for mentors

In turn, the providers run mentor focus groups for the mentors. Such meetings provide an opportunity for mentors to discuss concerns, to gain further knowledge or skills training and to network generally with other mentors on the programme. Again, mirroring the overall logic of the programme, a number of exemplar focus groups are being run by the central team which serve a quality assurance, development and training function for the mentors in terms of their supervisory needs. The process involves mentors working in pairs or small groups and discussing issues around their mentoring process and practice in order to receive:

- mentoring on their own practice;
- the time to explore techniques and help with their problems;
- an opportunity to reflect on their own practice;
- help and support if they feel out of their depth;
- support with ethical issues.

In addition to these focus groups, each mentor is invited to attend up to three supervision sessions per annum, lasting between 2 and 3 hours, provided by the provider organizations. These tend to be group supervisions.

Although this programme is a voluntary mentoring programme, it has attracted a large number of experienced professional helpers. These voluntary mentors on the whole tend to be in the reflective and reflexive categories when we compare their experience with our simple heuristic. However, what our analysis reveals is that there may be a relative lack of challenge embedded in the supervisory processes that have been developed, which is particularly important for very experienced mentors to experience. Rather the emphasis of the interventions is to support knowledge sharing and psycho-social support for participants. Whilst this sort of challenge may not be a pressing need in the minds of the mentors or the providers, there is a clear imperative to avoid any complacency or collusion on the part of either group, if the scheme objectives are to be met. The implications of this for mentoring supervision will be considered below.

## Evaluation of the approach

Despite the 'blurring' of hard and fast distinctions between the labels of coaching and mentoring, mentoring still has associations with the use of personal experience and with the whole person and their values. The importance of personal experience is evident in the NWDA scheme. As with most business-to-business mentoring programmes, managers in small businesses tend to learn better and see the value in help from someone who has, to use the colloquial expression 'been there, done that and worn the t-shirt' (see Clutterbuck and Megginson 1999). This tendency has some important implications for mentoring supervision.

As many novice mentors will say, one of things that they find most difficult initially is resisting the urge to give advice and to tell the mentee what they know.

As well as providing the generic support functions described above, we have found that the supervision processes can be particularly helpful in helping the mentors find a suitable amount of professional distance from their own experience and practice. This seems to enable them to be more resourceful as mentors by avoiding the 'pendulum effect' of either pushing their experience onto the mentees or completely withholding their experience from the mentee. Also, our experience of those working in small businesses as entrepreneurs suggests that many of these have healthy egos and often, irrespective of gender, espouse a tough guy/macho (Deal and Kennedy 1982) culture within their organizations. Supervisors also need to pay careful attention to the importance of challenging dominant assumptions about business and organizations with the mentors. Hence, it is important that mentoring supervision in this scheme enables mentors to balance themselves and to offer their experience to the mentees on the one hand, but at the same time to prevent them from either consciously or subconsciously developing clones of themselves on the other!

Research on mentor supervision lags behind research on coaching supervision for a number of reasons. First, mentoring as a label is more likely to refer to more informal unpaid helping relationships than coaching does, which can mean that mentoring supervision, in turn, is likely to get less formal attention and recognition than coaching. Second, due to mentoring being more often a voluntary and unpaid activity the majority of mentors do not have access to supervision, resources or financial incentives to support their supervision activities.

Whilst this argument also holds true for manager-coaches within organizations, the image of coaching (rightly or wrongly) being more performance focused means that such managers are more likely to get organizational support and supervision for their performance coaching of staff rather than their mentoring activities.

## Learning more

As argued above, there is relatively little research on mentoring supervision in particular. However, Megginson et al.'s (2006) edited book on mentoring in action contains several case examples of mentoring programmes and how mentors are supported in their practice, across a wide range of contexts. Gopee's (2008) book focusing on mentoring and supervision is also helpful, although care must be taken to avoid confusing mentoring supervision with clinical supervision in the NHS. Finally, for an excellent critical text on mentoring in context and the challenges facing mentors and their development, Colley's (2003) book on mentoring for social inclusion is worth examining.

To conclude, there are several critical questions that need to be explored further in the context of mentoring supervision:

1   What sort of supervision do mentors need when helping people?
2   How can mentors be supported in achieving an effective balance between using their knowledge to help the mentee and allowing the mentee to become self-reliant?

3   Is mentoring supervision distinct from coaching supervision due to its different markets, contexts and participants?

# References

Barrett, R. (2002) Mentor supervision and development – exploration of lived experience, *Career Development International*, 7(5): 279–83.

Blasé, J. and Blasé, J. (2002) The micropolitics of instructional supervision: a call for research, *Educational Administrative Quarterly*, 38(1): 6–44.

Clutterbuck, D. and Megginson, D. (1999) *Mentoring Executives & Directors*. Oxford: Butterworth-Heinemann.

Colley, H. (2003) *Mentoring for Social Inclusion*. London: Routledge Falmer.

Deal, T. and Kennedy, A. (1982) *Corporate Cultures: The Rites and Rituals of Corporate Life*, 3rd edn. Cambridge, MA: Perseus Books.

Dryden, W. (1991) *A Dialogue with Arnold Lazarus: It Depends*. Buckingham: Open University Press.

Garvey, B. and Alred, G. (2000) Educating Mentors, *Mentoring & Tutoring*, 8(2): 113–26.

Garvey, B., Stokes, P. and Megginson, D. (2009) *Coaching and Mentoring*. London: Sage Publications.

Gopee, N. (2008) *Mentoring and Supervision in Healthcare*. London: Sage.

Hawkins, P. and Shohet, R. (2002) *Supervision in the Helping Professions*. Buckingham: Open University Press.

Kram, K. (1983) Phases of the mentor relationship, *Academy of Management Journal*, 26(4): 608–25.

Kram, K. (1985) *Mentoring at Work: Developmental Relationships in Organizational Life*. Glenview, IL: Scott-Foresman.

Kutter, P. (2002) From the Balint method toward profession related supervision, *The American Journal of Psychoanalysis*, 62(4): 313–25.

Lawton, B. and Feltham, C. (eds) (2000) *Taking Supervision Forward*. London: Sage.

Maidment, J. and Cooper, L. (2002) Acknowledgement of client diversity and oppression in social work student supervision, *Social Work Education*, 21(4): 399–407.

Marrow, C.E., Macauley, D.M. and Crumbie, A. (1997) Promoting reflective practice through clinical supervision, *Journal of Nursing Management*, 5: 77–82.

Megginson, D., Clutterbuck, D., Garvey, B., Stokes, P. and Garrett-Harris, R. (2006) *Mentoring in Action*, 2nd edn. London: Kogan Page.

Merrick, L. and Stokes, P. (2003) Mentor development and Supervision: a passionate joint enquiry, *International Journal of Coaching and Mentoring* (e-journal), 1. www.emccouncil.org (accessed 6 June 2011).

Merrick, L. and Stokes, P. (2011) *A Schema for Mentor Development and supervision*.

Stokes, P. (2003) Exploring the relationship between mentoring and counselling, *British Journal of Guidance and Counselling*, 32(1): 25–34.

Willis, P. (2005) European Mentoring and Coaching Council, Competency Research Project: Phase 2, June. www.emccouncil.org (accessed 18 July 2011).

# 17 Supervision for organization consultants

*Erik de Haan and David Birch*

## Introduction

Organization Development (OD) consultants are increasingly benefiting from the supervision of their consulting and executive coaching work. Supervision is making an important contribution to the professional development and quality assurance of consultants and is becoming a key differentiator in the marketplace. With the growing professionalism of the OD field, supervision is making an important contribution to many formal qualifications in organization consulting. As more consultants work independently or as 'sole practitioners' in many of their assignments, there is a growing need for time and space to reflect in a supervisory relationship. In this chapter we look at the various forms of consulting supervision, and reflect on the pros and cons of different approaches. We end with a few dilemmas that may arise for the OD supervisor. We argue that consulting supervision is a distinctive field in its own right, however, the issues it faces are also of relevance to coaching supervisors.

We see organization consulting, or OD consulting, as a broader field than executive coaching or coaching supervision, comprising larger scale organizational interventions such as process consultation, team and organization development, strategic conferences and whole-system methodologies (Checkland 1981; Schein 1987; Weisbord and Janoff 1995). It is precisely the broader reach of these consulting interventions that make consultants work closer with the organization's agenda and with their clients or 'client systems' within the organization. Supervision, although similar to executive coaching mostly organized off-line, nevertheless acquires a broader reach and a deeper view of the organization as a whole. Organization supervision is therefore more complex and multilayered as we will attempt to show in the following examples and models. It is for this reason that organization supervision also branches out into wider areas of the professional's role, encompassing more frequently (1) the way the consultant or supervisee interacts with other consultants within the context of larger-scale assignments; and (2) the consultant's or supervisee's home base or consulting organization, with significant dynamics around the acquisition of assignments or the progression towards more senior roles. In other words, some good OD consulting supervision is not focused on the supervisee's client work at all, but rather on the supervisee's relationships with their direct peers and managers, but always in service of their learning and effectiveness as a consultant.

## The varieties of consulting supervision

OD consulting supervisors and supervisees can decide to work together in three different modalities or contracts:

### Individual consulting supervision

This is fully focused on the individual consultant and her practice. The advantage of this approach is that the supervisor is not part of the organizational system and is therefore well placed to attend to the interplay of transference and counter-transference (Searles 1955; Ledford 1985) in the supervisory relationship. Because the supervisor has not had any direct experience of the consulting environment, the supervisor's impressions are shaped by the way the supervisee is describing their work. By playing back to the supervisee what they are observing in them and how they are feeling, the supervisor is able to help the supervisee to inquire into the assumptions, prejudices and associations that they make with respect to their clients, their consulting practice and themselves.

## Case illustration

*Roger is a consultant working for a niche consultancy, participating in organization-development assignments and tailored executive education. The firm has five partners (owners) and fifteen senior consultants. Roger is seen as someone who may be able to become a partner over the next five years or so, although this has not been made explicit to him. The firm pays for him to meet with a supervisor (who is a clinical psychologist) at least quarterly, plus an occasional session if he feels he needs one. Although they talk about his client work Roger is preoccupied with the dynamics within the firm, where differences of opinion between the partners are repressed and played out unconsciously by the senior consultants. The partners maintain an impression of always being in agreement. They meet every month and although the whole firm knows when those meetings are, they don't know much about what is being discussed there. Symbolically, this is represented by the door to the main library, which is normally open, being shut during partner meetings. Roger regularly feels criticized by one of the partners, whereupon another partner stretches out a hand to comfort him. He also feels that he is in competition with one or two of the other senior consultants who are also aspiring to partnership. The work with clients can be intense, but having to face these put-downs and rivalries in the firm is much harder for Roger. As an outsider to the organization, the supervisor 'holds up the mirror' in a way that helps Roger to appreciate his part in the dynamics more clearly. He learns how some of his own reactions are understandable in terms of his own family dynamics, and from the fact that he feels quite exposed and vulnerable in the firm whilst he feels much more impactful and confident when working with his clients. Through his work in supervision, Roger manages to keep a steady course, not to escalate any of the tensions too far, and eventually he is invited to join the partnership. It is not until then that he experiences the more open power struggles among the partners and not surprisingly he finds it useful to continue working with his supervisor at about the same frequency.*

## Shadow consultancy

This is working as a shadow consultant (Schroder 1974) to one or a group of consultants; in other words supporting a consultancy project in an 'off-line' supervisory role. Like individual supervision, the client does not encounter the supervisor, except perhaps as a name on a contract or invoice. The supervisor works away from the glare of the client engagement, 'in the shadow' of the consulting team, attending to the resonances within the team as it works on the assignment. This distance from the client system and the presence of inter-consultant dynamics enables the supervisor to pick up still more patterns of transference/counter-transference, or what is often called parallel processes (Searles 1955).

In this way of supervising, the supervisor is usually attached to a team of consultants working on a specific project, but shadow consulting can also take place in mixed groups of consultants or within a consulting portfolio.

## Case illustration

*A shadow consultant had just started supervising a team of change consultants working at a financial services organization. As the group session progressed, she noticed that whenever the project leader was speaking her mind wandered. Even when she forced herself to listen, she was only able to follow what was being said for a few minutes at most. When others in the team spoke, she found it easier to concentrate, but was concerned about the quality of her supervision because she had not fully followed the project leader's contribution. When the same thing happened during the second session she decided to share her experience with the group in a way that avoided criticizing the project leader. She asked whether others felt the same way and whether this might be a reflection of their work with the organization in some way. To her astonishment several team members admitted that they too found it hard to follow their project leader's thought process. The leader was initially embarrassed, but with the help of the group came to realize that their key client, the CEO, was isolated and remote from his colleagues, who also seemed to only half-understand what he was trying to communicate. The supervisor pointed out that the team's experience of the project leader was in fact a classic example of a parallel process; in other words a replication of what was happening in the client system.*

*The supervisor then helped the team think through what the project leader could do differently and how this insight might also be relevant to the CEO. This resulted in a profound shift in the team's effectiveness, as they learned to share what might be construed as negative feedback in a spirit of mutual inquiry rather than criticism. The CEO was similarly defensive when the project leader shared their observations but was astonished at their accuracy when he sought feedback from his closest colleague. Here again we see how – unlike coaching supervisors – an organization supervisor working purely with the consulting team and their interactions, can have a profound effect on the outcome of consulting interventions in the client organization.*

## Peer supervision

This involves working actively as a peer supervisor within a consulting team. Sometimes team members may take it in turns to play the role of supervisor, so that each team member moves back and forth between consulting and supervising roles. The advantage of this approach is that the peer supervisor has their own direct experience of the client organization, which means they can test certain hunches and ground them in the reality of their own experience. This may however compromise their ability to pick up on parallel processes, and in our experience a peer supervisor will need more individual supervision for himself or herself to process the conflicts of straddling the boundaries between supervision, consulting and participation in client organizations.

For us the most effective method of peer supervision involves the peer supervisor remaining somewhat detached from the work of their supervisees, making time and space for the supervision meetings away from the client. Groups of consultants will work best if there is clear contracting between them about the purpose and roles of supervision.

## Case illustration

*A team of 15 consultants working on a culture change project at a government department were grouped into five peer-supervision groups, or 'trios' as they were referred to. Each trio met for an hour once a fortnight, with colleagues taking it in turns to play the role of the supervisor. In one trio, a colleague was concerned about the management style of one of the senior client staff, which they felt was unnecessarily aggressive and bullying. With the help of their peer supervisor and the third member of the trio, they explored their feelings and reactions, including their unacknowledged prejudice associated with the person's educational background. This helped them empathize with the individual and re-evaluate their critical stance. Rather than confront the person as they had been intending to, they decided that they would try and build a closer relationship with the person and if necessary influence from a position of support and respect.*

## What makes working as a consulting supervisor different?

As we have seen in the examples above, the distinguishing characteristic of consulting supervision – as compared to coaching supervision – is that the consultant's internal relationships with peers and managers become more prominent and provide unique material to help supervisee and supervisor learn about the relationships and dynamics in the client organization(s). The parallel process per se is prominent in all supervision, but this ability to carry the *systemic* back into the *system* is distinct and very powerful.

Supervision for organization consultants is an expanding field because of the growing recognition that practitioners need to attend to the dynamics that shape their responses and relational patterns. As argued above, supervisors are in an excellent position to detect, explore and assess organizational dynamics. It is interesting to compare these patterns to Lewin's well-known 'force fields' (Lewin 1951) and to some of the supervision case examples in Hirschhorn (1988).

The degree to which the patterns that the supervisor picks up are amplified or reduced depends on an aspect of the personality of consultants and supervisor called personal 'valency' (Bion 1961). A person's valency for picking up unconscious patterns is strongly related to their personality and personal experiences in life. Patterns we are able to pick up consciously are patterns we are able to experience and observe. Patterns we tend to pick up unconsciously are patterns that somehow 'stir' us up, moving us emotionally because they remind us of other earlier patterns that we could not quite (allow ourselves to) experience and which are thus handled less consciously.

In such a way individual supervisors can pick up important determining patterns (blocks to change, opportunities for new change, etc.) that are normally below the level of conscious awareness, but they can only do so within a specific and limited spectrum of valencies. The phenomenon is comparable to the phenomenon of 'resonance' in physics, where an object can only pick up and amplify particular frequencies of, for example, sound waves, and not others.

Each of the different modes of consulting supervision offers a unique potential for picking up organizational patterns. The consultants/supervisees act as 'lenses'

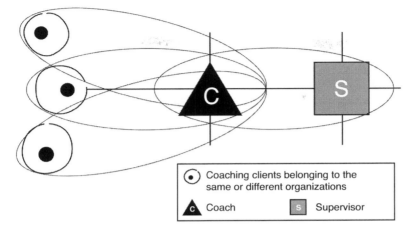

**Figure 17.1** Schematic depiction of executive coaching supervision for one individual coach
*Note:* The vertical lines represent other client relationships that the consultant and supervisor will have. The horizontal line to the right of the supervisor connects to their supervisor.

for picking up patterns and issues in the organization(s) and in the process the supervisor also spots issues with the lenses themselves. In the *coaching supervision* process (see Figure 17.1) the situation is most straightforward, because the supervisor has only one lens and no direct access to the client organization(s) that are being discussed. This offers a clear-cut window onto the coaching relationship and behind that the organizational dynamics. There is relatively little room for amplification or resonance, and the coach's valency has a modest place in the exploration.

In *individual consulting supervision* (Figure 17.2) there is more room for picking up patterns, as the consultant has been directly exposed to organizational dynamics *between* people working for the organization. We can see that the consultant has a broader role in the organization than the coach in Figure 17.1, and will pick up more organization dynamics from direct exposure, and may even become relatively 'native' or 'immersed' within the organization.

In *shadow consulting* (Figure 17.3), the supervisor is exposed to a much 'richer' dynamic between consultants, with more 'antennae' towards organizational patterns. In our experience dynamics between consultants working in teams may reflect, or mirror, strong and unconscious organizational dynamics. This is shown in some of the examples above and in Hirschhorn's example of a deputy director who is under intense pressure and works with a pair of organization consultants who are in turn supervised by the author (Hirschhorn 1988: 40).

Finally, in *peer supervision* (Figure 17.4), the supervisor has access to a still wider pattern of dynamics, including their own direct experience. The situation is still

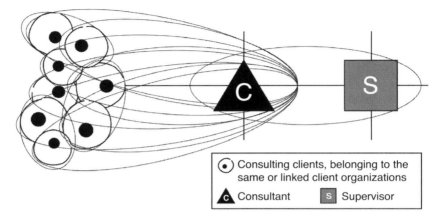

**Figure 17.2** Schematic depiction of OD supervision for one individual consultant working on a single assignment
*Note:* The vertical lines represent other client relationships that the consultant and supervisor will have. The horizontal line to the right of the consultant connects to his/her supervisor.

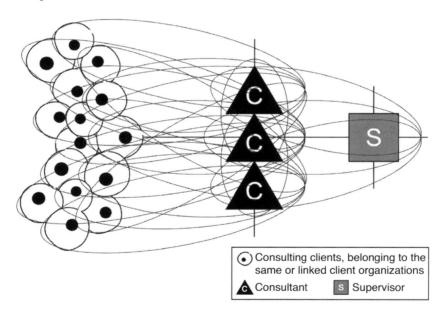

**Figure 17.3** Schematic depiction of 'shadow consultancy' supervision for a team of OD consultants working on a single assignment
*Note:* The vertical lines represent other client relationships that the consultant and supervisor will have. The horizontal line to the right of the consultants connects to their supervisor.

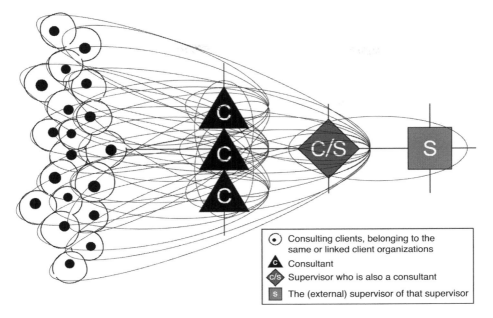

**Figure 17.4** Schematic depiction of peer supervision for a team of OD consultants working on a single assignment
*Note:* The vertical lines represent other client relationships that the consultant and supervisor will have. The horizontal line to the right of the supervisor connects to their supervisor.

richer, but also 'messier', as the supervisor will be less clear about what she is picking up is attributable to. The supervision of the peer supervisor is particularly important as a way of grounding certain ideas and observations, and to become aware of patterns that are now no longer accessible.

The peer supervisor is picking up patterns that are sometimes four layers deep. Firstly, organizational patterns which are manifest in patterns of individual client behaviour. These then influence the relationship between consultant and client, which is finally experienced in the 'here and now' by the peer supervisor. Only then do these patterns become available for conscious processing. It is precisely because of the 'free response' enabled by the supervisor's valency, that these patterns can be picked up in the first place. Valuable as they are, they will be biased or coloured by the personal experiences they went through before being consciously detected.

# A case illustration

Having looked at the modes of consulting supervision and the types of contracts that we have ourselves engaged in both as clients and as supervisors, we shall now review a recent case illustrations, anonymized for publication. This was a one-off shadow consulting engagement which illustrates some of the complexities involved in consulting supervision, including how the consulting 'system' and the client 'system' can influence each other in unexpected ways.

## Shadow consulting

*Graham was part of a consulting team engaged by a prestigious university to help revitalize and engage the professoriate in its research strategy. As the assignment progressed he became aware that he was avoiding contact with another consultant called Helen, which troubled him as they usually worked extremely well together. He felt that Helen was disinterested in him and his ideas and seemed intent on pursuing her own agenda with the client. This was exacerbated by the close relationship that Helen had established with a senior professor at the university who had an outstanding international track record as a research leader.*

*Graham knew that he ought to raise his concerns with Helen but felt strangely anxious at the prospect of doing so. He was convinced that Helen would ridicule or humiliate him if he brought the subject up, so he played safe and chose not to share his growing feelings of resentment with his colleague. Not only was he feeling shut out, he was also aware of a growing anxiety that he was somehow failing in Helen's eyes, and that she was privy to some critical feedback from the client about his contribution to the project.*

*Eventually it was Helen who brought the topic up with Graham, concerned that her colleague had grown so distant over recent weeks. Graham remained reluctant to engage with her but agreed that it would be a useful topic to take to the next meeting with the team's shadow consultant.*

*The shadow consultant supervisor helped Graham and Helen discover how they had come to identify with their respective client contacts in the institution. Helen had a rapport with the senior professor, who was highly influential in shaping the university's research agenda. Graham meanwhile had established a bond with a less prominent academic, who the professor often expected to take on the less interesting administrative tasks. Graham had grown accustomed to hearing their complaints about how the professor showed little interest in their ideas and contributions and felt generally used and abused by them. The supervisor suggested that they might be participating in a 'parallel process', where the dynamics present in the relationship between the two clients was being recreated between Helen and Graham.*

*The supervisor suggested that an exploration of the parallel process might yield some useful clues about how Helen and Graham might work more effectively together and within the client system. With the shadow consultant's help, they each role-played the client who they felt closest to, using their experience and intuition to explore how their clients were feeling about one another and the strategizing process. To Graham's surprise, Helen was adamant that 'her' professor would have been horrified to know that his colleague was so angry with him, which opened up a discussion about how they could help the two professors become more aware of their unconscious patterns of behaviour. They decided to work with this theme soon afterwards in a facilitated workshop where the clients were encouraged to actively listen and inquire into one another's thinking. Following a process review, the professors agreed that this more searching and robust conversational process should become a regular feature of their strategic process.*

*Graham meanwhile felt relieved that his strong relationship with Helen had been restored and acutely aware of how an exploration of his supposedly personal feelings in supervision had unexpectedly provided such a powerful insight into how he might best serve his clients in the future.*

This case study illustrates how a shadow consulting supervisor can play an important role in helping consultants 'step back' from the drama of the assignment and inquire into the assumptions, prejudices and unconscious processes that can interfere with their ability to think clearly about their clients or their own teamwork. The shadow consulting supervisor needs to listen carefully to their clients' narratives, without actually believing them to be the 'whole truth'. As she listens, the supervisor reflects on the potential relationship between the consultants' narratives and the organizational process that they are immersed in with their clients. The supervisor's role is to help the consultants reframe these narratives; they are able to do this only when they understand how their participation in the client system has distorted their capacity to think and respond clearly and appropriately.

## Dilemmas for OD consulting supervisors

Although the different modes of supervision are quite distinct from one another, the potential approaches open to the supervisor are broadly similar, whatever the mode or the client context. In particular, supervisors tend to experience a number of dilemmas, which crop up again and again when working with clients. In the following paragraphs we hope to capture some of those, and to convey something of how it feels to work as an OD consulting supervisor.

In the first place as human beings and as supervisors we feel the limits – and hidden promises – of our valencies quite acutely. We become aware of our own counter-transference (Ledford 1985) without necessarily knowing what it is about: we feel unease, discomfort, distraction, displaced anger, boredom, or other feelings that feel real but may be a manifestation of the client/consultant dynamics that are experienced by the consultants being supervised. In other words we feel the sensation in our 'antennas' before we can even begin to make sense of the signal. And if we attend to the sensation we become aware of the inadequacy of our measuring equipment in this area, which is so strongly entwined with our own unresolved issues and transferential patterns. This dilemma begins as discomfort, then emerges as a choice whether to attend or not, and may become a huge doubt about whether what we feel is of any use to our supervisees.

Second, if we then move closer to reflecting back and communicating some of our observations, we can feel dilemmas about how impactful we should be, or how tentative. Of most benefit to the supervisee is usually to be *both*

    a.   impactful: concise, sharp, challenging, new, original, focused; and

    b.   tentative: as an invitation to further reflections rather than as the final word on any matter the consultant(s) is bringing.

Furthermore, when addressing or opening up new client material we will experience dilemmas as to how much to set the tone. Is it more useful to our clients and ultimately to the organization to work in an emergent way, i.e. similar to how an executive coach or OD consultant might work[1]? Or is it important to be directive and map all aspects of the 'case' more actively, working more like an expert consultant?

Similarly we may have dilemmas around when to work in conversation, i.e. reflectively, and when to work more in a 'playful' way, for example by recreating the organization's dynamics in role play, 'two chair' work, psychodrama and organization constellations. Emergent, playful ways of working may provide a stronger lens into unconscious dilemmas within the client organization, because in these interventions the supervisees will be less able to censor their material.

Next, we have experienced dilemmas and concerns in terms of the role we play for the client organizations. Ultimately, the client organization should be the main benefactor and the ultimate client of our work, but they are – usually – one step removed from the supervisory relationship. We have noticed that we struggled at times to be aware of our own engagement with the organization. On the one hand we know we need a certain level of detachment to begin picking up organizational patterns that were not noticed by the consultant. On the other hand, we aim to be impactful in the consultants' client organization. As an organization supervisor one finds oneself in a similar predicament to that of a wildlife documentary filmmaker, where one's observing presence will at some stage, unknown to them, begin to have an impact on the ecosystem observed. The scrutinizing lenses of consultants and supervisors are not just passively observing, they are also present objects in the field of view of the organization's employees, and so they may become a yardstick for measuring progress in the organizational domain. The presence of a coach supervisor is usually much more at a distance to their supervisees' client organizations, such that this dilemma does not occur.

Finally, we have experienced dilemmas about the normative aspect of supervision as well. If a consultant's manager is only interested in revenue or billable days as a 'measure of success', their supervisor is in a much better place to hold meaningful performance conversations with consultants. However, such conversations hold an intrinsic risk of the supervisor becoming a surrogate 'performance manager' the consultant.

Some consultancy firms have internal 'mentors' working alongside external supervisors, whose task it is to hold those performance conversations that go beyond billable days and who report directly to the consultant's line manager.

## Evaluation of this mode of supervision

On the whole, OD consultants have to work within an organization whilst holding on to their outsider's perspective. They have to apply their knowledge, experience and intuition as they engage with the organization, acquiring, as they do so, an insider's perspective on the organization's issues. Such a stance of being an 'outsider within' is not straightforward at all, and carries with it all sorts of temptations, risks and limitations (De Haan 2006). On the one hand, there is a risk in staying overly analytical and detached, which often results in observations, ideas and solutions that are more relevant for the consultant – or for their previous clients – than for the case in point. On the other hand, consultants risk becoming over involved if they identify too strongly with the organization's agenda and issues. One could call this the dilemma of 'aloofness versus collusion'.

However, supervision can be of great benefit to organization consultants as it can help to maintain a balance between these opposing risks and temptations. A supervisor stays – as much as possible – outside of the client engagement, and is much freer to comment on what might be going on for the client and within this client–consultant relationship. Supervision can have an immense formative effect on consultants, not to mention the value it has in a normative and restorative sense (Proctor 2008). Organization consultants often experience anxiety and stress as they try to balance a very diverse portfolio with competing obligations to clients and colleagues. Supervision can help to reduce the stress by helping the consultant to reflect on and understand their own reactions and responses. The supervisor is in an ideal position to provide some 'normative' feedback on a consultant's practice, based on a respectful appreciation of the complexities and challenges that they face. The supervisor's understanding is often better than that of the consultant's line manager or even the consultant herself. We are excited by the prospect of further development and professionalism of consulting supervision so that it can take up its rightful place in the support and quality assurance of organization consultants and expert consultants alike.

## Learning more

The following activities are to enable further reflection about the rich profession of consulting supervision:

1   Ask two clients or friends who work for the same organization to engage in a short conversation about the challenges that they face over the next couple of weeks. Notice not only which challenges they choose to address

but also how they speak about these challenges. Very often the way in which they conduct their conversation will tell you something about the challenges themselves. After the short conversation you may ask them how their responses were 'typical' for their organization's culture. Then you can share your own observations about how they spoke with each other and how these apparent dynamics between them may relate to the issues that they discussed.

2   Make a timeline of all the employers that you have worked for, including yourself if you have been self-employed. Try to find at least one aspect that all these organizations have in common. Then ask yourself what your choice of employers may tell us about you. What are the themes or patterns that you are likely to pick up quite quickly with clients because of your previous organizational experience?

3   Take some time after your next supervision session to map out the dynamics at play. Describe the interaction at that supervision session on four different levels: within the client organization, between the supervisee(s) and clients in that organization, between the supervisee(s) and you, and between you and you (i.e. in your own mind) when you come out of the session. See if you can find any overlap between these patterns of interaction, and try to understand which of the four levels this key pattern comes from, i.e. where are its origins?

The following three texts are useful further reading:

Larry Hirschhorn (1988) *The Workplace Within: Psychodynamics of Organizational Life*. From an anonymous Amazon book review that we concur with: 'Don't let the title of this fine book scare you off. Hirschhorn's *The Workplace Within* is one of the finest tools available for the executive who wishes to deepen his or her understanding of what goes on in organizations today. When read carefully, thoroughly and critically, this book can be a wonderful tool for extending one's social sensitivity in the workplace.'

Marjan Schroder (1974) *The Shadow Consultant*. Schroder's short article is one of the earliest recognitions of some of the specifics of the task of the (internal) organization supervisor. With great sensitivity and powerful examples Schroder demonstrates how even a peer OD consultant can do a good job supervising their consulting colleagues.

Peter Hawkins and Nick Smith (2006) *Coaching, Mentoring and Organizational Consultancy – Supervision and Development*. This is a practical resource book that examines the values and assumptions that underpin organizational consultancy and explores the vital importance of supervision to maintaining an ethically sound practice.

## Note

1   It is worth reminding ourselves here that an executive coach can also be seen as a 'supervisor': as the supervisor of the team that her client leads.

## References

Bion, W.R. (1961) *Experiences in Groups*. London: Tavistock.

Checkland, P.B. (1981) *Systems Thinking, Systems Practice*. Chichester: Wiley.

De Haan, E. (2006) *Fearless Consulting*. Chichester: Wiley.

Hawkins, P. and Smith, N. (2006) *Coaching, Mentoring and Organisational Consultancy – Supervision and Development*. Maidenhead: Open University Press.

Hirschhorn, L. (1988) *The Workplace Within: Psychodynamics of Organizational Life*. Cambridge, MA: MIT Press.

Ledford, G.E. Jr. (1985) Transference and counter-transference in action research relationships, *Consultation*, 4(1): 36–51.

Lewin, K. (1951) *Field Theory in Social Sciences*. New York: Harper & Row.

Proctor, B. (2008) *Group Supervision*, 2nd edn. London: Sage.

Schein, E.H. (1987) *Process Consultation*. Reading, MA: Addison-Wesley.

Schroder, M. (1974) The shadow consultant, *The Journal of Applied Behavioral Science*, 10(4): 579–94.

Searles, H.F. (1955) The informational value of the supervisor's emotional experience, *Psychiatry*, 18: 135–46.

Weisbord, M. and Janoff, S. (1995) *Future Search: An Action Guide to Finding Common Ground in Organizations and Communities*. San Francisco, CA: Berrett-Koehler.

# 18  Peer supervision for coaching and mentoring

*Tatiana Bachkirova and Peter Jackson*

## Introduction

Peer or peer-group supervision is becoming a popular mode of supervision in coaching communities. This is a sign of the increasing awareness of coaches of the value and importance of continuing professional development and the role of supervision in it, as we discussed in the Introduction to this book. Although supervision becomes more and more prominent it is apparent that it is not growing as fast as coaching practice, thus affecting the availability of supervisors. In this case, the obvious solution for coaches is to pair up or form peer-supervision groups to help each other in ensuring the quality of their practice. A common view that we have encountered is that this type of supervision is always available and affordable in the communities of coaches. However natural and positive the intention, the apparent simplicity of the peer-supervision mode may obscure the inherent challenges and the additional skills that are needed to practise it. In this chapter we will look at peer supervision from a number of angles to ascertain its potential benefits but also to elicit serious challenges that need to be considered by coaches and supervisors who are interested in this option.

The concept of peer help dates from before the rise of coaching, and valuable lessons can be drawn from its history in other domains. An early example emerged in the field of counselling as a supplementary movement of co-counselling in the early 1950s. It was pioneered in the USA by Harvey Jackins (1965) who founded a community of volunteers helping each other to work through their own issues. The central idea was one of reciprocal peer counselling: peers took turns in the role of counsellors using good listening skills and giving full attention to each other. All participants had some basic training to learn how to assist colleagues in exploring their issues and discharging painful emotions. This was further developed some time later by John Heron (see Heron 1998) who in 1974 founded a similar community – Co-counselling International – with a stronger principle of self-determination of the 'client' in peer work.

Another approach – 'Focusing Partnership' – was introduced in 1978 with the publication of the first edition of Eugene Gendlin's *Focusing* (1978, 2003). *Focusing* follows Gendlin's groundbreaking *Philosophy of the Implicit* and methodology of appreciation of and communication with the organism as a whole. Focusing is not considered to be a form of counselling, but rather a reciprocal form of providing unobtrusive companionship and attention to a focusing 'partner'. The process of focusing employs 'a body-sense of meaning' to work with current experiences. This process may also involve what Gendlin (2003) calls 'Thinking at the Edge' – a sequence of steps that helps to articulate something new in the field in which one works (2003: ix).

Ladyshewsky (2010) describes a similar process in relation to peer coaching that began to develop extensively in early 1980s as part of teacher development in Australia. Classroom teachers were able to get non-evaluative feedback from their peers regarding their teaching effectiveness and new developments that they were trying to implement. It was followed by similar movements in the business and organizational context (Kram and Isabella 1985; Peters 1996; Ladyshewsky 2007) as an adjustment to management development programmes to promote 'transfer of training' (Ladyshewsky 2010: 284). These movements seem to be voluntary and locally based, non-monitored or monitored only by those who were interested in the original training delivery.

Coming to the present, it seems, in the light of the many informal arrangements being made between coaches – arrangements which look for all the world like peer supervision – that there is much to be learned from its predecessors. Certainly, we can observe that movements that have a solid and recognized theoretical basis can attract more participants. Movements that are supported and organized by a reasonably formal body are more sustainable and can create a pool of those who wish to be part of it. However, the quality and the benefits of this work depend hugely on individual members of such communities. In spite of the effort of overseeing bodies to provide relevant training, it is difficult to ensure the safety and effectiveness of this work as well as manage the expectations of those involved. Those professional bodies, coaching companies or other organizations who are interested in promoting this mode of supervision on a wider scale may be particularly interested in the lessons of these predecessors.

## Description of the peer-supervision mode

The need for coaching supervision is associated first and foremost with the fact that the coach may influence the coaching process just as much unintentionally as they do intentionally. Supervision is intended to ensure that 'the coach maintains an appropriate degree of awareness as well as due diligence with relation to the impact they have on the client at both the surface and "deep" levels' (SGCP guidelines for coaching psychology supervision 2007, http://www.sgcp.org.uk/sgcp/in-practice/supervision.cfm). This primary focus remains the same for peer supervision. Enhancing the long-term professional development of the coach is a secondary function. Whether peer supervision meets these priorities, and if so, how, are the two questions that underpin our discussion in this chapter.

### Forms of peer supervision

In terms of the process there seem to be many formal and informal arrangements which can fall into the category of peer supervision. The obvious options are one-to-one peer supervision and peer-group supervision. Another form is a chain peer supervision of say four coaches: A supervises B, B supervises C, C supervises D and D supervises A. The role of peer supervision in the overall supervisory arrangement of each coach may also vary. Some coaches choose to have peer supervision as their main or even the only mode of supervision. Many others, despite choosing to be supervised by a qualified supervisor, still value the opportunity to add peer supervision arrangements to the more formal process. Peer supervision provides an additional value for them.

*One-to-one peer supervision* involves two peers providing supervision to each other taking the role of a supervisor in turn and giving equal time to each other in each role. We would argue that it is important that the peers in this case are already experienced coaches and both have sufficient competencies as coaching supervisors. Although one-to-one peer supervision is likely to be particularly attractive to less experienced coaches who may still be in the process of building a business, there are issues that are made more complex by the peer relationship. For example, contracting, mutual commitment, and the lure of collusive dynamics in the relationship.

*Peer supervision in a group* is an option also for experienced coaches who choose to meet regularly and provide supervision to each other on a reciprocal basis. (This is distinct from *group supervision* where the group would be led by an appointed supervisor.) In addition to the elements of contracting that are already implicit in supervision and in groups, the peer-group context requires agreement on arrangements such as criteria for membership and how group supervision is going to be managed. These agreements also need to be reviewed periodically. The set of competences required by group members is similarly extended to include group facilitation skills.

*Chain peer supervision* requires more attention to logistics before the whole chain of supervision can start working, but once this is done should resemble the one-to-one peer-supervision relationship. Sometimes the chain chooses to rearrange the order to benefit from working with different people. There is also a much better chance for success if all members of the chain are experienced and knowledgeable as supervisors as well as coaches.

### Supervisory competences

In all the above forms of peer supervision we have suggested that those involved in it should already be experienced coaches. The value of peer supervision among coaches at the beginning of their career will be limited and can have serious downsides: for example, creating a false sense of security that supervision is in place, while missing opportunities for development and quality control that may be beyond the capability of inexperienced coaches/supervisors. Despite the attraction for developing coaches, this is a particular risk if this form of supervision is the only one practised.

Furthermore, we would argue that competent supervision requires skills and perspectives over and above coaching experience. While there can always be benefits from viewing our practice from the fresh angle a professional colleague can bring, this does not amount in itself to adequate supervision of practice. There is still a risk of collusion and that valuable insights into issues of quality might be missed. Many buyers of coaching are also aware of this. Based on assessment processes we have supported, buyers are already inclined to check the supervisory arrangement of the coaches they employ and are seemingly unsatisfied if the coach relies solely on peer supervision.

What sort of supervisory competences should peer supervisors have? They need to be skilled in all the following areas that are considered important and specific for effective supervision of coaching:

- contracting and issues associated with legal and ethical arrangements of coaching in various contexts;
- models of supervision with underlying theoretical background;
- nature, models and dynamics of one-to-one relationships in the context of supervision, including issues of power in coaching and supervision;
- models and theories of individual development in different contexts, including development of coaches;
- a range of approaches to assessment and evaluation of the coaching process depending on the context and nature of coaching;
- supervision of complex coaching situations including ethical, mental health and diversity related issues.

We can only add to this fairly generic list that peer supervisors may need to pay particular attention to contracting and the dynamics of relationship in the process of supervision, as these are the areas that will be challenged by the nature of the peer relationship. It is also important for peer supervisors to be honest about the limits of their competence and be open with each other if they encounter issues they do not feel confident to deal with. They should regularly discuss their development as supervisors and engage in the CPD of those supervisory skills as well as their coaching.

On the whole it may appear impossibly burdensome for some coaches to invest so much energy in peer supervision; some may be thinking by this point, why bother? Perhaps it is easier to have 'normal' supervision arrangements in any case? We believe, however, that there are good reasons for not giving up on peer supervision. For example, it is an excellent way to add more perspectives/diversify the orientation and theoretical basis of the professional input into our practice. It is also an excellent exercise in honing supervisory style and skills.

## Role and function of peer supervisors

The primary role of a coaching peer supervisor is the same as in any other supervision. Two main functions are in focus: to ensure that the needs of the coaching clients are met in the most effective and appropriate manner; and that the coach is developing further as a professional. The process provides a structure and the environment for a coaching practitioner to reflect on the ways in which they are meeting the needs of the clients and continually develop as practitioners.

## Issues and opportunities

There could be many different issues that need to be considered when setting up peer supervision. It may be helpful to think of these under the following headings: issues of peer supervision 'in groups' and 'of groups'; peer supervision between internal coaches; and psychological issues of one-to-one peer supervision.

### Issues of peer supervision in groups

The group context can deliver all the functions typical for one-to-one supervision. In addition, it can also help to develop interactional skills of leadership, assertion and receptivity. However, if we accept one of the main functions of supervision as 'helping the coach to see more than they currently see in their work' (Bachkirova 2008: 17), it becomes more complex when working with groups. There is simply much more *to see* in a group situation. Therefore all facilitators in a peer supervision group need to combine skills of facilitating the exploration of coaching cases with skills of understanding and managing group dynamics. Addressing group processes can be extremely challenging, yet ignoring them can undermine the work done by the group on specific coaching cases.

### Peer supervision between internal coaches

Many organizations are interested in developing a coaching culture and opt to train their own internal coaches. In some cases, peer supervision of internal coaches is a natural process that follows. It has been argued by one of us, however, that a good option in this case is to have an independent supervisor leading a peer-supervision group (Bachkirova 2008). On the one hand, this can help coaches *to see through* the specifics of organizational culture and to keep in sight a perspective that is wider than immediate organizational needs alone. On the other hand, it could allow for a valuable knowledge of the organizational context to be used and accumulated through working with peers.

### Issues of psychological nature in one-to-one peer supervision

There are potentially great strengths that emerge from the peculiarities of a peer-supervision relationship. It is likely that peers will already know each other and have selected each other for peer supervision on the basis of their existing trust and rapport. We would also argue that by playing both roles (supervisor/supervisee) attention is drawn to process and dynamics in a way that can provide considerable development. As Congram has commented in Chapter 9 'In supervision the more the supervisor and coach can meet within an "I-thou" dialogue the greater the potential for learning'. Unsurprisingly, these very assets also have downsides. We would alert peer supervisors to the following issues.

First, it is very likely that partners in peer supervision will also have presuppositions about each other and about the process of supervision. We may have a high opinion of our partner's skills, or authority and may – paradoxically – feel less able to negotiate relationship issues than if the same person were taking responsibility *as supervisor* for the supervision relationship. Without explicit attention, it may be that one partner becomes hampered by this power differential. Similarly a peer-supervisor who considers themselves the 'junior partner' may be inhibited in their supervision practice: a kind of performance anxiety. Performance anxiety in coaching practice would normally be a topic for supervision. It is by no means impossible, but may be difficult to discuss this with a peer supervisor who is 'part of the problem'. It may also be very time consuming.

Issues also arise where there are multiple relationships between the peer-supervision partners (a situation we may avoid elsewhere, but we may well be working with someone in peer supervision who we know for some other reason). It may, for example, be difficult for the partner acting as supervisor to manage the 'supervisory stance' in a flexible way, that is to say, to switch appropriately between different relational strategies to suit the need in hand. To some extent this is handled naturally in a relationship where there is rapport, but it may be difficult – depending on the particular dynamics of the relationship – to switch to a more assertive challenging stance, say, or even a deeply empathetic one where these stances may be inconsistent with other ongoing relationships between the partners. Negotiating endings would be affected in a similar way.

It seems to follow that a conscious engagement by both partners with these issues should form part of the contracting process and that their successful negotiation may take more time, attention and psychological flexibility than would be the case where the respective roles are fixed.

## Case illustration

It is evident from our argument that the key differences between peer supervision and other arrangements centre around contracting and the ongoing negotiation of relationship. There is no systematic difference in content or process in peer supervision compared to other modes. An account of the supervision itself would not therefore illustrate the peculiarities of peer supervision. However, it is worth illustrating the kinds of conversations that can demand more attention in peer coaching than they would in other relationships. Here, then, we have drawn on a selection of reflections of our own and of colleagues using peer supervision. We are grateful for their permission to include them in this chapter.

> 'Part of the awkwardness that I feel in switching roles is moving from what I feel as a kind of "abandonment" as client (in a nice way – i.e. openness to where the process will take me), to a kind of 'responsibility' (what can I say or do that might help?). I feel this can be a bit confusing

*and may be subject to a certain interference from preformed expectations of our relative status and power. I had a stronger than usual urge to share similar experiences. Don't really know why. Am I trying to undermine any appearance of authority?'*

*'What would happen if you genuinely thought your peer supervisor wasn't a good enough supervisor or practitioner for you to work with? I know some people feel they definitely need someone who really understands first hand the level and context in which they're practising – i.e. a more "senior" practitioner. How can someone who is in this position do peer-supervision?'*

*'One of the most difficult issues for me has been stopping myself from being too helpful. With a client, it's relatively easy to step back and maintain an objective distance. With a peer coach, there is more pressure to help by providing ideas or new perspectives, rather than allow them to emerge in the space between us. On the positive side, I find that I have greater permission to challenge with peer coaches. We expect each other to pose uncomfortable questions and welcome them.'*

*'As far as peer supervision in organizations is concerned, my current experience would indicate that, although people set off with good intentions of getting together to sustain and practise their coaching skills, it rarely happens. There has to be either a strong framework requiring it to happen, or sustained effort from a group of individuals working in a congenial culture. People today tend to be time poor and there is always some organizational fire burning that takes priority over reflection in action, let alone reflection on action. My current view is that peer supervision needs to be "insitutionalized" in some way or it ain't going to happen.'*

*'If we share the same stage of meaning-making with our peer, we are both subject to the same lenses and can only work within this frame of reference – broadly speaking; although our different experiences will produce some different perspectives on challenges to our shared meaning-making systems which may help us both to test the limits of these and potentially undergo developmental shifts. Shifts which may or may not be recognizable as changes in meaning-making: they might simply be developments in tacit knowledge and behaviour as a coach.'*

## Evaluation of the peer supervision mode

As noted previously, the practice of peer supervision as a mode of supervision will depend heavily on the characteristics, quality and choices of those who are involved in it, for example, the partners' preference of theoretical tradition. It is unlikely that the quality of supervision will be better than the quality of practice by each individual peer. However, the issue of improvement is also in their own hands. Peer supervisors can choose to make use of other theoretical traditions of coaching/supervision if they are interested in these schools of thought or decide to become more knowledgeable/experienced in these traditions. They can choose to apply any model of supervision from the range discussed in this book if they know them or are prepared to learn and experiment with them. The only limitation to such experimenting could be the mutuality of the contract between the peers and consideration of appropriateness to the particular coaching case, situation and the context. The overall understanding of the benefit and challenges of the peer-supervision arrangement should also be carefully considered by the pair or a group.

### Potential benefits and challenges of peer supervision

Peer-supervision can bring particular benefits as a mode of supervision. It is often the case that coaches choose to pair for supervision with those people who they know well, respect as professionals and trust on a deeper level. With such a background to relationship, it is possible that the insight into each other's style, blind-spots and particular strengths that this relationship might afford, could be invaluable for overall development and learning. Each partner might be more open to the critical suggestions of the other because of the trust they have already developed. Another factor that may enhance peer supervision compared to formal and paid supervision is that currently official supervisors are often asked to provide references about their supervisees. This might consciously or subconsciously make supervisees less open about most difficult cases or particular issues that could show them in unfavourable light in the eyes of their formal supervisors.

On the other hand, the process of peer supervision may create an image of false simplicity, leading to underestimation of serious challenges that could undermine the effectiveness of peer supervision. We have already mentioned the potential for collusion, because peers may have an impetus to 'be there' for each other and to be helpful rather than challenging. Peer supervision is also by nature a 'dual relationship'. Peer supervisors are supervisors and supervisees at the same time. Quite often they are also colleagues, friends or even more than friends. This inevitably implies issues that may complicate the working relationships. One of them is simply skipping through some important elements of contracting and processes just because of the assumption that 'we all know the rules of the game'. Peer supervision may also simply become low priority in busy periods and fall of the diaries because peers may be over-sympathetic towards each other. It has to be said, however, that many of these disadvantages could be minimized by the genuine attempt to keep an eye on these factors and by regular discussions about these issues in an open and honest manner.

## Learning more

Every coach can learn to become a better peer in a peer-supervision mode. If we want to enhance this ability we can start from an honest evaluation of our strengths as peer supervisors and what we are still missing. We suggest starting your peer-supervision engagement with this exercise, and to help each other in a best coaching tradition to find a best way to develop peer-supervision skills as part of your contract. You can help each other in this process by asking for and providing honest feedback about how you are doing as a peer supervisor. Some good questions to regularly ask each other in this process are:

- What changes do you notice in me as your peer supervisor?
- How do they affect you in this work?
- What other changes in my peer-supervision approach would you welcome?

There are currently no texts which focus specifically on peer supervision. You may find it useful though to look at two books that address two sides of the peer-supervision function separately.

This is a good text to look at if you wish to become a better supervisee:

Carroll, M. and Gilbert, M. (2005) *On Being a Supervisee: Creating Learning Partnerships*, self-published manual.

And this is the book that discusses various issues of being a supervisor:

Hawkins, P. and Smith, N. (2006) *Coaching, Mentoring and Organizational Consultancy: Supervision and Development.* Maidenhead: Open University Press.
In combination they can provide useful information and questions for further thinking and development as a peer supervisor.

# References

Bachkirova, T. (2008) Coaching supervision: reflection on changes and challenges, *People and Organisations at Work*, Autumn edition, p. 17.

Gendlin, E. (1978) *Focusing*, 1st edn. New York: Everest House.

Gendlin, E. (2003) *Focusing*, rev. edn. London: Rider.

Jackins, H. (1965) *The Human Side of Human Beings*. Seattle, WA: Rational Island.

Heron, J. (1998) *Co-Counselling*. Auckland: South Pacific Centre for Human Inquiry.

Kram, K. and Isabella, L. (1985) Mentoring alternatives: the role of peer relationships in career development, *Academy of Management Journal*, 28: 110–32.

Ladyshewsky, R. (2007) A strategic approach for integrating theory to practice in leadership development, *Leadership & Organization Development Journal*, 28(5): 426–43.

Ladyshewsky, R. (2010) Peer coaching, in E. Cox, T. Bachkirova and D. Clutterbuck (eds) *The Complete Handbook of Coaching*. London: Sage, pp. 284–96.

Peters, H. (1996) Peer coaching for executives, *Training and Development Journal*, 50(3): 39–41.

# 19 E-supervision: application, benefits and considerations

*Julie Hay*

## Introduction

I consider e-supervision to be any form of supervision that uses technological transmission of sound, whether that is via VOIP (Voice over Internet Protocol) that converts sounds into digital signals, or telephone that converts sounds into electrical, and nowadays digital, signals, or digital or analogue recordings of the supervisee's practice or the supervisor's feedback. VOIP is often accompanied by the transmission of sight, with cameras being low cost additions or standard additions to computers.

Asynchronous e-communication, such as via exchange of emails and audio or video recordings, has of course been available for many years. Its benefits and downsides are covered well by Clutterbuck and Hussain (2010) so I will concentrate here on synchronous e-supervision.

Below I present some thoughts on why synchronous e-supervision is significant and a brief history of its antecedents. I continue with a review of the opportunities it provides, including the potential for a global impact on coaching standards and the pragmatic benefits of avoiding the need for travel. I consider how the challenge of physical separation can also be of benefit, providing the e-supervisor adjusts their expectations about how they process stimuli from the supervisee. Several brief examples are included to demonstrate e-supervision in action and the chapter concludes with some suggestions for background reading and a recommendation that the best way to progress is to start practising.

## The significance of e-supervision

Within the therapeutic context I still experience mixed reactions to the notion of e-supervision but the coaching community has long had e-coaching so the move into e-supervision is not so alien. Those who express doubts often do so because of lack of familiarity with the current functionality of technological communication. This is understandable because it is not easy to keep up with the rapid advances. We have email, Internet and intranets, wikis, blogs, twitters, webinars, social networks – the list goes on. We no longer even need computers as many phones can access these features. We cannot afford to ignore progress but we do need to ensure that it serves rather than rules. It is encouraging that Li and Bernoff (2008) title their book about the rise of the Internet *Groundswell* to make the point that developments are being driven by the users; they also write 'the technologies are not the point . . . *concentrate on the relationships, not the technologies*' (2008: 18, original emphasis).

We can view the distinction between face-to-face supervision and e-supervision as a difference in environment and dynamics rather than a difference in context or approach. In other words, the functions and processes of supervision are the same, the context remains whatever emerges from the mix of contexts of supervisor, supervisee and client, and there need be no change to the theoretical approach. Clearly some elements of the environment are different because the parties are not in the same location, and a change from visual to auditory channel of communication may change the dynamics.

In my opinion, therefore, e-supervision is a change in context rather than mode, so can be used for coaching supervision in organizations, for groups, for mentoring and between peers. It can also utilize the models explored in Part 1 and theoretical approaches in Part 2, insofar as these use dialogue.

## A brief history

E-supervision of coaching brings together the 'histories' of supervision, coaching and the Internet. Clinical supervision began as far back as the 1920s, associated with classical psychoanalysis, and has since spread across the range of helping professions to include coaching. Coaching itself has no doubt been practised since time immemorial although in its current identity it also dates back to the last century. The Internet as we now know it is the new entrant; Bacigalupe (2010) points out that in 2001 social networking did not exist and the Internet was more of a collection of information. Within a decade it has changed into a virtual world and accessible networking platform. Bacigalupe may have overlooked the impact of Thomas J. Leonard within the coaching sphere. This founder in 1964 of the International Coach Federation had previously set up Coach University in 1992 (still there as Coach U 2010) and teleclass.com in 1998 (no longer there, perhaps because Leonard died in 2003).

Without the developments of the Internet, it seems unlikely that e-coaching and e-supervision would be experiencing the growth they are. Although telephone coaching was being used fairly extensively, there were still significant costs involved if this was being done long distance. The advent of services such as Skype (2010), which allow us to have auditory and visual contact, at no cost above that already incurred to access the Internet, has brought this format into general reach.

---

The author has no commercial connection with Skype beyond being registered as a user.

# E-supervision practice considerations

I do not intend to describe various technologies, mainly because they change so fast that whatever I write may well be out-dated by the time this chapter is published. The key distinction is that e-supervision is done at a distance using technological communication systems rather than the traditional face-to-face direct communication. Some systems are free when using existing Internet connections, such as Skype, which describes itself as 'software that enables the world's conversations'. Conference calls are also possible for group supervision. Many of the systems will also provide visuals, so that although we may be limited in how much can appear on our screen, we can see the supervisee(s) and can even observe live practice. Software is available that allows us to record sessions (sound and visual is possible) so that those taking part can listen again – and the supervisor can take it to their own supervision.

An extension of e-supervision can have the supervisee submitting material beforehand. For instance, they might record a session with a client, select an extract containing a seemingly significant interaction sequence, and send the supervisor that extract plus a transcript with their own analysis. The supervisor can review this before a supervisory discussion or can send feedback to the supervisee, possibly also using recording instead of typing up their comments.

## Opportunities and issues

The long-distance reach of e-supervision provides a significant opportunity for raising professional standards of coaching in areas of the world where coaches might otherwise have limited access to professional development. For example, in some countries I have noticed a tendency to position coaching as a status symbol charged for by the hour – the more hours, the greater the status for the client and the coach. Supervisory prompting about contracting related to client (and organization) outcomes has stimulated supervisees to challenge cultural norms and introduce a more professional approach to evaluation of their services.

Associated with this, we now have the potential to 'make a difference' at a global level. We are seeing more and more examples of how worldwide e-communication is challenging power structures. Governments attempt to prevent their citizens accessing the Internet. The US Government sought to stop Wikileaks from publishing classified documents, and Wikileaks supporters responded by using software that enabled them to close down (albeit temporarily) specific websites by bombarding them with access attempts. Whether we view such events as autocratic governments stifling e-dissent or rebels causing political mayhem, such uses of the Internet have a significant impact on the 'world order'. Translating this into the world of coaching and coaching supervision, we can do more than raise coaching standards – we can contribute to the increased autonomy (Berne 1964) of coaches and through that to the increased autonomy of their clients, and hence to changes to the political cultures of countries. This opportunity does of course come with responsibilities to ensure that we are fostering genuine autonomy and not merely passing on our own political opinions.

E-supervision also provides significant pragmatic opportunities due to the ease of e-contact compared to the travel associated with working face-to-face. As I was working on this chapter, the UK had its heaviest snowfall for years and much travel became impossible. Although living in an area that missed the worst, I was unable to travel to keep appointments elsewhere within the UK, and my flight to Eastern Europe was cancelled. However, my distance contacts were unaffected, and I acquired a few more appointments with supervisees who would normally have made the journey to see me. And I was still able to have my own supervision with a supervisor in France, yet struggled to reach another supervisor who practised only 30 minutes away by car (but 2 hours by train). This also has benefits in terms of the ecological impact of travelling.

Such travel may not be needed if supervisor and supervisee are in the same location. However, this raises potential problems when both parties share similar perspectives within the same or related contexts. E-supervision allows us to have a global reach. For no extra cost or time spent travelling, supervisors can supervise coaches in different organizations, different areas of the country, and even in different countries. We can have contact with many practitioners who live in countries where they have no easy access to supervisors, either because there are none or because the national professional community is small and they are all colleagues and often friends. Many of these countries are in the 'financially-disadvantaged' category so supervisees cannot afford to pay travel costs, even if they had the time to make the journeys.

### Benefits and challenges

In my opinion the lack of face-to-face contact that is generally quoted as the principal challenge to e-supervision is also the dynamic that creates the most significant benefit. This is because the lack of face-to-face contact encourages both supervisee and supervisor to stay in the present rather than experiencing the full impact of transference and/or counter-transference (Casement 1985). It feels different when we are sitting in separate locations rather than together. This effect of distance is also reinforced because the kinaesthetic connection is being modified or filtered by the technology. The supervisee is less likely to engage in strong emotional reactions or expect the supervisor to take over the problem. Instead the supervisee is more likely to stay grounded, continue thinking and talking even when experiencing emotive insights, and take responsibility for their own input to the supervision process – and to the piece of work being supervised. The supervisor is less likely to feel drawn into rescuing (or persecuting or being victimized by) (Karpman 1968) the supervisee. There will be less of a pull into a parent-child or co-dependency mode.

An alternative explanation of this phenomenon is to consider the context as the provision of an environment in which mindfulness can occur more readily. Passmore and Marianetti (2007) propose that coaching practice is enhanced if the coach uses mindfulness as a preparation tool. This 'practice of being present with the immediate experience of our lives' (Aggs and Bambling 2010) can be facilitated during the e-supervision process and at the same time will enhance the supervision process itself by decreasing the likelihood of the supervisee unwittingly regarding the supervisor as a parent figure.

The other main challenge is that the supervisor may need to change their channel of communication or lead representational system (Bandler and Grinder 1979). Many of us are accustomed to take in information predominantly through sight, with fewer people using auditory as their main channel. However, unless we have a physical impairment, we will process both visual and auditory stimuli – plus of course kinaesthetic, which using simplified neuro-linguistic programming (NLP) theory means anything to do with the rest of our senses, so includes body sensations, physical reactions, emotional and psychological responses. Working electronically means that we will focus much more on what we are hearing, including the words and what they might represent, tone of voice, any hesitations, sighs, laughter, the 'music behind the words', and what is not being said. Working face-to-face may result in us paying a lot more attention to what we are seeing, including noticing facial expressions, skin tones, body language, gestures, body movements, what such observable factors might represent, and what the lack of them might mean.

Hence, if our own lead representational system is auditory we may function within each supervision session just as we do face-to-face. If our lead system is visual, we may need time and practice to pay more attention to our auditory channel; fortunately our neurology is such that we have the spare brain capacity to set up the necessary new neural pathways. In either case, we can still take in information through our kinaesthetic channel, although some of us will find that this is usually stimulated via our visual or auditory channel and may not serve us as well until we get used to the shift required.

## Roles and responsibilities of the supervisor

I mention roles and responsibilities only briefly because they are largely the same with e-supervision as with any other supervision. Whichever definition or description we prefer (e.g. Hess 1980; Proctor 1986; Bachkirova et al. 2005; Hawkins and Smith 2006), the functions remain an amalgam of normative, formative and supportive (Hay 2007 adaptation of Proctor 1986) and the responsibilities include the management of the supervisory dynamics. E-supervision adds to that the need to take into account the potential impact on supervisees who may have some difficulty in relating to the supervisor via technology, or may simply struggle with using technology.

The supervisor may also need to be more cautious about the potential for a values-based impact on supervisees. The ease of communicating with supervisees who exist within very different national cultures requires that we pay particular attention to the sociological content that we maybe incorporating into our focus on professional norms.

## E-supervision in action

In the following examples, names have been changed to preserve confidentiality. Content details are provided to illustrate how e-supervision can function as well as face-to-face supervision in terms of the identification of underlying issues and the analysis of the supervisory process.

> *Lydia operates as a psychotherapist as well as an external coach. Before commencing e-supervision, Lydia had attended a few transactional analysis (TA) training sessions run in her country; we had met on the two occasions that I have been leading these workshops and I had given her face-to-face supervision in a group setting. The stated aim for e-supervision was Lydia's ongoing professional development as a coach; we agreed that she would identify specific issues for each session and I would be responsible for monitoring to alert her to any themes that became apparent. Because Lydia was intending to obtain formal qualifications in TA, we also clarified that there was a multi-cornered contract that included the European TA Association. In other words, as a teaching member of that association I would have a responsibility for monitoring her ethical practice of TA.*
>
> *During sessions, we have to date applied several TA concepts to increase Lydia's awareness of the client's own dynamics and context, as well as checking for possible parallel processes (Searles 1955). In line with Hawkins and Shohet's (2000) seven-eyed model, we have also reviewed our own dynamics within the sessions and the different cultures within which we operate (Hay 2007). What emerged more gradually was a theme of confusion of roles. Lydia felt strongly that she wanted a warm, close relationship with clients but this appeared to manifest as a blurring of the boundaries between coaching and therapy. Instead of talking about the impact of childhood experiences on the client's current behavioural skills, and focusing on how to develop such skills, Lydia was feeling overwhelmed when the client began sharing intimate information about current personal relationships.*
>
> *As this theme emerged, I realized that it paralleled our own process in that we had not contacted clearly enough about whether I was providing coaching or supervision; it was also resonating with my own alternative persona as a psychotherapist. I was able to adopt a relational supervisory style (Fowlie 2010) in order to bring this to Lydia's awareness. This led to much clearer contracting and a shared understanding of the differences between coaching, supervision and therapy. It also meant that supervision content was extended to include the opportunity for Lydia to review the overall balance of her coaching and therapy services and how these met her own needs for relationship – and the latter was taken for discussion within therapy.*
>
> *Alex provides a simpler example. Alex was operating as an internal coach in a country where coaching has only fairly recently been introduced. As with Lydia, our*

*contract was focused on professional development as a coach. Although this was a simple two-party contract because Alex paid for his own supervision, it soon became clear that the employment context was significant because Alex was attempting to coach his own subordinates without any awareness of the implications of the organizational culture and hierarchy. This required more of a cognitive supervisory style as I prompted Alex to recognize that the organization had very autocratic senior management which had been the norm in the country generally until recent years, so his subordinate junior managers were wise to be reluctant to adopt the more democratic style that Alex [now] preferred. I also encouraged Alex to review how the existing contracts of employment meant that he was creating a double-bind in that they could not please both Alex and senior management – and the latter held the power over their appraisals and salaries.*

Lydia and Alex both spoke good English but I often work with coaches using interpreters. The interpreter may be in the room with the coach but often they are somewhere else and we use a conferencing connection. A more complex example concerns a group of coaches who come together into two groups, with an interpreter in a third location. We schedule the time allocated to each person; each has their supervision slot in turn whilst the others listen in. The interpreter translates for me what the supervisee says and for the group what I say. Just as when working face-to-face, it is sometimes necessary for the interpreter to remind one of us to pause whilst translation is being done.

Supervision in these circumstances is often better managed by supervisees than when face-to-face because they are less inclined to exhibit involuntary verbal reactions and their physical reactions cannot be seen by the supervisee currently working. After each supervision slot has finished, we have a process review during which participants can comment on or ask questions about the way I did the supervision. This is also the opportunity for them to share any of their own reactions and consider whether these might be transferential, and if so what further action they might need to take.

A final example to show the range of options is of a trainee supervisor in one country supervising a coach colleague in another country whilst I am in a third country. So three national cultures and legal contexts, three varied experiences of coaching and coaching contexts, three national associations as well as three regional associations (Europe, Pacific, North America) – and a fantastic opportunity for each of us to experience what it means to be part of a global coaching profession.

## Evaluation of the approach

An Internet search at the end of 2010 for e-supervision research provided references only to studies related to helping professions other than coaching, such as nursing and psychotherapy. This is clearly an area for future attention. In the meantime, we have case studies such as that in this chapter and those collated by Clutterbuck and Hussain (2010). A review of the growth of e-counselling by Finn and Barak (2010) also seems relevant due to the similarities between counselling and coaching. Finn and Barak quote others to show how various psychotherapeutic approaches are being used; we can cautiously extrapolate this to support the notion that e-supervision can do the same. The authors also reference research studies that demonstrate successful establishment of online therapeutic relationships and alliances, including consumer satisfaction results at the same level as for face-to-face counselling. Again, we can cautiously expect that this would apply to e-supervision relationships. Finally, Finn and Barak's own study surveyed e-counsellors and found an overall attitude of satisfaction with the effectiveness of e-practice: another possibly relevant finding although this could of course have reflected the fact that their respondents were those who chose to opt into their survey.

For those who have doubts about the 'virtual reality' nature of e-supervision, Goffman's (1974) material on frames and presence can aid understanding of the process. Goffman proposes that we employ frames or schemata of interpretation that are socially shared and culture specific. Even coaches and supervisors who are unfamiliar with Internet communications will already have frames about telephone interaction and these will include the 'real' presence of the parties involved even though they are in different locations. The key is to add our frames of reference about supervision to the mix so that we become engrossed in the supervisory process and take for granted the technology and software that are allowing us to connect. When technical problems interrupt that connection, we will be forced to shift to frames about the connection process and may need time to get our focus back onto supervision once we are re-connected. Effective use of e-supervision may, therefore, depend on the flexibility of our frame-making.

## Learning more

If you are already undertaking e-supervision, as supervisor or supervisee, hopefully the above will have stimulated new thoughts for you. If you have not yet engaged in this process, I hope this chapter will have gone some way towards reassuring you and stimulating you to explore your options. The technology becomes easier to use by the day and the opportunities are there to engage in professional development activity with colleagues you would be unable to meet face-to-face. You too can become part of a worldwide community that has the capacity to raise professional standards whilst incorporating the benefits of international diversity.

In the same way that we have not learned coaching by reading books, there is no substitute for practice. If you prefer to do your learning before engaging in e-supervision itself, there are plenty of options for social networking with friends and colleagues until you have become familiar with the technology. However, provided one of you is comfortable with e-contact, I suggest that it will not matter whether this is the supervisor or the supervisee. Supervision is a process between colleagues; although it is often taken for granted that the supervisor is more experienced at coaching than the supervisee, there is no real need for the supervisor to be the expert in all spheres of the relationship. Just as a supervisee might make the arrangements for a meeting room, they can also handle the technological arrangements if necessary.

As background reading, I recommend *Groundswell* by Li and Bernoff, as referenced above. Although some of their material, such as when they write about how to grow your business, may seem unrelated to those of us who are coaches and supervisors rather than business people, Li and Bernoff provide a very clear explanation of how the Internet and related processes are operating. Social technology has been described as an unstoppable force and we need to understand it and how it will be impacting on our profession as it spreads and develops.

Another useful text is *Virtual Coach, Virtual Mentor*, edited by David Clutterbuck and Zulfi Hussain and also referenced above. This book provides a wide variety of perspectives on using electronic media to enrich coaching and mentoring, including both organizational and individual case studies. Although not directly related to e-supervision, there are two chapters on this alongside much else that will stimulate your thinking based on the experiences of others.

# References

Aggs, C. and Bambling, M. (2010) Teaching mindfulness to psychotherapists in clinical practice: the Mindful Therapy Programme, *Counselling and Psychotherapy Research*, 10(4): 278–86.

Bachkirova, T., Stevens, P. and Willis, P. (2005) *Coaching Supervision*. Oxford: Oxford Brookes Coaching and Mentoring Society.

Bacigalupe, G. (2010) Supervision 2.0: e-supervision a decade later, *Supervision Bulletin, Family Therapy Magazine*, 9(1), January/February. http://socialtechnologiesresearch.com/2010/02/04/supervision-2-0-e-supervision-a-decade-later-by-bacigalupe/ (accessed 1 January 2011).

Bandler, R. and Grinder, J. (1979) *Frogs into Princes*. Moab, UT: Real People Press.

Berne, E. (1964) *Games People Play*. New York: Grove Press.

Casement, P.J. (1985) *Learning from the Patient*. New York: The Guilford Press.

Clutterbuck, D. and Hussain, Z. (eds) (2010) *Virtual Coach, Virtual Mentor*. Charlotte, NC: Information Age Publishing.

Finn, J. and Barak, A. (2010) A descriptive study of e-counsellor attitudes, ethics, and practice, *Counselling and Psychotherapy Research*, 10(4): 268–77.

Fowlie, H. (2010) *Philosophy of Relational Supervision*. http://www.relationalta.com/Resources/resources.php (accessed 31 December 2010).

Goffman, E. (1974) *Frame Analysis: An Essay on the Organization of Experience*. New York: Harper Row.

Hawkins, P. and Shohet, R. (2000) *Supervision in the Helping Professions*, 2nd edn. Buckingham: Open University Press.

Hawkins, P. and Smith, N. (2006) *Coaching, Mentoring and Organizational Consultancy: Supervision and Development.* Maidenhead: Open University Press.

Hay, J. (2007) *Reflective Practice and Supervision for Coaches.* Maidenhead: Open University Press.

Hess, A.K. (1980) *Psychotherapy Supervision: Theory, Research and Practice.* New York: Wiley.

Karpman, S. (1968) Fairy tales and script drama analysis, *Transactional Analysis Bulletin*, 7: 39–43.

Li, C. and Bernoff, J. (2008) *Groundswell: Winning in a World Transformed by Social Technologies.* Boston, MA: Harvard Business Press.

Passmore, J. and Marianetti, O. (2007) The role of mindfulness in coaching, *The Coaching Psychologist*, 3(3): 131–7.

Proctor, B. (1986) Supervision: a co-operative exercise in accountability, in A. Marken and M. Payne (eds) *Enabling and Ensuring: Supervision in Practice.* Leicester: National Youth Bureau/Council for Education and Training in Youth and Community Work.

Searles, H.F. (1955) The informational value of the supervisor's emotional experiences, *Psychiatry*, 18: 135–46.

Skype (2010) Quotation cited from http://about.skype.com/ (downloaded 6 December 2010).

# Part IV

# Practical case studies in supervision

# 20  Mentoring supervision in the NHS

*Rebecca Viney and Denise Harris*

## Introduction and context

The National Health Service (NHS) is in a constant state of change, with new government policies, reorganizations and reduction in NHS funding making it a challenging environment in which to work (Steven et al. 2008). Coaching and mentoring can have a significant impact on staff members' capacity to function in this environment. Support of this nature is relatively new in the NHS, although development of coaching and coaching supervision is increasingly seen as a priority by the Department of Health. This is reflected in ongoing funding for coaching development from the NHS National Leadership Council and the emphasis on the importance of Clinical Leadership (National Leadership Council 2010).

For all doctors there have been some particular career challenges. In recent years they have faced uncertainty in their career structure following the introduction of Modernising Medical Careers (MMC), the need to prepare for revalidation (Abbasi 2008) and the reform of the NHS (DH 2010a). Furthermore, the structure of medics' training has changed, with trainees feeling less supported as they are in more fluid teams with no clear support structures (Temple 2010: vii and 38). In response to this, the London Deanery, which is responsible for development and training for postgraduate doctors and dentists, launched a Mentoring Service in May 2008 to support doctors and dentists working in London.

The importance of this support has since been highlighted by specific recommendations regarding the use of mentoring for doctors. Sir John Temple identified that 'Newly appointed consultants require mentoring and support' and that 'Mentoring and support for trainees must be improved' (Temple 2010: vii and 38). The Department of Health also specifically identified Mentoring as an important aspect of support for doctors, in regard to both developing women doctors and in protecting the health of doctors (Deech 2009; DH 2010b).

This chapter will examine the development of supervision for the mentors in the London Deanery service and discuss the challenges that presented.

## London Deanery Coaching and Mentoring Service

Funding for mentoring through the London Deanery was provided for doctors and dentists in transition. This referred to those managing change in their role, speciality, position, health or place of work.

A network of trained mentors was developed. All the mentors were doctors or dentists and had an educational responsibility. The Deanery undertook to train, assess and support the mentors, individually match mentee to mentor, and fund mentoring for those eligible. The Deanery also committed to provide mentoring for other London doctors who did not fall into the funded groups but were able to access funding from their Primary or Secondary Care Trust or to self fund.

Until recently, the term 'mentoring' has been used in preference to 'coaching' in medical and dental circles, and often mentoring has been perceived as a remedial intervention. There is however a significant overlap in the skills and principles underlying both activities (Connor and Pokora 2007: 6; Viney and McKimm 2010) and the European Mentoring and Coaching Council have recommended that the term 'coaching/mentoring' be used. Therefore in early 2010 the Mentoring Service was renamed the 'Coaching and Mentoring Service' to reflect this and to recognize that the skills the mentors learned were coaching skills.

The London Deanery Coaching and Mentoring Service was set up and managed by a GP educationalist. It is unusual in that all the mentors are doctors or dentists and in a teaching role. The rationale for this was based on the recognition that in addition to supporting the mentees, the mentors would be able to utilize the skills in their educational and clinical roles. Mentoring would support development of clinical and management leadership for the mentors and could be used with their students and teams. The skills could also be used to help patients become more empowered to manage their own health.

Recruitment of mentors aimed to include representatives from each speciality and from all primary and secondary care trusts in London. This supported the process of embedding a culture of coaching and mentoring throughout the NHS in London.

## Mentor supervision and development

In planning and setting up the service, the London Deanery sought expert advice from a number of existing and successful medical and dental schemes in order to model best practice. In addition, the importance of providing supervision and continuing professional development was highlighted by Foster-Turner (2006) as essential for good practice. Therefore, as well as funding the coaching training and mentoring time, it was necessary for the Deanery to organize and fund the mentors' ongoing professional development and supervision.

Development opportunities included half day 'skills boosters' events for small groups of mentors who set the agenda by identifying issues from practice. Mentors had access to 'mentor forums' providing them with new skills and techniques. This provided opportunities to update and learn new skills, to network and receive supervision on their practice. They were also offered the opportunity to undertake a certificate or diploma in Coaching and Mentoring for Leadership with the Institute of Learning Management (ILM), which included access to a peer mentor and a personal supervisor who provided telephone supervision. The mentors responded to the opportunity for further development and the workshops were well attended.

When determining the most effective method of providing supervision, a number of factors were considered. The mentors represented a significant variety of cultural and learning styles and some groups of doctors were unfamiliar with the concept of supervision. They needed to engage with and make suggestions regarding supervision in order that it was seen as accessible and that they 'owned' it. They were consulted and their feedback and comments influenced the development and structure of the supervision that was offered. This helped to ensure that the mentors remained engaged and saw it as something they should prioritize, even when they had other pressures on their time or did not feel the need to attend.

The mentors who coached 'doctors in difficulty' had access to supervision and support by telephone provided by Mednet, a confidential self-referral service for doctors and dentists experiencing emotional difficulties. However, for the majority of the mentors group supervision was identified as the preferred model. This decision was influenced by the experience of an existing mentoring supervision scheme that had used an action learning set model for supervision. In addition, by offering supervision in groups the sessions could be combined with development of the community of mentors within the London Deanery.

The outcomes that were identified for the supervision included providing support for the new mentors, facilitating reflection, providing opportunity for action learning and providing feedback to the Deanery about the service.

## Supervision case description

The organization of the supervision groups evolved and changed in response to the mentors developing understanding of what they needed from supervision. This was divided into three phases.

In the first phase the Tavistock clinic, an existing provider of supervision training for doctors and dentists, facilitated group supervision at a central location in the evening. The four supervision groups were run by psychotherapist facilitators every eight to ten weeks using the psychodynamic model. Mentors were allocated to the groups by geographical area. In response to requests from mentors an additional group was run in the afternoon. However, the attendance was patchy and this group did not continue.

The second phase took place after about six months in response to the mentors' request to meet nearer their homes. The Tavistock Clinic continued to facilitate the two groups in North London. Mentors from the Maudsley Hospital in South London facilitated the two groups in South London with support from a lay professional coach and a highly skilled medical director.

During this phase NHS London offered telephone supervision, although due to funding constraints they were only able to support six of the mentors at that time. Few mentors accessed this, possibly due to the telephone supervision already available for those who were undertaking the ILM post graduate certificate. In addition, most mentors were already established in supervision groups and may not have seen themselves as needing access to a limited resource.

The Mentoring Lead continued to review the supervision regularly, meeting with the facilitators and taking feedback from the mentors. After 18 months of the second phase a major review of the format was undertaken. The mentors were invited to attend a central supervision evening. For the first hour the groups were allocated a facilitator, not their usual supervisor, who invited them to identify what they had found most useful, what went well and what went less well. As expected, there was a great variety of responses and a number of points emerged. There was mixed success for the supervision groups that were meeting in the localities. The numbers attending two of the groups were very small and the group membership changed from month to month; this meant that they struggled to form bonded learning groups. Most mentors in these groups felt that they had insufficient mentees to warrant an evening away from their families after a day's work. In addition, booking a suitable venue to meet was a challenge.

The other two groups were more successful. They benefited from good group bonding and the opportunity to try out skills in a safe environment, as well as getting feedback on the use of those skills. One of these groups had a facilitator who although not a mentor was a very experienced supervisor and psychotherapist. They made use of their supervision skills and the expertise within the group to ensure the participants found the sessions beneficial. Most of the group members found the psychodynamic approach helpful and this group had the most consistent attendance. However, the approach did not suit everyone, and it was recognized that trying different models of supervision in the groups should be considered: for example the seven-eyed model (Hawkins and Shohet 2007). In addition, at the next meeting the 'fish bowl' technique was used to explore the thinking behind supervision and to consider further the future provision of supervision. This was conducted with the supervisors on the inside and the mentors on the outside of the 'bowl'.

In response to the evaluation, the third phase included a number of elements. It was agreed to meet centrally again, to try out different models of supervision and ways of organizing the supervision groups, new techniques and to look at competencies. The mentors used the time to network; share news; disseminate mentoring service information; run a coaching and mentoring book club; and review a different area of the EMCC and ICF competency framework at each meeting.

## Learning from the experience

Within two and a half years the London Deanery Coaching and Mentoring Service had grown to include over 86 mentors, supporting more than 750 mentee applications. It is possible that one of the reasons for this was that it was run by and for a specific staff group. A report on the first two years of the service included the following comments from mentees: 'It's the truthful objectivity which stuns me – and a sense that solutions often lie within the so-called problem'; 'Mentoring has refreshed the aims of my medical career' (Viney and Paice 2010: 36–7).

Providing development and supervision for the mentors, however, has presented some challenges and learning points.

It was important to offer a variety of options of both modes and models of supervision. It has also been important to continually review and amend what is on offer. This has helped the organizers to modify the supervision to meet the variety of needs represented by the mentors. It has also provided opportunities for the support to change in response to the developing understanding of mentoring and supervision by the mentors.

Mentors have responded well to development opportunities and are enthusiastic about attending events that offer them training in new skills. However, few medical specialities have previous experience of supervision, and this has presented some challenges when endeavouring to provide effective and accessible supervision opportunities. Some mentors have a negative perception of supervision; they view it as implying they are not doing their mentoring well enough and that they need to improve. The cultural context also has an impact on their use and perception of supervision. Medical and dental staff are not used to admitting to or examining their weaknesses in a public arena or group. They are used to being the expert who has to know the answer.

In addition to these barriers, understanding how to use supervision time has been challenging. Feedback provided by the supervisors indicated that the mentors continue to learn how to use supervision and what it is for. Coaching supervision is an unfamiliar method of learning for them and they need expert support to use it effectively. The nature of medical and dental interventions means that the mentors can find it difficult to use the time appropriately:

> The environment in which coaches and mentors are working with doctors and dentists is very active, 'doing' and evidence based. Time out for reflection (especially where this uses whole system reflexivity as the approach) may seem a bit like 'doing nothing' and there is a challenge around making time for supervised reflexivity in a coaching setting.
>
> (Supervisor A)

For doctors and dentists, remaining focused on the coaching process and skills during supervision is a challenge. There has been a tendency to focus on the problem of the client rather than helping the mentor (coach) to develop their skills and expertise. They can fall into the trap of talking about 'cases', as this is how they have learned and developed clinical expertise during their training and medical career. In addition, as clinicians they are inclined to look at the deficit model and want to identify solutions for their clients. They can forget that the client (mentee) is not ill or broken and therefore has potential to solve their own problems and dilemmas and to be resourceful: *'they may be over focused on problem solving* [rather than] *listening and helping the mentee work out their own solutions'* (Supervisor B); *'Letting go of the notion of needing to be "the expert" is an ongoing challenge in a professional context where this is normally a "given"'* (Supervisor C).

Another challenge that emerged was the risk of breaching confidentiality when discussing 'cases'. The community of medical staff in London is relatively small and there is a risk of people being recognized. This also means that the group may be more inclined to problem-solve and advise the mentor rather than remaining focused on the coaching process. The facilitators need to be aware of this and to make use of different models of supervision to help ensure the process is effective. An additional benefit of this is that the mentors will feel safer to explore and develop their coaching and more able to be open about their learning needs with regard to developing coaching skills.

For the majority of the mentors the skills of coaching and mentoring are new. The issues that have been brought to supervision therefore reflect the developmental aspect of the service. Doctors are used to knowing what the right answer is, and struggle with mentoring where there is no need for correct answers. This is understandable in light of the active and evidence-based nature of the medical model identified above. They have also brought concerns around their competence as mentors and the effectiveness of their mentoring skills. Other issues have been around clarity of the similarities and differences between mentoring, coaching, supervision and clinical interventions.

It is possible that access to telephone supervision would have ensured that all mentors made use of supervision from the beginning of the service. However, this was not considered when the service was set up in 2008 as it was seen as a luxury. If a similar service were to start now we would recommend a combination of telephone supervision with forums for mentors to network and develop skills. Individual supervision would also help to address the difficulty of retaining client confidentiality.

The emphasis on providing high quality development and supervision for the London Deanery mentors has been central to the service from the beginning. However, the professionalization of coaching is accelerating and the development of different forms of supervision specifically for coaching has grown exponentially over the past three years. It is essential therefore that the Deanery continue to review the format and organization of supervision at regular intervals. This should be done in partnership with the facilitators of the supervision and in response to feedback from the mentors. In addition other information including Foster-Turner's (2006) paper and the NHS Institute Coaching Framework will influence the ongoing development of the provision of supervision.

# References

Abbasi, K. (2008). Mentoring and the meaning of soul, *Journal of the Royal Society of Medicine*, 101(11): 523.

Connor, M. and Pokora, J. (2007) *Coaching and Mentoring at Work: Developing Effective Practice*. Maidenhead: Open University Press.

Deech, R. (2009) *Women Doctors: Making a Difference*. London: Department of Health.

DH (Department of Health) (2010a) *Equity and Excellence: Liberating the NHS*. London: Department of Health.

DH (Department of Health) (2010b) *Invisible Patients, Report of the Working Group on the Health of Health Professionals*. London: Department of Health.

Foster-Turner, J. (2006) *Coaching and Mentoring in Health and Social Care*. Oxford: Radcliffe.

Hawkins, P. and Shohet, R. (2007) *Supervision in the Helping Professions*. Maidenhead: Open University Press.

National Leadership Council (2010) *Clinical Leadership Interim Report*. London: National Leadership Council.

Steven, A., Oxley, J. and Fleming, W.G. (2008) Mentoring for NHS doctors: perceived benefits across the personal-professional interface, *Journal of the Royal Society of Medicine*, 101(11): 552–7.

Temple, J. (2010) *Time for Training: A Review of the Impact of the European Working Time Directive on the Quality of Training*. London: Medical Education England.

Viney, R. and McKimm, J. (2010) Clinical teaching made easy, *British Journal of Hospital Medicine*, 71(2): 107–9.

Viney, R. and Paice, E. (2010) *The First Five Hundred: A Report on London Deanery Coaching and Mentoring Service 2008–2010*. London: London Deanery.

# 21 Mentoring supervision with the Danish Association of Lawyers and Economists

*Else Iversen*

## Introduction

The Danish Association of Lawyers and Economists (Djoef) is a trade union whose membership is made up of graduates mostly from social sciences. In 2010 the membership was 70,000, including some 19,000 student members. For many readers it will be a new thought that a trade union offers mentoring to its membership. Djoef has done so since 2002.

Djoef considers professional and personal development as equally important for development of labour market rights and increase of salary. Mentoring is in our perception an efficient tool for professional as well as personal development for both mentors and mentees and that is why it has been offered to our managerial and leadership members. In 2010 our leadership mentoring programme had about 175 mentors, who had the capacity to take on about 220 mentees.

To become a mentor in our leadership programme one must have considerable experience as a high level manager/leader in either the public or private sectors. We offer a short joint training session for new mentors and mentees. The programme is assessed regularly by our research department, and the matching is done by trained staff, who have solid knowledge of our membership and their labour market. The purpose of these activities is to continuously develop the programme and to do our best to make every pairing a successful one.

## The background for and the purpose of the initiative of supervision

To ensure a further growth of the programme hand in hand with maintaining the quality of it, in 2008 we decided to offer supervision to our mentors. At that time, our mentoring programme had been running for five years, and in order to support the further development of the mentors we took the initiative to offer supervision. The inspiration to offer supervision came from our participation in the EMCC Conference in Stockholm 2007 and what was discussed there on how to ensure that the quality of mentoring when the number of participants was increasing year on year. In order to retain mentors and to create a higher awareness of their task and their own personal development through supervision, we decided to set up a pilot project offering supervision to a small group of ten mentors.

## The supervisors

The set-up for the pilot project was an internal joint venture between the mentoring team handling the matching and training of mentors and a business psychologist from our career centre. We saw it as important that the supervisor knew the membership and their challenges, but had no affiliation with the mentoring programme. We were well aware that strict confidentiality in the conversations between mentor and supervisor was of utmost importance.

Having a member of staff who could provide professional supervision as a business psychologist allowed us to initiate this service. We were confident that the supervision was work oriented. What we had in mind for setting up supervision was a kind of mentor's mentor. We wanted to make a setting and a space in time that invited the mentor to reflect on the role and task he performed as mentor and at the same time invite him to reflect on that as a part of his personal and professional development. When our psychologist left Djoef in the spring of 2010, her task was taken over by a colleague, who is not a psychologist, but is a very experienced coach.

We had no specific topics in mind that we thought the mentors would want to put on the agenda. The initiative was created as a means to strengthen the quality of conversations between mentors and mentees. This is not to say we had concerns or doubts about the existing level of quality in the mentoring conversations. It was more an initiative to give our mentors the chance to 'step back metaphorically . . . so that you can take a meta-perspective or broader view of your practice' – to quote Hay (2007: 4).

## The supervisors' approach

Both supervisors in this project describe their approach to supervision as eclectic, relying on methodologies stemming primarily from systemic, narrative, solution-focused coaching, and to some extend from protreptic.[1] The latter has its strength among others in working with values and concept understanding. In the realm of protreptic it means that the supervisor focuses on digging into the mentor's profound understanding of values and how he expresses that in concepts. Therefore it is useful for working on the meta-level of mentoring, as that is what the mentor will be doing when the relationship with the mentee is well established and the level of confidence is sufficiently deep.

Both of them have started their sessions with an approach that is very similar to coaching: agenda setting, agreeing on the time frame, and setting the boundaries.

An issue at least in the first meeting has been to 'establish the room' as something that is not psychological and does not have the purpose of mending something wrong, but to create a reflective space, in which it is possible to create if not symmetry in the relation then as close as you can get to that in such a situation. When they achieve it, the supervisors stress that it provides an opportunity for the session to be an explorative learning process for both.

An approach very central to both supervisors has been to work with changing positions or perspectives – primarily of course the position the mentor takes in relationships with the mentee. Changing perspective during a supervision session is a very intense learning situation for the supervisee, and it can become a model for the mentor to use in their own mentoring sessions. One of the supervisors underlines that in her supervision she has been very explicit in creating transparency between herself and her supervisee in order to show the supervisee what it means to be emotionally present with the supervisee. At its best, it helps the mentor to speak honestly to himself and reach a deeper insight in the barriers he creates for himself. The supervisor also establishes a role model to the mentor to be emotionally present with the mentee.

As in a mentoring session the supervisor at times will go beside the supervisee and at others she will go ahead. She determines when to change by following the supervisee's discourse. Is it consistent and coherent? Is the supervisee sufficiently searching in their dialogue? If so, you can keep going ahead, if not – go beside the supervisee and make her follow you again.

Both supervisors emphasize that they were supervising mentors who are very results-oriented in their daily work. Their impression was that supervisees perceive themselves as development oriented, but in reality of supervisory conversations it appears that development is seen only as instrumental rather than an issue of self-awareness and personal growth. In the supervision sessions, they typically seem to take few chances and are reluctant to show weaknesses. When they do open up, it is the result of very high trust and confidence in the relationship between supervisor and supervisee, and this takes time to create.

## The supervision – what did we do?

At the beginning it was a pilot project that offered supervision to ten mentors – first come, first served. We wanted to give our mentors an opportunity to reflect and develop personal and professional competencies and understand themselves better in their role as mentors and subsequently as managers/leaders. The purpose of individual supervision was to give the mentor an opportunity to reflect upon their practice and challenges, to integrate and develop personal and professional competencies and to create new lines of action.

The offer was announced at the annual meeting for mentors. The aim of that meeting was to support the network between mentors and raise their awareness of the process and how they can stimulate good mentoring conversations. We introduce mentors to their potential mentees and usually invite an expert to give a talk or a short course on a specific topic. In 2009 the expert was Lis Merrick from

Sheffield Hallam University, who talked on supervision in mentoring and who also joined us in a case study on the supervision pilot project. This is described in our learning results further on.

We offer our mentors who choose to be supervised three individual meetings with the supervisor. The agenda and timing of the meetings is set exclusively by the supervisee when meeting the supervisor.

## Results from the sessions

How was the offer received? Despite a population of curious mentors, uptake of supervision was low. Perhaps because, like so many top level executives and managers, they are busy and have difficulty in finding time for their own personal and professional development, only 20 mentors have taken up supervision in two years of the scheme.

Those who were supervised and participated in the survey gave us very interesting feedback. In general the topics they chose to be supervised on were within the following categories:

- the task of being a mentor, rather than an oracle;
- how to use a broad selection of their own experiences in a constructive way with the interests of the mentee in mind;
- how to maintain and develop the joy of being a mentor;
- balance of support and challenge.

These topics show growing awareness of the role and the tasks of the mentor. However, we are not alone in involving in our programmes mentors, who are not completely comfortable with the fact that they are not advisors. We see them and describe them much more as partners in a reflection process, the origin of which is 'owned' by the mentees. This is particularly important since our programmes are focusing on development – the personal development of the mentee. At the same time these conversations suggest that these mentors are on the right track.

When it comes to what the mentors have gained from being supervisees two main themes emerge from the data:

- development of the mentor on a personal (self-awareness) level: 'I've become more aware of myself – it is a step forward in my self development';
- development of the mentor on a practical or process level: 'I have more diverse means and methods to provide a better job in my mentoring'.

### Self-awareness

The self-awareness theme is underlined by the following additional statements in the case study:

'I have become more proactive/motivated.'
'You get better informed about yourself.'
'I was forced to reflect on my practice.'

'It is a method to achieve greater self-insight – a mirror to yourself.'

'I got helpful insight on my managerial problems.'

'Supervision is a process that develops in line with one's own development as a mentor.'

'I saw myself with new eyes.'

'I've become aware how a mentee can give me more good input and thus how the programme can be fantastically useful to me.'

What is important for us as programme managers and developers is that their responses show a deeper self-understanding and development on a personal and professional level as well as mentors. The fact that they reflect on their development as mentors and as individuals and link these two together reinforces our belief that a good mentor is a person with high self-awareness and self-esteem.

## Practical and process level

On the development of the mentor on a practical or process level the quotes from our supervisees show the following results:

Understanding the programme: 'I've gained insight into what the mentoring programme is meant to yield';

Learning not to take mentee's problems on: 'I have learned not to take on my mentee's problems. I'm not there to find the solutions to his/her problems.' 'My role is to guide him/her to find his/her own solutions';

Practical help: 'Help in solving practical problems – finding a practical angle to help the mentee.' 'The knowledge I've gained I have been able to use, e.g. contracting for a certain number of meetings.'

Learning how to manage endings and understanding issues of dependency: 'I've learned to make processes stop, meaning that I've become clearer and wiser how to discontinue them.' 'Before supervision I've found it difficult to end relations with my mentees.' 'It has been difficult not to make my mentees dependent on me.'

Improved boundary setting: 'The knowledge I have gained, I have been able to use ... I made it clear from the beginning that it was a process consisting of a number of meetings and there will be a beginning and the end of the process.'

Keeping 'fresh' as a mentor: 'I tested some new angles on how to vary the programme in order not to get bored with it.'

Two-way learning: 'I've become aware how a mentee can give me good input.'

Development as a mentor: 'Supervision is a process that supports being a mentor.' 'I've got help in becoming more specific.' 'I have become better at bringing myself forward.'

Providing feedback: 'It's a way to receive feedback.'

Important learning for us as programme managers is that the mentors, even if they are experienced in the role, need inspiration and reassurance. We provide training, but not every one participates. And even if they do participate in the training and in our follow-up sessions, this is not a substitute for direct and personal feedback from a one-to-one relationship between supervisee and supervisor. The legitimacy for raising personal issues in that context will never be replaced by a training situation where many mentors participate.

The examples of topics raised here show the level of self-awareness and a readiness among the mentors that is highly rewarding to observe. Development is a relentless predator – and you become bigger when you gain inspiration from others. The more mentors we have who are motivated by using the role to further their own development, the more satisfied the mentees will be, and the better the effects and reputation of our programme.

## Why the reluctance?

Having offered supervision to our mentors for two years now, we of course are pondering the reasons for the reluctance among the rest of our mentors to make use of this offer. We are well aware of the time pressures mentors have, and the fact that devoting time to be mentors is in itself a challenge to their busy schedules. On the other hand, those who have set time aside to take the offer are not necessarily the ones that have the most time. One hypothesis might be that if we can find the right way to communicate about the offer and the development it creates for the supervisee, we might attract more mentors to come forward.

## The next step

We have been considering offering group supervision to our mentors. When we did the case study, we addressed this issue in a focus group interview. The views received were:

- It could be a fast way of getting access to other mentors' experiences.
- It would cover more general themes and problems.
- You would learn a lot from the others.
- It would be more of an exchange of experiences.
- It is a broader forum and would focus on other things also.
- It would be less personal and intense than individual supervision.

So far we have decided not to pursue this. From our experience with working with around 500 mentors, we know that they are busy, competitive people, so group sessions where the group sets the agenda can be very difficult. Their knowledge of each other is limited, and at this time we do not perceive that there is sufficient trust and confidence among them to gain from group supervision.

We have taken another initiative instead. Six times a year we invite the mentors to a 'morning conference' on a topic related to mentoring. Some examples are: good beginnings, good endings (of a mentoring relation); competence feedback;

coaching in mentoring; and use of personal profile analysis in mentoring. Gradually we have passed to the mentors responsibility for suggesting topics. One or two mentors take the floor with a case as an example of how to deal with the topic. It has been quite successful and the attendance has been growing. We believe that is currently a better alternative to group supervision.

Our case study has shown that supervision is something we should continue. Although this case study involves a rather small sample, we are reassured that offering supervision to our members is giving our programme and our mentors valuable assistance in their development. From our experience, we know that we need more than one approach to retain our mentors and assist them in developing their mentoring skills. Our interest as programme managers is, of course, that we can keep using mentoring as a means of connecting our members as they develop as people and professionals. It is our view that good mentoring and good leadership go hand in hand.

We have also learned that using the experience of mentors in supervision is helping us recruit more mentors, through word of mouth. We have learned that our communication to the mentors needs to be frequent and make use of different communication channels.

We have also learned that we at some occasion should extend the offer to more than three sessions. We can rely on the supervisor's judgement, and if they find it beneficial to the supervisee to continue the supervision we will then let her make the decision.

## Note

1   The concept stems from the Greek philosophers. First articulated in ancient Greece in the fourth century, protreptic dialogue is a means of direct exhortation to pursue a just life by addressing core values: the good, the just, the true and the beautiful, and hence involving attitudes such as generosity, decency, honesty and empathy. See for instance Ole Fogh Kirkeby (2010) *The New Protreptic*, CBS Press.

## Reference

Hay, J. (2007) *Reflective Practice and Supervision for Coaches*. Maidenhead: Open University Press.

# 22 'Intervision': a group-based peer-supervision project by EMCC Switzerland

*Christoph Epprecht*

'In dialogue it is necessary that people be able to face their disagreements without confrontation and be willing to explore points of view to which they do not personally subscribe. If they are able to engage in such a dialogue without evasion or anger, they will find that no fixed position is so important that it is worth holding at the expense of destroying the dialogue itself. This tends to give rise to a unity in plurality of the kind we have discussed elsewhere.'

David Bohm (2003: 296)

## Introduction

Intervision is a supervision process involving a group of peers with the same professional focus, who cooperate in a goal-driven process towards finding solutions within a shared structural design. Mutually accountable volunteers give and receive learning and teaching without compensation (Lippmann 2009). Intervision has its origins in a variety of sources, including self-help groups, action learning sets, supervisor development groups (Proctor 2008: 215) and peer supervision (Hawkins and Shohet 2006: 164–8).

Established in 2006, EMCC Switzerland is one of the three major professional coaching and mentoring bodies in the German-speaking part of Switzerland. The EMCC Intervision Project was announced to the membership body in Autumn 2008. About 25 per cent or eleven members of the Swiss membership body registered to start the first Swiss EMCC intervision group with the first session scheduled on 4 November 2008. There were six women and five men, ranging in age from 45 to 68 years, with an average of 50. Eight group members were self-employed coaches; three worked within companies as internal coaches.

This chapter describes the concepts underpinning the intervision process and provides a practical example of it in action.

## Background to the case study

There were several reasons for the Swiss EMCC board to offer the membership body a structure of 'reflective space':

- members' need to review challenging client issues;
- providing a safe place to explore the personal and professional development of the practitioner;
- members wanting to explore issues of professional conduct;
- to enhance the market reputation of EMCC coaches generally;
- to attract new members;
- to differentiate EMCC from other professional bodies.

The pilot project lasted for one year, with six sessions involving six to ten participants. Participation was free for EMCC members; guests were welcome at no charge, but expected to apply for membership. All participants committed to strictest confidentiality. Cases/topics were presented in an anonymous form (e.g. pseudonyms of persons, situations, companies, context). Typically, two cases were presented in a three-hour session.

The objective of each intervision group session was to:

- highlight the case in focus by generating a variety of diverse views and approaches to practical solutions;
- offer the individual presenter or case owner new perspectives on their particular case;
- generate practical options for effective action in the case;
- review effective coaching approaches;
- explore feasible solutions.

The expected outcomes were:

- critical self-assessment of individual coaching styles;
- refined perception of self, mirrored by others through feedback;
- critical reflection of own coaching paradigms;
- strengthening of own professional identity;
- enhancement of professional competence;
- resolving other specific issues coaches bring to the group.

Most of the Swiss EMCC members operate as coaches for senior executives, working primarily on issues of performance and behaviour. So the Swiss EMCC board decided that the intervision would be more effective, if the learning process were facilitated by a board member in the role of facilitator. This would demonstrate the EMCC's authority and commitment to quality assurance in executive coaching (e.g. contracting, evaluating). Another point in favour of facilitation was the fact that our board didn't expect the same colleagues to attend all six sessions. As there was no budget available to appoint a paid supervisor, I was invited by the board to design and deliver an intervision service that would be free to members.

The facilitator's job was to ensure that, despite the changing mix of participants, in all sessions the set rules were strictly followed. This was particularly important if the intervision relationship had to be contracted anew in every session, due to the changing mix of participants. The facilitator (sometimes called a moderator) was an observer of the second order (i.e. they observed both the case owner and the group). There was no expectation that the facilitator could hold an objective perspective on the group process and cases. They would be interpreting the situations as much as the other group members. To induce learning for the case owner and for the group, the moderator was expected to provoke diverse and discrepant perceptions on every presented case.

Intervision contracting was quite similar to 'supervision contracting' as defined by Hawkins (2010: 385–6). The contracting process included:

- practicalities (time, frequency, place);
- boundaries;
- working alliance;
- session format;
- the organizational and professional context – who else the intervision process needs to serve, including the organization that employed the coach, their coaches and their organization;
- the EMCC as the professional body to which the participants belong.

As a general rule we assumed that at least two cases could be worked on each session, giving each member an opportunity to present two cases a year. Given that members were mostly self employed running their own businesses, time slots were limited to working days from 6 to 9 p.m.

Since the purpose of the intervision sessions had a clear orientation towards exploring solutions for the case presenter, the emphasis was on the 'whys, whats and how to dos'. However, where the emotional domain of the coaches became subject to discussion there was still room for an inner halt. This has happened about with every third case. In such moments we always experienced appreciation, respect, thoughtfulness, and consideration for the emotional situation of the case owner by the participants. We can rightly say that in such moments without exception the group's attention spontaneously switched to the underlying emotional experience. On the other hand, we also learned that with more speaking time available the result had not necessarily led to more insight.

The main strands underpinning the concept of intervision, similarly to supervision, were drawn from 'humanistic psychology, psychology of the reflecting subject including the epistemological stance of constructivism' with some relationship to psychoanalysis and transactional analysis, communications theory and systems theory (Lippmann 2009). The structure of the process that the Swiss EMCC intervision scheme adapted had close similarities with 'the five-stage coaching model CLEAR (Contract, Listen, Explore, Action, Review) that can also be applied to the stages of supervision, or coaching the coach' (Hawkins 2010: 385).

## How intervision works

The function of intervision is to look at one's own reality from a distance in new ways. By exchanging different views on a particular case, intervision helps the case owner to be more effective in their *meaning-making* for a particular situation. And it helps the group to experience the effectiveness of joint *sense-making* in pursuit of potential solutions.

Intervision is almost free from pressures of any kind. On the other hand, there is the general expectation, implicitly shared by all, that any problem in any case should have at least one solution. Often, the situations in the presented cases are 'contingent'. There is never 'impossibility' nor is there any 'necessity'.

As in coaching, the intervision process starts with describing a situation: to verbalize the hitherto tacit, making the non-verbal knowledge explicit (Stojnov and Pavlovic 2010). By using words, distinctions can be drawn (Spencer-Brown 2009). By making distinctions, 'difference' may surface. From difference that makes a difference, learning can emerge (Bateson 1979; de Shazer 1991). Asking difficult questions rather than making 'statements' helps the case owner to explore new cognitive territories (Megginson and Clutterbuck 2009).

By using the language of solution-seeking, the pattern of the group process is as follows:

- denote something (verbalize);
- explore/explain its meaning (construct subjective reality);
- assess/evaluate 'meaning' whether it makes sense to others (context);
- re-construct meaning and/or sense (assimilation/accommodation).

For the case owner, intervision is a protected space to expand their own awareness with the respectful support of colleagues. Intervision is a structured group process. At its core are iterative sequences of meaning-making. The decision is made by each individual case owner whether to 'assimilate' or 'accommodate' in response to an unexpected outcome. When a situation is comprehended in words it serves as a springboard into action (Weick et al. 2005: 409).

## An example of intervision in practice

The following is an example of an actual issue brought to the group.

Roger is an executive coach. His client Alan is the new head of an international division. Alan is a shrewd thinker, eloquent speaker, flawlessly fitting his wording with consistent argumentation. In the last coaching session, Alan expressed concern that Fred, one of his reports, doesn't accept him as his new boss. Alan assumes that Fred would just pay lip service to what he expects him to deliver. Moreover, when Alan invited his team to an outside event, Fred made excuses declaring that he was scheduled to attend an important business meeting abroad. Although it was Alan's intention to convene all team members together to discuss his new vision, he could not find a reason not to accept Fred's excuse and had to 'swallow the toad'. This is why Alan is frustrated. Roger asked Alan: 'Does this mean that you failed to convince Fred to call off his trip abroad to take part in your team event? Isn't this avoiding conflict with reports instead of taking the risk to be assertive as a leader?' Alan explained that as the newcomer in the division he does not want to confront but rather to convince his reports. In the case of Fred, this has obviously failed.

Roger's question to the group was, 'How can I support Alan to become more assertive towards Fred'?

While Roger is listening, the group first exchanged some assumptions on Alan and his actual situation. Voiced questions were: 'Before knowing enough details of the new vision, are there fears in the team to lose personal status when giving away too much know-how?' 'Has this been a real team before Alan as new boss came on board?' 'Is there a cultural gap between Alan coming from culture X whereas the team represents culture Z?'

The group came up with questions for Alan who as a leader has to ask himself first in this situation: What has happened? How do I feel as the leader? What do I request from the team? How do I proceed with the team next time?

The group also raised questions on the resources of Roger as a coach:

Is Roger able to challenge Alan in the emotional domain? For example: admit his own vulnerability? Accept that his management style impacts on the performance of others? Not try to shift the blame for poor performance to others? Actively invite critical feedback from the team first, asking for positive feedback second?

Taking notes, Roger summarizes what he has learned from the group's discussion. In the next coaching session he will ask Alan four questions:

- Were Alan's expectations of the team sufficiently clear when he invited the team to the outside event?
- Was Alan's communication of the outside event clear and timely?
- Can Alan agree with Fred on an adequate solution next time with regard to absences before an outside event?
- How will Fred and Alan know that next time the three questions above have been treated accordingly?

## Outcomes of the intervision process

According to Hawkins (2010: 384) supervision has three main functions: D: 'developmental', R: 'resourcing' and Q: 'qualitative'. Participants reported positive outcomes in all three of these areas.

They evaluated the intervision outcomes on a scale from 1 = 'doesn't apply' to 10 = 'fully applies' as follows:

- 'Developmental' (8 to10): differentiating perception of self, strengthening of own professional identity; enhancement of professional competence;

- 'Resourcing' (4 to 7): self-critical analysis of posture including personal coaching style;
- 'Qualitative' (4 to 7): critical reflection of own coaching paradigms.

## Lessons from the pilot

One of the recurrent issues considered by the group was the challenge faced by internal coaches in balancing their roles as both HR manager and internal coach.

The internal coach runs the risk of replicating 'blind spots' in the organization, for example, by implicitly respecting the (mostly invisible and unspoken) 'power horizon' inherent in corporate regulations and norms. As a result, the internal coach may be less able to raise the awareness of internal clients. Widening gaps between what management say they do and what management actually do can cause role conflicts between HR and internal coach. Based on evidence from their personal experience, the group concluded that the challenge for the HR coach is to make explicit both perspectives – as HR and as internal coach.

Other specific learning for the group was that often there are several potential approaches to an effective solution of the client's issues. The varied backgrounds and experience of the participants created greater awareness in the case presenter of this wider choice of effective solutions for the client.

Another lesson was that the client's context (mostly relating to their workplace) increases the complexity of both the coaching process and the intervision process. Issues brought forward by the case owners were often ambiguous. It was helpful to explore systemic patterns to see more clearly where the case owner could likely expect an effective response on their planned intervention with the client.

I was always impressed by the quest for meaning and for sense-making of the 'constructed' insights by the group. Despite time limitations, there was a high degree of emotional involvement in almost every case. The engagement of the group was characterized by listening respectfully, trying to get the full picture, trying to understand the connections, to explore the impacts of the presented situation more deeply, by the joy of making shared discoveries about the 'iceberg' under the surface, and by the empathic and powerful containment in critical emotional moments of colleagues.

## Challenges for the facilitator

My own reflections on the process, in my role as facilitator, include the following:

- Sometimes it is difficult to combine a neutral, independent, respectful and fair attitude with the posture of being authentic and transparent.
- Trying to honour the ideas and contributions of each participant, to acknowledge diversity and balance diverse meanings in the group can sometimes be a challenge.

- There may be a time conflict between the need of the case owner to take away insights and learning and the right of each of the other group members to speak up.
- Equally challenging is disciplining participants to stick to questions that enhance understanding rather than suggest solutions. Apparently, when not in coaching mode, even coaches may slip into giving advice. The art of 'not knowing' also requires a continuous effort when attending to intervision.
- Recognizing and working with my own limitations, especially when struggling with 'moments of disconnect' (Clutterbuck 2008), emerging from critical moments (de Haan 2008) is very important.

## Recommended reading

de Haan, E. (2005) *Learning with Colleagues: An Action Guide for Peer Consultation*. Basingstoke: Palgrave Macmillan.

Hay, J. (2007) *Reflective Practice and Supervision for Coaches*. Maidenhead: McGraw-Hill.

Heilsbronner Modell (2011) https://www.kollegiale-beratung.net/p365354134 _406.html (accessed 14 March 2011).

Lippmann, E. (2009) *Intervision, Kollegiales Coaching Professionell Gestalten*, 2nd edn. Heidelberg: Springer.

## References

Bateson, G. (1979) *Mind and Nature: A Necessary Unity (Advances in Systems Theory, Complexity, and the Human Sciences)*. Cresskill: Hampton Press.

Bohm, D. (2003) *The Essential David Bohm*, ed. Lee Nichols. London: Routledge.

Clutterbuck, D. (2008) *Moments of Disconnect*, Essay: Understanding and interpretation of supervision processes, European Mentoring & Coaching Council, annual conference, Prague, 4 December.

de Haan, E. (2008) *Relational Coaching: Journeys Towards Mastering One-to-one Learning*. Chichester: Wiley & Sons Ltd.

de Shazer, S. (1991) *Putting Difference to Work*. London: Norton and Company.

Hawkins, P. (2010) Coaching supervision, in E. Cox, T. Bachkirova and D. Clutterbuck (eds) *The Complete Handbook of Coaching*. London: Sage.

Hawkins, P. and Shohet, R. (2006) *Supervision in the Helping Professions*, 3rd edn. Maidenhead: Open University Press.

Lippmann, E. (2009) *Intervision, Kollegiales Coaching Professionell Gestalten*, 2nd edn. Heidelberg: Springer.

Megginson, D. and Clutterbuck, D. (2009) *Further Techniques of Coaching and Mentoring*. Oxford: Elsevier Butterworth-Heinemann.

Proctor, B. (2008) *Group Supervision: A Guide to Creative Practice*, 2nd edn. London: Sage.

Spencer-Brown, G. (2009) *Laws of Form*, 5th edn. Leipzig: Bohrmeier Verlag.

Stojnov, S. and Pavlovic, J. (2010) An invitiation to personal construct coaching, *International Coaching Psychology Review*, 5(2): 129–39.

Weick, K.E., Sutcliffe, K. and Obstfeld, D. (2005) Organizing and the process of sensemaking, *Organization Science*, 16(4): 409–21.

# 23 Supervising maternity coaches

*Jennifer Liston-Smith*

## Introduction

This case study looks at my work as supervisor of corporate maternity coaching and the models, processes, tensions and discoveries applied and brought to light through this. It covers supervising a team of external coaches serving client organizations (with elements of a dual role for me as supervisor); and providing supervision and development to internal coaches within client organizations.

Maternity coaching works with a specific transition or series of transitions in the life of a working woman going on maternity leave, giving birth and returning to work. The sponsoring employers' aims include:

- improving return rates from maternity leave;
- smoothing handover and return to the benefit of coachee, colleagues and clients;
- encouraging good communication;
- enhancing confidence and sense of support;
- retaining talented employees through the parent transition.

Assuming focused support will enhance loyalty and performance in the coachee (e.g. Bussell 2008), clients and coaches regarded the coaching as a necessary (though not sufficient) element in female talent retention and in increasing female representation in senior leadership roles (e.g. Gratton et al. 2007). They saw supervision as an element of coaching best practice.

The coaching used Managing Maternity's *Maternity Project*™ *Questionnaire and Model* (Liston-Smith 2009b, 2010a) and, later, My Family Care's *Maternity Coaching Framework* (Liston-Smith 2010b). Both tools suggest a model of maternity coaching which encourages the coachee to explore the aspirations and needs of self and other stakeholders; at work and home. The implications of adopting a central model will be explored in relation to supervision.

## Organizational context

All the maternity coaching considered here took place in the UK offices of global law, accountancy and investment banking firms between 2005 and 2010. Commissioning clients were highly selective in appointing a provider, seeking best practice and learning from what works in other organizations. They turned to me as a recognized practitioner and supervisor in a relatively new field.

Clients were reluctant to specify behavioural objectives for coaching or measure progress on a developmental trajectory as might be expected in performance coaching or leadership development. Clients and coaches favoured an empathic, humanistic approach combined with a research-informed model of maternity coaching. They were not seeking counselling or open-ended, person-centred support and emphasized planning the individual's return to work, and holding win-win conversations with managers.

Still, the coaching addresses highly personal matters within demanding corporate environments. All parties were aware from the outset that maternity coaching was somewhat counter-culture in the sense of opening up and encouraging conversations in the workplace that were not otherwise happening and also attempting to 'buck the trend' on the maternity transition as a moment when some women may otherwise leave the organization or stall in their career progression.

## Supervision case context

Since an overall coaching framework and research base was offered, there was a delicate line between training and supervision, particularly for internal coaches. However, though the framework was fixed, the coaching agenda and intervention style were fluid and coaches adopted a broad range of approaches. Their backgrounds included cognitive-behavioural coaching, positive psychology, gestalt, psychodynamic, and co-active coaching (Whitworth et al. 1998). The coaches were practitioners of several years' experience and almost without exception were women or parents; mostly both.

For internal coaches, the format involved group supervision reviewing case material in the light of models, research knowledge and experience, with provision for occasional one-to-one supervision. Group supervision was favoured partly on cost considerations but largely so that organizational learning could be shared confidentially. Objectives included enhanced confidence, best practice knowledge and relevant skills in the coaches.

There was mutual learning from appreciating and comparing the impact of different approaches and thereby an important balance between mentoring on the part of the supervisor and purely facilitating, enabling and supporting. Starting with a specific case, discussions generally became 40 to 50 per cent focused on coach development, spurred by issues within the case in question.

For external coaches there was a regular mix of project team (those engaged with a specific client) and wider team (across clients) supervision along with one-to-one sessions. Group supervision was usually by telephone due to geographical spread of coaches, with approximately twice-yearly face-to-face team supervision. Coaches were invited to complete forms to reflect immediately on coaching sessions and to prepare for supervision. The team agreed that outcomes should include that coaches feel confident, resourceful and empowered, and that supervision has performed the three functions described in the next paragraph.

We explicitly adopted a commitment to supervision being 'formative, restorative and normative' (Proctor 1988). Of the different versions of these three functions identified by Hawkins and Smith (2006: 151), Proctor's counselling-derived nomenclature was chosen: its memorability made it easier to carry out quick checks on progress. We echoed Hawkins and Smith's view that the processes of coaching supervision are probably best stated as developmental, resourcing and qualitative, though we recognized that the sense of responsibility that can come with maternity coaching does speak to the supportive 'restorative' benefit of supervision, which may not be fully captured in the idea of resourcing, since coaches may view 'resourcing' as adding tools to their repertoire.

We used the seven-eyed model (Hawkins and Smith 2006) as a framework with which we all became familiar. So coaches would say 'Well of course, at mode 4, this is triggering all kinds of reactions in me'. In modes 4, 5 and 6 and in the overarching context of mode 7, we would grapple with:

1   my own vested interest as a supervisor who was also a director of the consultancy being engaged by the client to deliver results (examined further under Challenges, below);
2   whether the impartiality of our coaching is affected by our wishes not only for the coachee but also for their family and for corporate social responsibility ideals beyond talent retention;
3   the fact that these interventions were taking place when employers such as investment banks were under intense public scrutiny through the global financial crisis, from 2007. Like witnesses in a court of law, coaches were influenced consciously or otherwise, by media coverage.

Setting boundaries on our areas of influence, we tended to return to a balance expressed as 'supervision is there to serve not only the profession, but also the developmental needs of the coach/supervisee, the individual coachees that the coach is coaching, and the client organizations that employ the coach' (Hawkins 2010: 384).

## Supervision case description

We made a group contract covering how we would listen to each other, be bold and honest and hold confidentiality in the spirit of the various codes of ethics the different coaches adhered to.

The maternity coaching models (above) were used in supervision to offer guidance for a way of working (normative/formative – transfer of best practice); a checklist for reviewing cases (normative/restorative); and suggesting a range of possible interventions (mode 2 of the seven-eyed model, above).

In group supervision, both for external and internal coaches, one or two coaches would bring a case and share in detail their observations particularly of the coachee at mode 1, the relationship they had formed with the coachee at mode 3 and their own reactions and responses at mode 4.

Part of our group contract involved an intention not to dive in with an alternative approach or handy tool (mode 2), but that we would hold back sufficiently to see and understand the wider system. Then when we arrived at mode 2, we found real value in cross-fertilization.

Sometimes a coach presented a case to me as supervisor, with others observing then joining a wider discussion; sometimes one or two other coaches would engage with the presenting coach from the start. Occasionally, I prepared a fictionalized case study as a less emotive, yet quite telling, way of revealing the different viewpoints created by coaches' differing backgrounds. We sometimes used a process called intervision (see Chapter 22), where several peers offer observations one after another following a coach's initial exposition. Having heard them all, the coach can consider which offers the most fruitful way forward. This requires a presenting coach to feel quite robust and adventurous.

A condensed transcript follows with six coaches considering a common challenge: supporting coachees to communicate their needs and aspirations to their managers.

**Coach A:** [having filled out detail on how the coachee presented at mode 1] I'm so frustrated with this one and feel a bit useless about *what* to offer. X's manager clearly would rather she just left quietly and didn't come back. What's the point of coaching her to communicate effectively with him when he won't even set a meeting to discuss her working pattern?'

**Coach B:** It sounds as though it's quite challenging for you personally, and frustrating [offering empathy, expressing the person-centred core of our group contract]. Do you want to say more about how you're experiencing that because you look more tense in the shoulders than I've seen you before? (mode 4)

**Coach C:** Yes, we mostly find this area of addressing the unwilling manager challenging I guess, and we can only work with the one person who's in the room being coached, or at least we can only work directly through their bit of the system anyway. One of the things I find is we need to notice if we're getting drawn into a drama triangle [Karpman 1968], rescuing the poor coachee from her bad manager! (mode 3)

**Coach D:** For sure, yes, it's frustrating and y'know you've got a bit of a monkey on your back there. Maybe not be so hard on yourself, eh? When you sit there in front of your coachee, what are the automatic negative thoughts going through your head? Whatever core beliefs are you triggering in yourself to end up telling yourself you're useless? [e.g. Ellis et al. 1997] (mode 4)

**Coach E:** Have you tried Perceptual Positions [e.g. Bostic St. Claire and Grinder 2001]? You consider a situation from the perspective of yourself (that's the 1st position), the other person (2nd position) or from a 'fly on the wall' view (3rd position). Could you use that to help her work out what he's feeling vulnerable about, then at least she would know how to pitch a business case for her flexible working request; if she's stood in his shoes? (mode 2)

**Coach F:** Yes, if I could add, from my Non-Violent Communication perspective [Rosenberg 2003], if we understand what are the other person's unmet needs then it makes sense of their negative feelings and we're more motivated to work out what their behaviour is trying to request of us. How would you get that to emerge for her? (mode 2)

**Coach A:** Phew! (pause) You're right D – I'm such a perfectionist that I should be able to make it all right for her and magically 'fix' her manager in some remarkable non-directive, enabling way showing what an amazing coach I am (laughs). OK, it's a fair cop. And it's good to hear others struggle with this one. I guess it feels as though we're on the line as maternity coaches here because this is the big issue, isn't it? But there I go again just getting revved up for another boost of anxiety through talking up the pressure. (mode 4)

**Supervisor:** We've talked about 'shift in the room' [e.g. Hawkins and Smith 2006] before. What's changed for you so far?

**Coach A:** Well, I'm not suffering in silence all on my professional own with this issue now. And yes, I'm more relaxed – my shoulders have dropped, haven't they, B? But thank goodness you don't get so hooked into fixing me here as I get for my coachee, eh! (mode 5)

**Supervisor:** And what's your hunch as to what's needed now to transform this live in supervision as we've committed to doing? Given where you've already got to, what else can we do here live for the benefit of the wider coaching system you're returning to? (mode 5)

**Coach A:** That three perceptions exercise that you talked about E – how do I do that? (mode 2)

[**Coach E** gains permission to lead the group through a demonstration, encouraging Coach A to move to different locations and explore the perspective of each. Coach A concludes that she can offer this exercise live in coaching and that even if it can't make a meeting take place, it might inform the way X writes out her business case for flexible working to email to her manager, requesting a discussion from a more empathic point of view.]

**Supervisor:** That's really brought that to life, thanks E. The tension I had in my chest has relaxed, too (mode 6). I'm also thinking that in terms of the anonymous organizational feedback we pass on, we could suggest including this approach in the managers' programme (mode 7).

## Some themes and outcomes of supervision

We emphasized humanistic core conditions: this area of coaching unearths profound life transition issues and their resonances in ourselves as coaches. We were also frequently reminded of the powerful motives we bring to this work as coaches. Many practitioners in the field of women's leadership are also activists of a kind, aligning with the view that 'there are considerable dangers in seeing private troubles merely as troubles – and not as public issues' (Mills 1943: 534). Alongside holding lightly our wish to change the world through maternity coaching (!) we became more alert to (and also relaxed about) the temptation towards advice-giving in parent coaching; and the coachees' requests for it ('yes, but how *did* you get yours to sleep through?').

Those who put themselves forward as maternity coaches will often have opinions on how things 'should' be, from their own experience both as employees and managers and also as parents and children. It is vital to explore these. Might we find coaches 'rescuing the victim' from her organization (Moyes 2009: 168), or wishing a certain future for her or her children along Robert Kegan's cautioned lines 'Among the many things from which a practitioner's clients need protection is the practitioner's hopes for the client's future, however benign and sympathetic these hopes may be' (Kegan 1982: 296; Liston-Smith 2009a).

It appeared to be highly developmental for coaches to be able to air these in front of trusted peers, to increase their flexibility of response and confidence in their ability to work with and contain these tensions.

Naturally a great deal of practical know-how emerged, including the consistency of themes for coachees: (how to get away at 5 p.m., progress one's career, talk with one's manager *and* home partner, accept one's changed identity, ask for and accept support) and some tried and tested approaches to these challenges, as well as a healthy shared suspicion of always bringing the same approach to the same concern. We signposted information on identifying and responding to peri-natal depression and a referral list of helping agencies, including detailed knowledge of any Employee Assistance Programme provided by the employer organization.

Coaches expressed that they most of all appreciated:

- the contextual knowledge;
- the confidence that came through opening up their practice to peers in a supportive learning environment.

Beyond this immediate learning, a large body of organizational feedback was generated through taking anonymized themes of supervision and feeding these back to HR and Diversity teams by agreement. In this way, certain areas could be tackled at an organizational level such as producing clear guidelines for managers to encourage consistency across divisions. Coaches could work on enabling the coachee to play her part in the system in a diplomatic win-win way, while the organization attempted to support managers to 'raise their game' as well.

## Challenges faced

Beyond the maternity-coaching specific learning above, another more general insight arose. In supervising internal coaches, there is a question to be held in mind as to a 'team' of coaches' readiness for genuine group supervision (and indeed the supervisor's capacity for this too). There are powerful group dynamics unleashed and a high need for trust and investment. Some participants have complicating dual roles and other agenda; and they all have to get on with each other around other meeting room tables (Liston-Smith and Donaldson-Feilder 2010).

Whether an internal team or a group of external coaches vying for the next project, there is naturally pride, competition, vested interests and systemic noise played out in group supervision, as well as all the warm, supportive forces.

Sometimes there is confusion or conflict about the purpose of supervision itself. Internal coaches may wish it would lead to a qualification; a bankable form of professional development. External coaches could experience it as quality control, coercive enough to draw out defences and pretended competence.

I noted above my dual role for external coaches: I was supervisor and client-facing company director. Crucially, I did not have line management responsibility for our team of external coaches at the time of this study, and in supervising my dual role was to some extent offset by:

(i)   my not having sole power to select coaches for projects (so coaches were not on their 'best behaviour' in supervision);
(ii)  group supervision being sometimes led by an independent, trained supervisor. However, in this format, we were contending with the different and perhaps no less intrusive dynamic of myself participating in the group.

We saw that the alternative was separate group supervision without my participation. However, we decided overall to tackle the issues through inclusion and explicit recognition – rather than exclusion – in order to achieve the mutual learning we would otherwise have missed.

As supervisor of internal coaches, I recognized a felt urge to demonstrate Return On Investment in this ironically competitive niche area of women's leadership development. It seemed important to be explicit about bringing a combination of didactic input and facilitation and to clarify in advance the organization's objectives and expectations which can then enter the group contracting process.

A further memorable learning is captured by Marsden et al. (2010) who point out that we may well get what we look for, depending on whether we see the world through the spectacles of a psychologist, business strategist or HR professional, for example. There was transformational learning through highlighting the bias we bring to reading a situation, as well as to intervening. Seeing ourselves more clearly as constrained in this way is very helpful in the area of maternity coaching where some of the material at issue for coachees concerns challenging unconscious bias in oneself and others.

Corporate maternity coaching offers a testing crucible for supervision. Attention must be paid to the very private realms of motherhood, life transitions and – usually – coupledom, yet there is an ever-present organizational objective relating to retention and effective return to work and this within some of the most demanding performance-driven (and in popular myth, testosterone-fuelled) workplace environments. This sharp juxtaposition makes it easier to surface supervision's rich enquiry as to who is the client; and the need to hold multiple layers of clients in our attention!

# References

Bostic St Clair, C. and Grinder, J. (2001) *Whispering in the Wind*. Weybridge, VT: J & C Enterprises.

Bussell, J. (2008) Great expectations: can maternity coaching affect the retention of professional women?, *International Journal of Evidence Based Coaching and Mentoring*, special issue (2): 14–26.

Ellis, A., Gordon, J., Neenan, M. and Palmer, S. (1997) *Stress Counselling: A Rational Emotive Behavioural Approach*. London: Cassell.

Gratton, L., Kelan, E. and Walker, L. (2007) *Inspiring Women: Corporate Best Practice in Europe*. London: London Business School/The Lehman Brothers Centre for Women in Business.

Hawkins, P. (2010) Coaching supervision, in E. Cox, T. Bachkirova and D. Clutterbuck (eds), *The Complete Handbook of Coaching*. London: Sage, pp. 381–93.

Hawkins, P. and Smith, N. (2006) *Coaching, Mentoring and Organizational Consultancy: Supervision and Development*. Maidenhead: McGraw-Hill.

Karpman, S. (1968) Fairy tales and script drama analysis, *Transactional Analysis Bulletin*, 7(26): 39–43.

Kegan, R. (1982) *The Evolving Self: Problem and Process in Human Development*. Cambridge, MA: Harvard University Press.

Liston-Smith, J. (2009a) Protect us from our supervisors' best intentions! An exploration of the scope for coaching supervisors to 'bracket' our 'hopes for the client's future'. Unpublished dissertation. Oxford Brookes University Business School.

Liston-Smith, J. (2009b) Maternity insights: maternal leadership and the MPQ™, *Managing Maternity Newsletter*, May.

Liston-Smith, J. (2010a) Becoming a parent, in S. Palmer and S. Panchal (eds), *Developmental Coaching: Life Transitions and Generational Perspectives*. Taylor & Francis Psychology Press: London, pp. 91–114.

Liston-Smith, J. (2010b) Maternity Coaching Framework. Coaching materials in use with My Family Care clients (unpub).

Liston-Smith, J. and Donaldson-Feilder, E. (2010) Grow your own: how do external supervisors see the internal talent coach's role? *Coaching at Work* 5(6): 38–42.

Marsden, H., Humphrey, S., Stopford, J. and Houlder, D. (2010) Balancing business empathy and psychology in coaching practice, *The Coaching Psychologist*, 6(1): 16–23.

Mills, C.W. (1943) The professional ideology of social pathologists, *American Journal of Sociology*, 46(3). Reprinted in I.L. Horowitz (ed.) (1963) *Power, Politics and People: The Collected Essays of C. Wright Mills*. New York: Oxford University Press.

Moyes, B. (2009) Literature review of coaching supervision, *International Coaching Psychology Review*, 4(2): 162–73.

Proctor, B. (1988) Supervision: a co-operative exercise in accountability, in M. Marken and M. Payne (eds), *Enabling and Ensuring*. Leicester: NYB and CYETYW, pp. 21–23.

Rosenberg, M.B. (2003) *Nonviolent Communication: A Language of Life*. Encinitas, CA: Puddle Dancer Press.

Whitworth, L., Kimsey-House, H. and Sandahl, P. (1998) *Co-Active Coaching: New Skills for Coaching People Toward Success in Work and Life*. Davies-Black, Mountain View, CA: Davies-Black Publishing.

# 24 Beyond quality assurance: the Deloitte internal coaching supervision story

*Christine K. Champion*

## Introduction

This case study sets out to provide an overview and background to the context for coaching within the case study organization and then to explore the decision to invest in the provision of a coaching supervision programme for internal coaches. The set up and implementation of this programme within the organization is explored and from the feedback and reflections of key stakeholders, individual and organizational impacts are drawn.

As the lead supervisor in the programme, I then identify emergent themes and insights, making links with the relevant recent literature and highlighting the future areas for enquiry and further research into this developing field.

## Setting the context

This case study is set in Deloitte LLP. Deloitte LLP ('Deloitte') has over 12,000 professionals and is the UK member firm of Deloitte Touche Tohmatsu Limited,[1] which is the world's largest private professional services network. As an early adopter of coaching, the building of a coaching culture in Deloitte has now become a key part of the talent and leadership strategy. Deloitte have been working towards effective interventions over a period of time and have received external recognition in some instances.

Originally coaching had been used as a more limited, remedial intervention to support Directors and Partners with challenging assessment and development experiences. An 18 strong team of internal coaches was developed within Deloitte in 2003, with members mainly drawn from the HR and Learning functions. The intention was to develop and grow the internal coaching base and capacity to create a viable alternative to external coaching provision.

This move to develop internal coaching also reflected the competitive business market conditions for professional service firms where the opportunity for differentiation through developing the softer skills of emotional and social intelligence was seen as a means to build better quality relationships with all stakeholders including clients. The internal coaching team was set up to support the transition of key Deloitte people from technically excellent practitioners to effective leaders, relationship builders and client managers in order to support Learning strategy and drive improved performance, thus reflecting key business priorities.

The coaching process has become more formalized over time beginning with a needs analysis to identify the developmental objectives, to determine the suitability for coaching and to facilitate the matching process. Individual coaching programmes include a tri-partite contracting process at the start to ensure alignment around objectives, clarity around roles and responsibilities, and to confirm ethics and boundaries including confidentiality. The progress of coaching programmes is monitored internally via a centralized tracking tool and the evaluation process includes feedback and evaluations from key stakeholders.

## The drive to set up internal coach supervision

Before the set-up of the formal coaching supervision programme, internal 'intervision' groups ('intervision' is Deloitte's own term for peer learning groups) were set up as a form of action learning set to support the development of coaches through case, skills and knowledge sharing.

During this period, as the internal coaching practice developed within Deloitte, the emerging drive for the further professionalization of coaching was noted in the coaching literature (Grant and Cavanagh 2004). The introduction of supervision was seen by Deloitte as an opportunity to further build the credibility and the expertise of the internal coaches. The intention was that the introduction of supervision would demonstrate the commitment to building internal coaching capacity and capability as a viable, cost effective alternative to external coaches through enhancing the quality, competence and professionalism of internal coaches.

Since Deloitte did not at the time possess expertise or experience of supervision, four known external providers were selected, engaged and briefed to provide formal design proposals including costings for the internal supervision programme. Following this the supplier selection process included a meeting with each supplier to further review the proposals and the provision of a sample one-to-one supervision session.

The procurement process was a journey into unknown territories for Deloitte, since the team was relatively new to supervision and there is a lack of formal guidance or robust criteria on best practice in the selection of supervisors in this context. However, the process itself provided an immediate opportunity for learning more about the role, purpose and the process of supervision through discussions with suppliers and the sharing of best practice and experiential insights. The decision on the choice of supplier was felt to be important and highly significant since it would impact on the professional growth and development of the coaching team and their internal clients, hence influencing the credibility and effectiveness of internal coaching at Deloitte. The relational aspects of matching were reported as key in supplier selection with the building of trust playing an important role as the relationship with prospective suppliers developed through the procurement process.

The two proposed definitions of supervision noted below from the Cedar Talent Management proposal provide insight into the breadth of the supervision approach adopted at Deloitte.

> the formal process of professional support, which ensures continuing development of the coach and effectiveness of his/her coaching practice through interactive reflection, interpretative evaluation and the sharing of experience.
>
> (Bachkirova et al. 2005)

and

> The process by which a coach, with the help of a supervisor, can attend to understanding better both the client and their wider system and themselves a part of the client-coach system, and by doing so, transform their work and develop their craft.
>
> (Hawkins and Smith 2006: 147)

## Implementation

The bespoke programme was designed to include an offsite 'kick off' event for all coaches, as well as face-to-face group sessions of three hours (three per year) and one (annual) 90-minute individual session. The programme design and frequency was based on Cedar's perceptions of the evidence from best practice on the appropriate ratio between supervision and coaching hours, taking into account the existence of 'intervision' sessions with Deloitte at the time. This aligns with Birch's (2010) recommendation of a minimum of five sessions per year, depending on the individual coach's workload. Engagement with supervision was determined as mandatory for all coaches in order to continue working as an internal coach.

The objectives for the interactive 'kick off' event were to introduce the two supervisors and to engage the whole group in discussions around the role and purpose of supervision at Deloitte and to begin the process of contracting around the supervision. An introductory workbook was developed to support these activities and the preparation for future supervision sessions. The 18 members of the coaching team were divided into four groups, based loosely on geography and each supervisor was allocated two groups.

A list of the potential tasks of supervision were drawn from Hawkins and Smith (2006) and included in the workbook. These were explored with the groups with a view to providing more clarity and understanding around the process. The intention was to reduce uncertainty about the supervision process and create a readiness for supervision.

The 'seven-eyed-model' of supervision, reviewed in detail earlier in Chapter 2 in this book, was chosen as the basis of the process approach to provide a systems view of the interrelationships in coaching and the context for reviewing the supervision process. This seemed to provide a good fit with the client culture, organizational complexities and the multi stakeholder context. The model also provided a robust framework for supervision and appealed to the intellectual curiosity of coaches.

Themed qualitative insights into the impacts of supervision have been drawn from the feedback and reflections of the coaches, supervisors and other organizational stakeholders in the coaching supervision process. I have grouped individual impacts in line with the primary foci of coaching organizational supervision developed by Hawkins and Smith (2006) as 'Developmental', 'Resourcing' and 'Qualitative'. Organizational impacts are grouped according to the themes that I identified from the data.

## Individual impacts

### Developmental (skills, knowledge, understanding and capacities)

The early development of a wider range of questions and questioning approaches was reported. The coaches confirmed experiencing a 'huge amount of learning and development', including how to prepare for and engage effectively with the supervision process. They demonstrated and noted the development of skills in reflective practice, and through this the development of an awareness of the conscious choice made by the coach during the coaching process. The supervision provided an opportunity to link theory to practice through the inclusion of a 'mentoring' approach by sharing articles, further reading and exercises around the issues emerging. There was increased exposure to a range of effective coaching approaches thereby widening each coach's perspectives. This contributed to the further appreciation of a wide range of approaches and the options for the application of different tools and techniques, rather than coaches expecting there to be one 'right' approach.

### Resourcing (attending to emotional impacts)

Supervision was perceived as a positive reward and a supportive, affirmative experience which further developed the connections between coaches and reduced the feelings of isolation. Coaches reported greater confidence around the application of coaching tools, techniques and the management of the coaching process. There was a developing awareness of the opportunity to be conscious of and an openness to work with the emotions of the coachee and to explore the impacts on the coach during supervision. This led to the increased knowledge and awareness around self as coach. The supervision further validated the professional standing of the coaching team and as a result built the individual coach's commitment and motivation for internal coaching.

## Qualitative (ensuring appropriate interventions within defined ethical standards)

Supervision provided the opportunity for benchmarking best practice and for feedback from colleagues and the supervisor around practice. There was further clarity around the boundaries of coaching, how to identify the limits of competence of the individual coach and insights around when to refer to the additional specialized support available. Explorations in supervision provided insights into the role and responsibilities of the internal coach and the boundaries and relational complexities where role duality existed. Coaches reported an appreciation of the safe, reflective space provided for self-exploration during the sessions. Over time individual coaches experienced improved coaching resourcefulness and effectiveness in practice as indicated by the feedback from clients.

# Organizational impacts

Many of these contribute to the development of a coaching culture over time within Deloitte.

## Coaching capability and capacity

Supervision contributed to the development of a more cohesive team of coaches and provided a mechanism for collecting further insight into the capacity and capability of the team. As stories of success emerged from client experiences this contributed to an increased demand for internal coaching and ensured a more resource efficient approach compared with the cost of external coaches. The stories of success also created a virtuous cycle of developing greater confidence, capacity and competence of the internal coaching team through the generative dialogues.

## The development of coaching within Deloitte

Insights from the supervision process illuminated the opportunity for the next stage of skills development for the coaches. The successful track record and developing professionalism of internal coaches built organizational buy-in and the recognition of the value from internal coaching in supporting and driving learning strategy. This contributed to a developing readiness for coaching and a wider application of coaching in Deloitte, including triad developmental coaching, Transition coaching for maternity contexts and coaching at Partner level. There was a recognition that the internal coaching engagements supported individual and organizational change and transition in dynamic and uncertain internal and external environments.

## Organizational commitment to coaching

Supervision provided additional systemic insights contributing to organizational learning on cultural systems and to further opportunities for development within Deloitte. The evidence of success of coaching engagements contributed to the organizational commitment to invest in the development of an additional group of internal coaches to meet the growing demand for coaching within the organization. In addition investment was made available to develop an Advanced Coaching Skills programme for the established coaches.

## Reflections on the supervision process

At the start of the programme coaches reported an apprehension around the process and a certain level of performance anxiety and self doubt (Hindmarch 2008) as reflected in the comments below:

> 'I wondered what we would do for the three hour group session.'
> 'We don't know each other.'
> 'How will we add value for each other?'

This anxiety diminished over time as the coaches engaged with supervision and built their coaching hours. The diminishing of anxiety confirms De Haan's (2008) findings regarding the hierarchy of coach doubts that can emerge during practice and confirms the role for supervision in working with these through identifying critical incidents. At Deloitte as the learning was shared through the group process, feelings of individual isolation and uncertainty also lessened. A good example of this is provided by the opportunity to bring challenges and opportunities to the group relating to the broadening of coaching from a one-to-one to a team coaching intervention. Supervision provided a safe, reflective space to express anxieties, celebrate success, and to reflect on appropriate interventions to apply in this new context through the wider experiences of the group and the supervisor.

The dynamic development sequence in small groups identified by Tuckman (1965) was evidenced by the emerging levels of mutual trust within the groups over time. Interestingly, there was a noted absence of the 'Vanity Trap' investigated by McGivern (2009), which can present through the desire to demonstrate superior competence in front of colleagues, or of the game-playing indicated by Houston (1985), which can emerge in peer-group contexts. Indeed coaches demonstrated humility and generally remained reluctant to bring stories of success or to demonstrate their strengths in the group sessions, despite the supervisors encouraging this by confirming the legitimacy and validity of learning from successful encounters. This may suggest the future opportunity for engaging in more appreciative and positive based approaches to coaching supervision and reveals the potential for further research into practice (Linley and Harrington 2006).

The role of reflective practice in supporting coach learning and development is confirmed in this case study, as the coaches began to engage with this 'new' process guided by the supervisor. This was despite the counter-cultural environment within Deloitte reflecting a strong action orientation, where reflective space and time to think is scarce. There has also been evidence of the development of the 'internalised supervisor' (Casement 1985), with a capacity for spontaneous reflection in the moment. Coaches became more conscious of resisting the temptation to prompt or direct the coachee and developed more facilitative approaches, thus leaving space for the coachee to gain greater self-awareness and understanding.

Alongside this there has been a willingness in some of the coaches to move away from the focus on cognition as the basis for the coaching conversation, and towards engaging more with presenting emotions and working more holistically with the coachee. As confirmed by the research of Bachkirova and Cox (2007) the development of a readiness to recognize and to engage with emotion in coaching can add value for coaching as a means of developing effective leadership.

## Some early conclusions

The effectiveness of group supervision is clear in the case study with individual and organizational impacts confirming the weight of the advantages including increasing accountability and resource efficiency.

Despite there being some mixed views in the profession and in the literature regarding the freedom of choice in attending supervision, this did not appear to be an issue in Deloitte. This acceptance and commitment may be due to the regulated nature of the professional services sector. Indeed feedback suggests, and coach attendance confirms, that the commitment to attend, to support and learn from colleagues was viewed as a top priority, despite conflicting demands on the time of coaches due to their other roles and responsibilities.

The coaches welcomed diversity in practice and were not constrained by any one organizational model of coaching. The overarching Deloitte philosophy and organizational values provide the foundations for coaching while encouraging the freedom of choice for the individual coach development journey. The two qualified coaching supervisors have different backgrounds and approaches, which could be seen to demonstrate the efficacy of supervision irrespective of the particular model or approach being used by the supervisor.

At Deloitte it was held that a clear link has been demonstrated between supervision and the ongoing professional learning and development of the internal coaches. This reflects Lane's (2010) findings that supervision is a key contributor to the professionalization of coaching.

The value of the external coaching supervisor was appreciated in challenging and questioning organizational assumptions and the established ways of doing things. This externality can help to avoid the potential for 'consensus collusion'

(Heron 1975) by questioning established ways of working and opening up consideration of alternative approaches. In this case the external supervisor seemed better able to support the coaches on certain issues than an internal supervisor would have been. As predicted by St John-Brooks (2010), this was particularly significant when dealing with ethical dilemmas which arose from the complexities of internal coaching relationships, dual roles and multiple relationships.

## Next development steps

The credibility of internal coaches has been built within Deloitte as stories of success have circulated through word of mouth further embedding the coaching process and creating an appetite for coaching. However, the capacity for coaching and appreciation by the coaching team of the areas where internal coaches can add value may have accelerated faster than the general organizational understanding of the wider opportunities for coaching. This provides an opportunity for further education and communication of the potential for internal coaching at Deloitte.

As noted in this case study, the one-to-one supervision experience was highly valued, and facilitated the space for a more holistic and deeper exploration of self as coach, providing an opportunity to open up highly sensitive areas to the external supervisor, or as Gray (2010) describes it, a move from transactional to more transformational interventions.

There has been an opportunity through the review of coaching supervision to provide input into organizational learning and the evaluation of the coaching process and impacts. Indeed a key differentiator for coaching supervisors is the need to have knowledge, experience, insights and skills in understanding and working in the wider organizational context where the organization holds significant power and influence (Carroll 2006). Some organizational themes have been captured and fed back by the supervisors but there exists further future opportunity to formalize the capture of recurring issues and organizational themes (Hawkins and Smith 2006) outside of the actual supervision session, while still maintaining the essential boundaries of anonymity and confidentiality.

As the case study programme comes to the end of the second full year, it remains early days in the development of the theory and practice in organizational supervision with the need for further research into the value and impacts of supervision, how to select supervisors and how best to implement internal coach supervision programmes.

As I reflect on my journey so far as coaching supervisor in this context, informed by the feedback received from supervisees, a number of key insights stand out for me. I am reminded of the importance of the nature of the relationship between supervisor and supervisee, where trust, integrity and mutual respect are paramount in contributing to the effectiveness of supervision. Over time the commitments of all and the experience of supervision contributed to the belief in the efficacy of the supervision process. This has contributed to a virtuous cycle further strengthening commitment to the process and to each other. As a result of these factors and the dynamics of the group there was a developing willingness in the supervisees and myself to bring the whole self to coaching supervision and to take risks around professional self-development. In parallel to the supervisees, I have found rich ongoing opportunities for self-insight, learning and development through my work with Deloitte.

## Acknowledgement

As the Lead Supervisor in this case study, I would like to acknowledge contributions from colleagues, namely Caroline Flin and Gladeana McMahon, Coaching Supervisor.

## Note

1   Deloitte Touche Tohmatsu Limited is a UK private company limited by guarantee whose network of member firms are legally separate and independent entities. Please refer to www.deloitte.co.uk/about for more information.

## References

Bachkirova, T. and Cox, E. (2007) Coaching with emotions in organisations: an investigation of personal theories, *Leadership & Organisational Development Journal*, 28(7): 600–12.

Bachkirova, T., Stevens, P. and Willis, P. (2005) *Coaching Supervision*. Oxford Brookes Coaching & Mentoring Society.

Birch, D. (2010) Coaching supervision: quality assurance for executive coaches?, *Converse*, 7: 40–2.

Carroll, M. (2006) Supervising executive coaches. *Therapy Today*, 17(5): 47–9.

Casement, P. (1985) *On Learning from the Patient*. London. Routledge.

De Haan, E. (2008) Becoming simultaneously thicker and thinner skinned: the inherent conflicts arising in the professional development of coaches, *Personnel Review*, 37(5): 526–42.

Grant, A.M. and Cavanagh, M. (2004) Toward a profession of coaching, sixty-five years of progress and challenges for the future, *International Journal of Evidence based Coaching & Mentoring*, 2(1): 1–16.

Gray, D.E. (2010) Towards the lifelong skills and business development of coaches: an integrated model of supervision and mentoring, *Coaching: An International Journal of Theory, Research and Practice*, 3(1): 60–72.

Hawkins, P. and Smith, N. (2006) *Coaching, Mentoring and Organizational Consultancy: Supervision and Development*. Maidenhead: Open University Press.

Heron, J. (1975) *Six Category Intervention Analysis*. Guildford: University of Surrey.

Hindmarch, L. (2008) An exploration of the experience of self doubt in the coaching context and the strategies adopted by coaches to overcome it, *International Journal of Evidence Based Coaching and Mentoring*, special issue 2, November.

Houston, G. (1985) Group supervision of Groupwork, self & society, *European Journal of Humanistic Psychology*, XIII(2): 64–6.

Lane, D.A. (2010) Coaching in the UK – an introduction to some key debates, *Coaching: An International Journal of Theory, Research and Practice*, 3(2): 155–66.

Linley, P.A. and Harrington, S. (2006) Strengths coaching: a potential-guide approach to coaching psychology, *International Coaching Psychology Review*, 1: 37–46.

McGivern, L. (2009) Continuous professional development and avoiding the vanity trap: an exploration of coach's lived experience of supervision, *International Journal of Evidence Based Coaching and Mentoring*, special issue 3: 22–37.

St John-Brooks, K. (2010) Moral support, *Coaching at Work*, January/February, 5(1): 48–51.

Tuckman, B. (1965) Developmental sequence in small groups, *Psychological Bulletin*, 63(6): 384–99.

# Index